M000306074

STERLING
Test Prep

MCAT®
Practice Tests

Biological & Biochemical Foundations of Living Systems

6th edition

www.MasterMCAT.com

Copyright © 2019 Sterling Test Prep

We want to hear from you

Your feedback is important to us because we strive to provide the highest quality prep materials. If you have any questions, comments or suggestions, email us, so we can incorporate your feedback into future editions.

Customer Satisfaction Guarantee

If you have any concerns about this book, including printing issues, contact us and we will resolve any issues to your satisfaction.

info@onlinemcatprep.com

6 5 4 3 2 1

ISBN-13: 978-1-9475564-9-2

Sterling Test Prep products are available at special quantity discounts for sales, promotions, premed counseling offices and other educational purposes.

For more information contact our Sales Department at:

Sterling Test Prep
6 Liberty Square #11
Boston, MA 02109

info@sterling-prep.com

© 2019 Sterling Test Prep

Published by Sterling Test Prep

Dear Future Doctor!

Congratulations on choosing this book as part of your MCAT® preparation!

Scoring well on the MCAT is extremely important for admission into medical school. To achieve a high MCAT score, you need to develop skills to properly apply the knowledge you have and quickly choose the correct answer. Understanding key concepts, having the ability to extract information from the passages and distinguishing between similar answer choices is more valuable than simply memorizing terms.

This book is different from the majority of other MCAT science prep books. While other books either only superficially review science topics or provide practice questions with brief explanations, this book presents the science material in an MCAT-style test format and provides detailed explanations. These explanations discuss why the answer is correct and – more importantly – why another answer that may have seemed correct is the wrong choice. The explanations include the foundations and details of important science topics needed to answer related questions on the MCAT. By reading these explanations carefully and understanding how they apply to solving the question, you will learn important concepts and the relationships between them. This will prepare you for the MCAT and will significantly improve your score.

Our preparation materials will help you succeed by scoring well on the MCAT. All the content of our publications is prepared by our editors who possess extensive credentials, are educated in top colleges and universities and have been admitted to medical school with stellar MCAT scores. Our editors are experts on teaching, preparing students for the MCAT and have coached thousands of premeds on admission strategies.

We wish you great success in your future medical profession and look forward to being an important part of your successful preparation for the MCAT®!

Sterling Test Prep Team

Other MCAT products by Sterling Test Prep

MCAT Practice Tests

- *MCAT Physical & Chemical Foundations of Biological Systems + Biological & Biochemical Foundations of Living Systems (8 practice tests)*
- *MCAT Physical & Chemical Foundations of Biological Systems (4 practice tests)*

MCAT Practice Questions

- *MCAT Physics Practice Questions*
- *MCAT General Chemistry Practice Questions*
- *MCAT Biology & Biochemistry Practice Questions*
- *MCAT Organic Chemistry & Biochemistry Practice Questions*

MCAT Content Review

- *Physics Review*
- *General Chemistry Review*
- *Biology and Biochemistry Review*
- *Organic Chemistry and Biochemistry Review*
- *Psychology and Sociology Review*

Online CBT Testing

The practice tests included in this book are also available in an online format. Our advanced testing platform allows you to take the tests in the same CBT (computer based test) format as the AAMC's official MCAT.

We strongly advise you to use this feature for several reasons. Taking test on the computer (which you will do on test day) is a very different experience from working with a book. Our proprietary testing platform is designed to fully simulate the official MCAT®. Practicing the tests online, under timed conditions, helps you get accustomed to computer testing and have a smoother experience during the actual MCAT.

By using our online CBT testing, you will get a **Scaled Score** which is generated based on your performance compared with other test takers. You will also receive your personalized **Diagnostics Report**. This report includes detailed statistics on your individual performance on each test and categorizes the questions by topics and difficulty level. This will allow you to assess your knowledge of each subject and topic, identify the areas where you need to spend more time studying and compare your performance to the performance of other test takers.

> To access these and other online tests at a special pricing
> for book owners go to page 282 for access web address

- Assess your knowledge of different subjects and topics
- Receive a Scaled Score and Diagnostics Reports with your performance analysis
- Learn important scientific topics and concepts
- Improve your test-taking skills by simulating testing under time constraints
- Comprehensive and cost effective complete MCAT® science preparation
- Prepare and learn anywhere on your schedule

Our Commitment to the Environment

Sterling Test Prep is committed to protecting our planet's resources by supporting environmental organizations with proven track records of conservation, environmental research and education and preservation of vital natural resources. A portion of our profits is donated to support these organizations so they can continue their important missions. These organizations include:

 For over 40 years, Ocean Conservancy has been advocating for a healthy ocean by supporting sustainable solutions based on science and cleanup efforts. Among many environmental achievements, Ocean Conservancy laid the groundwork for an international moratorium on commercial whaling, played an instrumental role in protecting fur seals from overhunting and banning the international trade of sea turtles. The organization created national marine sanctuaries and served as the lead non-governmental organization in the designation of 10 of the 13 marine sanctuaries.

 For 25 years, Rainforest Trust has been saving critical lands for conservation through land purchases and protected area designations. Rainforest Trust has played a central role in the creation of 73 new protected areas in 17 countries, including Falkland Islands, Costa Rica and Peru. Nearly 8 million acres have been saved thanks to Rainforest Trust's support of in-country partners across Latin America, with over 500,000 acres of critical lands purchased outright for reserves.

 Since 1980, Pacific Whale Foundation has been saving whales from extinction and protecting our oceans through science and advocacy. As an international organization, with ongoing research projects in Hawaii, Australia and Ecuador, PWF is an active participant in global efforts to address threats to whales and other marine life. A pioneer in non-invasive whale research, PWF was an early leader in educating the public, from a scientific perspective, about whales and the need for ocean conservation.

Thank you for choosing our products to achieve your educational goals.

With your purchase you support environmental causes around the world.

Table of Contents

MCAT® Test-Taking Strategies

There are strategies, approaches and perspectives that you should learn to apply when taking the MCAT®. On the test, you need to think, extract information from passages, and analyze information quickly. This skill cannot be gained from a college course, a review prep course or a text book. But you can develop it through repetitive practice and focus.

General Strategies

Intimidation by information

Test developers usually select material for the test that will be completely unknown to most test takers. Don't be overwhelmed, intimidated or discouraged by unfamiliar concepts. While going through a question, try to understand all the relevant material available, while disregarding the distracter information. Being exposed to unfamiliar topics and terms is normal for the MCAT®.

As you read an unfamiliar passage, do not feel disappointed that you're not very familiar with the topic. Most other test takers are not familiar with it either. So, stay calm and work through the questions. Don't turn this into a learning exercise by trying to memorize the information (in a passage or question) that was not known to you before, because your objective on the test is to answer questions quickly by selecting the correct answers.

Find your pace

Everybody reads and processes information at a different rate. You should practice finding your optimal pace, so you can read quickly and still comprehend the information. If you have a good pace and don't invest too much time in any one question, you should have enough time to complete each section at a comfortable rate. Avoid the two extremes where you either work too slowly, reading each and every word carefully, or act panicky and rush through the material without understanding it.

When you find your own pace that allows you to stay focused and calm, you will have enough time for all questions. It is important to remember that you are trying to achieve optimal, rather than maximum, comprehension. If you spend the time necessary to achieve maximum comprehension of a passage or question, you will most likely not have enough time for the entire section of the test.

You should practice MCAT® tests under timed conditions to eventually find your optimal pace. This is why we recommend that you use the practice tests on our website, where you will get a scaled score and your personalized Diagnostics Report.

Don't be a perfectionist

The test is timed, and you cannot spend too much time on any one question. Get away from thinking that if you spent just one more minute on a question, you'll get it right. You can get sucked into a question to the extent that you lose track of time and end up rushing through the remainder of the test (which may cause you to miss even more questions). If you spend your allocated per-question time and are still not sure of the answer, select the best option, note the question number and move on. The test allows you to return to any question and change your answer choice. If you have extra time left after you answered all other questions on that section, return to that question and take a fresh look. Unless you have a sound reason to change your original answer, don't change your answer choice, as data shows that changing answers without reason often reduces a person's overall score.

You shouldn't go into the MCAT® thinking that you must get every question right. Accept the fact that you will have to guess on some questions (and maybe get them wrong) and still have time for every question. Your goal should be to answer as many questions correctly as you possibly can within the allotted time. Too much time on one question reduces the time left to answer other (maybe easier) questions.

Factually correct, but actually wrong

Often, MCAT® questions are written in a way that the incorrect answer choice may be factually correct on its own, but doesn't answer the question. When you are reading the answer choices and one choice jumps out at you because it is factually correct, be careful. Make sure to go back to the question and verify that the answer choice actually answers the question being asked. Some incorrect answer choices will seem to answer the question asked and are even factually correct, but are based on extraneous information within the question stem.

Narrow down your choices

When you find two answer choices that are direct opposites, it is very likely that the correct answer choice is one of the two. You can typically rule out the other two answer choices (unless they are also direct opposites of each other) to narrow down your search for the correct choice that answers the question.

Experiments

If you encounter a passage that describes an experiment, ask basic questions, including: "What is the experiment designed to find out?", "What is the experimental method?", "What are the variables?", "What are the controls?" Understanding experimental data helps you use the presented information to answer the questions associated with the passage.

Multiple experiments

The best way to remember the variations of the same experiment is to focus on the differences between the experiments. What changed between the first and the second experiment? What was done differently between the second and third experiments? This will help you organize the information in your mind.

Passage notes

Pay attention to the notes provided after a passage. The information in those notes is often necessary to answer questions associated with that passage. Notes are there for a reason and often contain information necessary to answer at least one of the questions.

Look for units

When solving a problem that you don't know the formula for, try to solve for the units in the answer choices. The units in the answer choices are your clues for understanding the relationship between the question and the correct answer. Review what value is being sought for in the question. Sometimes, you can eliminate some wrong answers because they contain improper units.

Don't fall for the familiar

When in doubt, it is easy to choose what you are familiar with. If you recognize a term in one of the four answer choices, you may be tempted to pick that choice. But don't go with familiar answers just because they are familiar. Think through the other answer choices and how they relate to the question before making your selection.

Don't get hung up on the passage

Read through the passage once briefly to understand what items it deals with and take mental notes of some key points. Then, look at the questions. You might find that you are able to answer some questions without using the information in the passage. With other questions, once you know what exactly is being asked, you can read through the passage more effectively, looking for a particular answer. This technique helps you save some time that you otherwise would have overinvested in processing information that had no benefit to you (not related to a question).

Roman numerals

Some questions present three or four statements and ask which of them are correct. For example:

      I.   Statement A
      II. Statement B
      III. Statement C

  A. I only
  B. III only
  C. I and II only
  D. I and III only

Notice that there is no answer choice exclusively dedicated to statement II. Therefore, it is likely that statement II is wrong and you can eliminate answer choice C. This narrows your search to three choices. However, if you are confident that statement II is part of the answer, you can disregard this strategy.

Extra Tips

• With fact questions that require selecting among numbers, don't go with the smallest or largest number unless you have a reason to believe it is the correct answer.

• Use the process of elimination for questions that you're not clear about. Try to eliminate the answer choices you know to be wrong before making your selection.

• Don't fall for answers that sound "clever" and don't go with "bizarre" choices. Only choose them if you are confident that the choice is correct.

• None of the strategies alone replace the importance of preparation. But knowing and using them helps you utilize your test time more productively and increases your probability for successful guessing when you simply don't know the answer.

MCAT® Practice Tests

Our guarantee – the highest quality preparation materials.

Be the first to report an error, typo or inaccuracy and receive a
$10 reward for a content error or
$5 reward for a typo or grammatical mistake.

info@onlinemcatprep.com

Biological & Biochemical Foundations of Living Systems

Practice Test #1

59 questions

For explanatory answers see pgs. 115-155

For CBT online format of this test that provides Diagnostics Report with performance statistics, difficulty rating of each question and other features visit:

www.MasterMCAT.com

Most questions in the Biological Sciences test are organized into groups, each containing a descriptive passage. After studying the passage select the one best answer to each question in the group. Some questions are not based on a descriptive passage and are also independent of each other. If you are not certain of an answer, eliminate the alternatives you know to be incorrect and then select an answer from the remaining alternatives. Indicate your selected answer by marking the corresponding answer on your answer sheet. A periodic table is provided for your use. You may consult it whenever you wish.

Periodic Table of the Elements

1 H 1.0																	2 He 4.0
3 Li 6.9	4 Be 9.0											5 B 10.8	6 C 12.0	7 N 14.0	8 O 16.0	9 F 19.0	10 Ne 20.2
11 Na 23.0	12 Mg 24.3											13 Al 27.0	14 Si 28.1	15 P 31.0	16 S 32.1	17 Cl 35.5	18 Ar 39.9
19 K 39.1	20 Ca 40.1	21 Sc 45.0	22 Ti 47.9	23 V 50.9	24 Cr 52.0	25 Mn 54.9	26 Fe 55.8	27 Co 58.9	28 Ni 58.7	29 Cu 63.5	30 Zn 65.4	31 Ga 69.7	32 Ge 72.6	33 As 74.9	34 Se 79.0	35 Br 79.9	36 Kr 83.8
37 Rb 85.5	38 Sr 87.6	39 Y 88.9	40 Zr 91.2	41 Nb 92.9	42 Mo 95.9	43 Tc (98)	44 Ru 101.1	45 Rh 102.9	46 Pd 106.4	47 Ag 107.9	48 Cd 112.4	49 In 114.8	50 Sn 118.7	51 Sb 121.8	52 Te 127.6	53 I 126.9	54 Xe 131.3
55 Cs 132.9	56 Ba 137.3	57 La* 138.9	72 Hf 178.5	73 Ta 180.9	74 W 183.9	75 Re 186.2	76 Os 190.2	77 Ir 192.2	78 Pt 195.1	79 Au 197.0	80 Hg 200.6	81 Tl 204.4	82 Pb 207.2	83 Bi 209.0	84 Po (209)	85 At (210)	86 Rn (222)
87 Fr (223)	88 Ra (226)	89 Ac† (227)	104 Rf (261)	105 Db (262)	106 Sg (266)	107 Bh (264)	108 Hs (277)	109 Mt (268)	110 Ds (281)	111 Uuu (272)	112 Uub (285)		114 Uuq (289)		116 Uuh (289)		

	58 Ce 140.1	59 Pr 140.9	60 Nd 144.2	61 Pm (145)	62 Sm 150.4	63 Eu 152.0	64 Gd 157.3	65 Tb 158.9	66 Dy 162.5	67 Ho 164.9	68 Er 167.3	69 Tm 168.9	70 Yb 173.0	71 Lu 175.0
†	90 Th 232.0	91 Pa (231)	92 U 238.0	93 Np (237)	94 Pu (244)	95 Am (243)	96 Cm (247)	97 Bk (247)	98 Cf (251)	99 Es (252)	100 Fm (257)	101 Md (258)	102 No (259)	103 Lr (260)

Biological & Biochemical Foundations of Living Systems
MCAT® Practice Test #1 – Answer Sheet

Passage 1

1 : A B C D
2 : A B C D
3 : A B C D
4 : A B C D
5 : A B C D

Passage 2

6 : A B C D
7 : A B C D
8 : A B C D
9 : A B C D
10 : A B C D

Independent questions

11 : A B C D
12 : A B C D
13 : A B C D
14 : A B C D

Passage 3

15 : A B C D
16 : A B C D
17 : A B C D
18 : A B C D
19 : A B C D
20 : A B C D

Passage 4

21 : A B C D
22 : A B C D
23 : A B C D
24 : A B C D
25 : A B C D
26 : A B C D

Independent questions

27 : A B C D
28 : A B C D
29 : A B C D

Passage 5

30 : A B C D
31 : A B C D
32 : A B C D
33 : A B C D
34 : A B C D
35 : A B C D

Passage 6

36 : A B C D
37 : A B C D
38 : A B C D
39 : A B C D
40 : A B C D

Independent questions

41 : A B C D
42 : A B C D
43 : A B C D
44 : A B C D
45 : A B C D
46 : A B C D

Passage 7

47 : A B C D
48 : A B C D
49 : A B C D
50 : A B C D
51 : A B C D
52 : A B C D

Independent questions

53 : A B C D
54 : A B C D
55 : A B C D
56 : A B C D
57 : A B C D
58 : A B C D
59 : A B C D

This page is intentionally left blank

Passage 1
(Questions 1–5)

An antibiotic is a soluble substance derived from a mold or a bacterium, and inhibits the growth of other microorganisms. Despite the absence of the bacterial beta-lactamase gene that typically confers penicillin resistance, there is a strain of penicillin-resistant pneumococci bacteria. Additionally, some of the cells in this strain are unable to metabolize the disaccharides of sucrose and lactose. A microbiologist studying this strain discovered that all of the cells in this strain were infected with two different types of bacteriophage: phage A and phage B. Both phages insert their DNA into the bacterial chromosome. The researcher infected wildtype pneumococci with the two phages to determine if the bacteriophage infection could give rise to this new bacterial strain.

Experiment 1

Two separate 25 ml nutrient broth solutions containing actively growing wild-type pneumococci were mixed with 15 μl of phage A and 15 μl of phage B. In addition, another 25 ml broth solution containing only wild-type pneumococci was used as a control. After 30 minutes of room temperature incubation, the microbiologist diluted 1 μl of the broth solutions in separate 1 ml aliquots of sterile water. These dilutions were plated on three different agar plates containing glucose, sucrose and lactose, respectively. The plates were incubated at 37 °C for 12 hours, and the results are summarized in Table 1.

Plates	phage A infected cells	phage B infected cells	wild-type cells
glucose	+	+	+
sucrose	+	−	+
lactose	+	−	−

(+) plates show bacterial growth; (−) plates show no growth

Table 1.

Experiment 2

10 μl of each of the broth solutions from Experiment 1 were again diluted in separate 5 ml aliquots of sterile water. These dilutions were plated on three different agar plates containing tetracyne, ampicillin and no antibiotic, respectively. The plates were incubated at 37 °C for 12 hours, and the results are summarized in Table 2.

Plates	phage A infected cells	phage B infected cells	wild-type cells
Tetracyne	−	−	−
Ampicillin	+	+	−
No antibiotic	+	+	+

(+) plates show bacterial growth; (−) plates show no growth

Table 2.

1. Which of the following best account(s) for the results of Experiment 2?

    I.   Wild-type bacteria have no natural resistance to either ampicillin or tetracyne

    II. Phage A DNA and phage B DNA encode for beta-lactamase

    III. Phage A and phage B disrupted the wild-type bacteria's ability to resist ampicillin

    IV. Phage A DNA and phage B DNA encode for enzymes that inhibit tetracyne's harmful effects

    A. II only   **C.** III and IV only

    B. I and II only   **D.** I, II and IV only

2. Plaques are transparent areas within a bacterial lawn caused by bacterial cell death. In which of the following cycles must phage A be able to produce plaques?

    A. S phase   **C.** lytic

    B. translocation   **D.** lysogenic

3. Which of the following best describes the appearance of pneumococci, a streptococcal bacterium, when stained and then viewed with a compound light microscope?

    A. spherical   **B.** rod   **C.** helical   **D.** cuboidal

4. Based on the results of the experiments, which statement is most likely true of phage A?

    A. Phage A reduced the ampicillin on the agar plates and therefore allowed bacterial growth

    B. Phage A inserted its DNA into the bacterial chromosome, rendering ampicillin ineffective against the bacterial cell wall

    C. Phage A inhibited the growth of the bacteria

    D. Phage A contained the viral gene that encoded for beta-lactamase

5. Which of the following conclusions is consistent with the data in Table 1?

    A. Phage A inserted its DNA into the bacterial chromosome region that encodes for the enzymes of glycolysis

    B. Phage A prevented larger molecules, such as lactose and sucrose, from passing through the bacterial cell wall

    C. Phage B utilized all of the sucrose and lactose and starved out the bacteria

    D. Phage B inserted its DNA into the bacterial chromosome region that encodes for disaccharide digesting enzymes

Passage 2
(Questions 6–10)

Water is the most abundant compound in the human body and comprises about 60% of total body weight. The exact contribution of water to total body weight within a person varies with gender and tends to decrease with age. Daily water needs are about 2.7 liters for women and about 3.7 liters for men.

Total body water (TBW) is distributed between two fluid compartments. These compartments contain the intracellular fluid (ICF) and extracellular fluid (ECF). The sum of ICF and ECF volumes equals TBW:

TBW volume = ECF volume + ICF volume

There are approximately 100 trillion cells in the human body. Intracellular fluid is the fluid contained within the membrane of each cell. ICF accounts for about 65% or about 2/3 of TBW. Extracellular fluid is the fluid surrounding the individual cells within the body. ECF, present outside of body cells, can be further divided into: interstitial fluid (IF), lymph fluid and blood plasma. Interstitial fluid and lymph fluid together comprise about 27% of the TBW. Blood plasma accounts for another 8% of the TBW.

Other extracellular fluids are found in specialized compartments, such as the urinary tract, digestive tract, bone and synovial fluids that lubricate the joints and organs.

Total body water (TBW) can be measured with isotope dilution. After ingesting a trace dose of a known isotopic marker, saliva samples are collected from the patient over several hours. The measurements are compared between experimental and baseline data. The calculation of body mass before and after the experiment provides a ratio of TBW to total body mass. The data is analyzed using the following formula:

Volume = Amount (g) / Concentration

6. In periods of low water intake, the renin-angiotensin feedback mechanism is used to minimize the amount of water lost by the system. The kidney works in conjunction with which of the following organs to excrete acidic metabolites and regulate acid-base buffer stores?

A. brain   **C.** heart

B. lungs   **D.** liver

7. In isotope dilution technique, a dose of approximately 7 milligrams of O^{18} labeled water was used as a tracer. If 21.0 M/L was the estimated particle concentration, what is the estimate of TBW?

A. 0.33   **C.** 0.33×10^{-2}

B. 33.3   **D.** 33.3×10^{-5}

8. The movement of water into the cell from the interstitial space to the cytosol is an example of:

     I. facilitated transport   III. osmosis

     II. active transport   IV. passive transport

A. I only   **B.** III only   **C.** I, III and IV only   **D.** I, II, III and IV

9. Edema is characterized by the presence of excess fluid forced out of circulation and into the extracellular space of tissue or serous cavities. Often, edema is due to circulatory or renal difficulty. Which of the following could be a direct cause of edema?

A. Decreased permeability of capillary walls

B. Increased osmotic pressure within a capillary

C. Decreased hydrostatic pressure within a capillary

D. Increased hydrostatic pressure within a capillary

10. An experiment is conducted to estimate total body water. According to the passage, which of the following must be true?

A. ECF comprises 35% of TBW and is estimated at 1/3 of body water

B. ECF comprises 65% of TBW and is estimated at 2/3 of body water

C. ICF comprises 50% of TBW and is estimated at 1/2 of body water

D. ICF comprises 35% of TBW and is estimated at 1/3 of body water

Questions 11 through 14 are not based on any
descriptive passage and are independent of each other

11. Which of the following compounds would most likely produce color?

A.

B.

C.

D.

12. Which of the following molecules of digestion is NOT transported by a specific carrier in the intestinal cell wall?

A. fructose
B. sucrose
C. alanine
D. tripeptides

13. Which of the following molecules would be a major product in the reaction of the molecule shown with a chloride anion in carbon tetrachloride (CCl_4)?

14. The nucleus of a tadpole myocardial cell is removed and transplanted into an enucleated frog zygote. After transplant, the frog zygote develops normally. The experimental results suggest that:

A. the zygote cytoplasm contains RNA for normal adult development
B. cell differentiation is controlled by irreversible gene repression
C. cell differentiation is controlled by selective gene repression
D. the ribosomes in the zygote nucleus are the same as in an adult frog

Passage 3
(Questions 15–20)

The Earth's atmosphere absorbs the energy of most wavelengths of electromagnetic energy. However, significant amounts of radiation reach the Earth's surface through two regions of non-absorption. The first region transmits ultraviolet and visible light, as well as infrared light or heat. The second region transmits radio waves. Organisms living on earth have evolved a number of pigments that interact with light. Some pigments capture light energy, some provide protection from light-induced damage, some serve as camouflage and some serve signaling purposes.

Polyenes are poly-unsaturated organic compounds that contain one or more sets of conjugation. Conjugation is the alteration of double and single bonds, which results in an overall lower energy state of the molecule. Polyenes are important photoreceptors. Without conjugation, or conjugated with only one or two other carbon-carbon double bonds, the molecule normally has enough energy to absorb within the ultraviolet region of the spectrum. The energy state of polyenes with numerous conjugated double bonds can be lowered, so they enter the visible region of the spectrum. These compounds are often yellow or other colors.

Certain wavelengths of light (quanta) possess exactly the correct amount of energy to raise electrons within the molecule from their ground state to higher-energy orbitals. For most organic compounds, these wavelengths are in the UV range. However, conjugated double bond systems stabilize the electrons, so that they can be excited by lower-frequency photons with wavelengths in the visible spectrum. Such pigments are known as chromophores and transmit the complimentary color to the one absorbed. For example, carotene is a hydrocarbon compound with eleven conjugated double bonds that absorb blue light and transmit orange light. The absorbed wavelength generally increases with the number of conjugated bonds. The presence of rings and side-chains within the molecule also affects the wavelengths of energy that the molecule absorbs.

Nucleic acids are biological molecules affected by light. DNA absorbs ultraviolet light and is damaged by UVC (electromagnetic energy with wavelength less that 280 nm), UVB (280-315 nm) and UVA (315-400 nm). UVA also stimulates the melanin cells during sun exposure, and there is an increasing amount of evidence that UVA damages skin.

Wavelength	Color
390 - 460 nm	violet
460 - 490 nm	blue
490 - 580 nm	green
580 - 600 nm	yellow
620 - 790 nm	red

15. The color-producing property of conjugated polyenes is dependent upon:

A. resonance

B. polarity

C. optical activity

D. antibonding orbitals

16. The four compounds represented by the electronic spectra below were evaluated as potential sunscreens. From strongest to weakest, what is the correct sequence of sunscreen effectiveness among these four absorption profiles?

I

III

II

IV

A. I, II, III, IV   **B.** II, III, IV, I   **C.** II, IV, I, III   **D.** IV, I, II, III

17. A chromophore is the moiety of a molecule responsible for its color. Two pigments differ in the lengths of the conjugated polyene chains. The first pigment transmits yellow light and the second transmits red light. What can be said about the sizes of the chromophores?

A. First chromophore is shorter

B. Second chromophore is shorter

C. One of the chromophores must be a dimer

D. Comparative lengths of chromophores cannot be determined

18. Many exoskeleton organisms produce a blue or green carotene-protein complex. What is the most likely cause of the color change from green to red when a lobster is boiled?

A. The protein is separated from the carotenoid pigment

B. Increase in temperature permits the prosthetic group to become partially hydrated

C. Heat causes the prosthetic group to become oxidized

D. The prosthetic group spontaneously disassociates

19. Why is a solution of benzene colorless?

    A. Benzene does not absorb light
    B. Benzene is not conjugated
    C. Absorption energy is too high for a frequency to be visible
    D. Absorption energy is too low for a frequency to be visible

20. The electrons that give color to a carotene molecule are found in:

    A. *d* orbitals
    B. *f* orbitals
    C. *s* orbitals
    D. *p* orbitals

Passage 4
(Questions 21–26)

Adenosine triphosphate (ATP) is the energy source for many biochemical reactions within the cell, including many membrane transport processes. However, several membrane transport processes do not use the energy liberated from the hydrolysis of ATP. Instead, these transport processes are coupled to the flow of cations and/or anions down their electrochemical gradient. For example, glucose is transported into some animal cells by the simultaneous entry of Na^+. Sodium ions and glucose bind to a specific transport protein and, together, both molecules enter the cell. A symport is a protein responsible for the concerted movement (in the same direction) of two such molecules. An antiport protein carries two species in opposite directions. The rate and extent of the glucose transport depend on the Na^+ gradient across the plasma membrane. Na^+ entering the cell along with glucose, via symport transport, is pumped out again by the Na^+/K^+ ATPase pump.

A medical student investigated a type of bacteria that transports glucose across its cell membrane by use of a sodium-glucose cotransport mechanism. She performed two experiments in which bacterial cells were placed in glucose-containing media that differed with respect to relative ion concentration and ATP content. Glycolysis was inhibited in the cells during these experiments.

Experiment 1:
Bacterial cells with relatively low intracellular Na^+ concentration were placed in a glucose-rich medium. The medium had a relatively high Na^+ concentration, but lacked ATP. At regular time intervals, the glucose and sodium concentrations were analyzed from the medium (Figure 1).

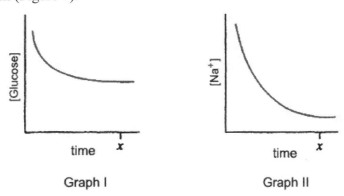

Figure 1. Glucose and Na+ concentrations in ATP-deficient medium

Experiment 2:
Bacterial cells with relatively low intracellular Na^+ concentration were placed in a glucose-rich medium. The medium had relatively high concentrations of both Na^+ and ATP. At regular time intervals, the medium was analyzed for the concentration of glucose, Na^+ and ATP (Figure 2). Over time, if radiolabeled ATP is used for the experiment, the majority of the radiolabel will be inside the cells in the form of ADP.

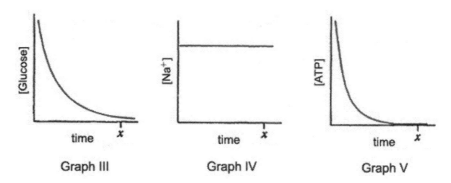

Figure 2. Glucose, Na⁺ and ATP concentrations in medium

21. Experiments 1 and 2 provide evidence that the cells take up glucose:

    A. in exchange for Na^+, if the ATP concentration is zero
    B. in exchange for ATP, if the extracellular Na^+ concentration remains constant
    C. together with Na^+, if the extracellular ATP concentration gradient is increasing
    D. together with Na^+, if a favorable sodium concentration gradient is maintained

22. From Experiments 1 and 2, the student hypothesized that the cells being investigated ultimately depend on energy to operate the sodium-glucose cotransport mechanism. Is this hypothesis supported by the data?

    A. Yes, because Figures 1 and 2 show that glucose crosses the cell membrane in exchange for phosphate
    B. Yes, because Figure 1 shows that a Na^+ gradient drives glucose transport, and Figure 2 shows that ATP maintains the Na^+ gradient
    C. No, because Figure 2 shows that extracellular glucose and ATP concentrations are independent
    D. No, because Figure 1 shows that glucose crosses the cell membrane indefinitely in the absence of exogenous energy

23. Based on the passage, the initial event in the transport of glucose and sodium into a cell is:

    A. direct hydrolysis of ATP in the cytoplasm by the sodium-glucose cotransporter
    B. direct hydrolysis of ATP on the extracellular surface by the sodium-glucose cotransporter
    C. binding of Na^+ to specific secreted proteins in the surrounding medium
    D. binding of Na^+ and glucose in the surrounding medium to specific membrane proteins

24. The result of Experiments 1 and 2 indicate that ATP promotes the cellular uptake of glucose by serving as a source of:

    A. monosaccharide
        C. metabolic energy
    B. enzymes
        D. inorganic phosphate

25. Within animal cells, the transport of Na^+/K^+ via the ATPase pump involves:

    A. facilitated diffusion
        C. osmosis
    B. active transport
        D. passive transport

26. According to Figure 1, as Na^+ concentration in the medium approaches the same concentration found in the cells, glucose concentration in the medium would:

    A. level off, because a sodium gradient is not available to drive cotransport
    B. remain at its original level, because sodium concentration does not affect glucose concentration
    C. approach zero, because glucose and sodium are transported together
    D. increase, because less glucose is transported into the bacterial cells

> Questions 27 through 29 are not based on any descriptive passage and are independent of each other

27. Which of the following structures is found in bacterial cells?

    A. nucleolus
        C. ribosome
    B. mitochondria
        D. smooth endoplasmic reticulum

28. Exocrine secretions of the pancreas:

    A. lower blood serum glucose levels
    B. raise blood serum glucose levels
    C. aid in protein and fat digestion
    D. regulate metabolic rate of anabolism and catabolism

29. What type of protein structure describes two alpha and two beta peptide chains within hemoglobin?

    A. primary   **B.** secondary   **C.** tertiary   **D.** quaternary

Passage 5
(Questions 30–35)

Thrombosis is the formation or presence of a blood clot, which may cause infarction of tissue supplied by the vessel. Although the coagulation factors that are necessary to initiate blood clotting are present in the blood, clot formation in the intact vascular system is prevented by three properties of the vascular walls. First, the endothelial lining, which is sensitive to vascular damage, is smooth enough to prevent activation of the clotting system. Second, the inner surface of the endothelium is covered with mucopolysaccharide (glycocalyx) that repels the clotting factors and platelets in the blood. Third, an endothelial surface protein known as thrombomodulin binds thrombin, the enzyme that converts fibrinogen into fibrin in the final stage of clotting. The binding of thrombin to thrombomodulin reduces the amount of thrombin that can participate in clotting. Also, the thrombin-thrombomodulin complex activates protein C, a plasma protein that hinders clot formation by acting as an anticoagulant.

If the endothelial surface of a vessel has been roughened by arteriosclerosis or infection, and the glycocalyx-thrombomodulin layer has been lost, the first step of the intrinsic blood clotting pathway (Figure 1) will be triggered. The Factor XII protein changes its shape to become "activated" Factor XII. This conformational change within the protein initiates a cascade of reactions that result in the formation of thrombin and the subsequent conversion of fibrinogen to fibrin. Simultaneously, platelets release platelet factor 3, a lipoprotein that helps to activate the coagulation factors. A thrombus is an abnormal blood clot that develops in blood vessels and may impede or obstruct vascular flow.

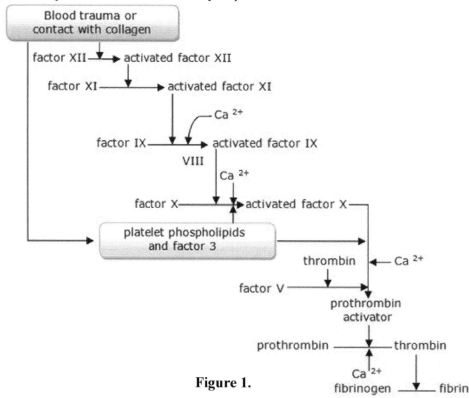

Figure 1.

An embolus is a thrombus that dislodges and travels in the bloodstream. Typically, an embolus will travel through the circulatory system until it becomes trapped at a narrow point, resulting in vessel blockage.

30. All of the following would cause prolonged clotting time in a human blood sample, EXCEPT:

A. addition of activated Factor X
B. removal of platelets or fibrinogen

C. addition of a calcium chelating agent
D. removal of Factor VIII

31. A physician injects small quantities of heparin in patients with pulmonary emboli histories to inhibit further thrombus formation. Heparin increases the activity of antithrombin III, the blood's primary inhibitor of thrombin. One possible adverse side effect of heparin administration is:

A. dizziness
B. minor bleeding

C. degradation of existing emboli
D. blood pressure increase

32. From the diagram in the passage, the function of Factor VIII in the activation of Factor X is that of a(n):

A. zymogen   **B.** substrate   **C.** enzyme   **D.** cofactor

33. The initial formation of thrombin in the intrinsic clotting pathway:

A. deactivates the blood factors
B. increases conversion of Factor XII to activated Factor XII
C. has a positive feedback effect on thrombin formation
D. causes a platelet reduction within plasma

34. Based on information in the passage, which of the following is the most likely mechanism of action of protein C?

A. Activation of Factors XII and X
B. Deactivation of activated Factors V and VIII
C. Accelerates formation of prothrombin
D. Negative feedback effect of thrombomodulin

35. Which of the following is most likely the origin of a pulmonary embolus that blocks the pulmonary artery?

A. Left side of the heart
B. The aorta

C. Pulmonary veins
D. Veins within the lower extremities

Passage 6
(Questions 36–40)

Fermentation is an anaerobic process that results in the conversion of high-energy substrates into various waste products. Fermentation harvests only a small amount of the energy stored in glucose. There are two common types: alcoholic fermentation and lactic acid fermentation.

Alcoholic fermentation (also called ethanol fermentation) is a biological process, whereby sugars (e.g. glucose, fructose and sucrose) are converted into cellular energy and produce ethanol and carbon dioxide as metabolic waste products. Because yeasts perform this conversion in the absence of oxygen, alcoholic fermentation is considered an anaerobic process. Anaerobic respiration is a form of respiration that uses electron acceptors other than oxygen.

Lactic acid fermentation is a biological metabolic process that converts glucose, fructose and sucrose into cellular energy and the metabolite lactate. It is also an anaerobic fermentation that occurs in some bacteria and animal cells (e.g. muscle cells). In homolactic fermentation, one molecule of glucose is converted into two molecules of lactic acid. By contrast, heterolactic fermentation yields carbon dioxide and ethanol in addition to lactic acid via a process called the phosphoketolase pathway.

In alcoholic fermentation, the conversion of pyruvic acid to ethanol is a two-step process. In heterolactic acid fermentation, the conversion of pyruvic acid into lactic acid is a one-step process.

Figure 1. Alcoholic fermentation and lactic acid fermentation pathways.

36. Lactic acid accumulates in muscles and is transported by the blood to the liver. What is the effect of lactic acid on respiratory rate?

    A. It decreases respiratory rate
    B. It increases respiratory rate
    C. It has no effect on respiratory rate
    D. Respiratory rate initially decreases and then quickly levels off

37. In lactic acid fermentation, pyruvate functions as an:

    A. electron acceptor for the reduction of NAD^+
    B. electron acceptor for the oxidation of NADH
    C. electron donor for the reduction of NAD^+
    D. electron donor for the oxidation of NADH

38. Fermentation differs from glycolysis, because in fermentation:

    A. glucose is oxidized
    B. NAD^+ is regenerated
    C. high-energy electrons are transferred to NAD^+
    D. ATP is produced

39. During alcoholic fermentation, pyruvic acid and acetaldehyde are, respectively:

    A. decarboxylated and oxidized
    B. decarboxylated and reduced
    C. reduced and decarboxylated
    D. decarboxylated and phosphorylated

40. During fermentation, the final electron acceptor from NADH is:

    A. an organic molecule
    B. alcohol
    C. NAD^+
    D. $\frac{1}{2} O_2$

Questions 41 through 46 are not based on any descriptive passage and are independent of each other

41. Which two atomic orbitals interact to form the D—D bond in D_2?

A. *s* and *s*

B. *p* and *p*

C. *sp* and *sp*

D. *sp*³ and *sp*³

42. During skeletal muscle contraction, which bands of the sarcomere shorten?

A. I and H bands

B. A and H bands

C. I bands and Z discs

D. Z discs

43. Human muscle cells behave in a manner similar to:

A. anaerobes

B. obligate aerobes

C. facultative anaerobes

D. strict aerobes

44. During the production of urine, the nephron controls the composition of urine by all of the following physiological processes, EXCEPT:

A. reabsorption of H_2O

B. counter current exchange with blood

C. secretion of solutes into urine

D. filtration for Na^+ to remain in blood

45. Which of the following molecules is NOT transported via Na^+ dependent transport?

A. bile acids

B. galactose

C. proteins

D. fatty acids

46. Which of the following characteristics of water make it the most important solvent on earth?

I.   Water is non-polar

II. Water is a Bronsted-Lowry base

III. Water is a Bronsted-Lowry acid

IV. Water forms hydrogen bonds

A. I and II only

B. II and III only

C. II, III and IV only

D. I, II, III and IV

This page is intentionally left blank

Passage 7
(Questions 47–52)

The reaction between alkyl bromide and chloride anion may proceed via any one of four possible reaction mechanisms. The observed pathway is a function of the solvent polarity. Although all four reactions involve substitution, each mechanism produces a distinct product.

Researchers calculated the free energies of activation (ΔG) in kcal mol^{-1} for the different mechanisms in two different solvents.

Figure 1.

The experiments demonstrated that the preferred pathway for the molecules in non-polar organic solvents is S_N2. However, as the solvent polarity increases, the difference in energy between the pathways narrows. In water, the preferred pathway, with a lower energy of activation, is S_N1.

Figure 2.

47. Which of the following is true regarding the reaction of (Z)-1-bromo-2-butene with the chloride anion in carbon tetrachloride?

    A. Reaction is unimolecular
    B. Reaction produces a racemic mixture
    C. Reaction is a concerted mechanism
    D. Reaction rate is independent of [Cl$^-$]

48. Which of the following molecules forms the most stable carbocation following the dissociation of the halide ion?

    A. (E)-1-chloro-2-butene
    B. (Z)-1-bromo-2-butene
    C. 1-chloro-3-methyl-2-butene
    D. no difference is expected

49. Regarding the reaction of 1-chloro-3-methyl-2-butene with Cl$^-$ in water, which of the following statements is supported by the passage?

    A. A strong nucleophile is required for the reaction to proceed
    B. A carbocation is formed
    C. The reaction occurs with an inversion of stereochemistry
    D. The reaction occurs with a single ΔG in the reaction profile

50. Which hypothesis explains the difference in the mechanism pathway (Figure 1) when the solvent is changed from CCl$_4$ to H$_2$O?

    A. Hydrogen bonding of the H$_2$O solvent stabilizes the transition state of the S$_N$2 pathway
    B. Hydrogen bonding of the H$_2$O solvent stabilizes the intermediate of the S$_N$2 pathway
    C. Hydrogen bonding of the H$_2$O solvent stabilizes the nucleophile of the S$_N$2 pathway
    D. Hydrogen bonding of the H$_2$O solvent stabilizes the carbocation intermediate of the S$_N$1 pathway

51. Which of the following reagents must be reacted with (E)-1-chloro-2-butene for a saturated alkyl halide to be formed?

    A. H$_2$, Pd
    B. 1) BH$_3$, THF 2) H$_2$O$_2$, $^-$OH
    C. 1) Hg(OAc)$_2$, H$_2$O 2) NaBH$_4$
    D. concentrated H$_2$SO$_4$

52. Which of the following reagents, when reacted with 1-chloro-3-methyl-2-butene will produce an alcohol with the hydroxyl group on C2?

    A. Lindlar
    C. Hg(OAc)$_2$, H$_2$O / NaBH$_4$
    B. BH$_3$, THF / H$_2$O$_2$, $^-$OH
    D. Grignard

Questions 53 through 59 are not based on any
descriptive passage and are independent of each other

53. How many amino acids are essential to the human diet?

A. 4　　　　　　B. 9　　　　　　C. 11　　　　　　D. 12

54. In eukaryotic cells, most of the ribosomal RNA are transcribed by RNA polymerase
[ ], major structural genes are transcribed by RNA polymerase [ ], and tRNAs are
transcribed by RNA polymerase [ ].

A. II; I; III　　　　B. II; III; I　　　　C. I; II; III　　　　D. I; III; II

55. Cellulose is not highly branched, because it does not have:

A. $\beta(1\rightarrow4)$ glycosidic bonds　　　C. a polysaccharide backbone
B. $\alpha(1\rightarrow4)$ glycosidic bonds　　　D. $\alpha(1\rightarrow6)$ glycosidic bonds

56. Which formula represents palmitic acid?

A. $CH_3(CH_2)_8COOH$　　　　C. $CH_3(CH_2)_{16}COOH$
B. $CH_3(CH_2)_{18}COOH$　　　　D. $CH_3(CH_2)_{14}COOH$

57. Lipids can be either:

A. hydrophobic or hydrophilic　　　C. amphipathic or hydrophilic
B. hydrophobic or amphipathic　　　D. amphipathic or amphoteric

58. Given that K_M measures the affinity of an enzyme and its substrate, without presence
of inhibitors, for the reaction rate to increase:

A. k_{cat} is must decrease　　　C. k_1 must decrease
B. k_{cat} must increase　　　D. k_{-1} must increase

59. Which amino acid-derived molecule transports amino acids across the cell
membrane?

A. S-adenosylmethionine　　　C. glutathione
B. insulin　　　D. γ-aminobutyric acid

Biological & Biochemical Foundations of Living Systems

Practice Test #2

59 questions

For explanatory answers see pgs. 157-196

For CBT online format of this test that provides Diagnostics Report with performance statistics, difficulty rating of each question and other features visit:

www.MasterMCAT.com

Most questions in the Biological Sciences test are organized into groups, each containing a descriptive passage. After studying the passage select the one best answer to each question in the group. Some questions are not based on a descriptive passage and are also independent of each other. If you are not certain of an answer, eliminate the alternatives you know to be incorrect and then select an answer from the remaining alternatives. Indicate your selected answer by marking the corresponding answer on your answer sheet. A periodic table is provided for your use. You may consult it whenever you wish.

Periodic Table of the Elements

1 H 1.0																	2 He 4.0
3 Li 6.9	4 Be 9.0											5 B 10.8	6 C 12.0	7 N 14.0	8 O 16.0	9 F 19.0	10 Ne 20.2
11 Na 23.0	12 Mg 24.3											13 Al 27.0	14 Si 28.1	15 P 31.0	16 S 32.1	17 Cl 35.5	18 Ar 39.9
19 K 39.1	20 Ca 40.1	21 Sc 45.0	22 Ti 47.9	23 V 50.9	24 Cr 52.0	25 Mn 54.9	26 Fe 55.8	27 Co 58.9	28 Ni 58.7	29 Cu 63.5	30 Zn 65.4	31 Ga 69.7	32 Ge 72.6	33 As 74.9	34 Se 79.0	35 Br 79.9	36 Kr 83.8
37 Rb 85.5	38 Sr 87.6	39 Y 88.9	40 Zr 91.2	41 Nb 92.9	42 Mo 95.9	43 Tc (98)	44 Ru 101.1	45 Rh 102.9	46 Pd 106.4	47 Ag 107.9	48 Cd 112.4	49 In 114.8	50 Sn 118.7	51 Sb 121.8	52 Te 127.6	53 I 126.9	54 Xe 131.3
55 Cs 132.9	56 Ba 137.3	57 La* 138.9	72 Hf 178.5	73 Ta 180.9	74 W 183.9	75 Re 186.2	76 Os 190.2	77 Ir 192.2	78 Pt 195.1	79 Au 197.0	80 Hg 200.6	81 Tl 204.4	82 Pb 207.2	83 Bi 209.0	84 Po (209)	85 At (210)	86 Rn (222)
87 Fr (223)	88 Ra (226)	89 Ac† (227)	104 Rf (261)	105 Db (262)	106 Sg (266)	107 Bh (264)	108 Hs (277)	109 Mt (268)	110 Ds (281)	111 Uuu (272)	112 Uub (285)		114 Uuq (289)		116 Uuh (289)		

	58 Ce 140.1	59 Pr 140.9	60 Nd 144.2	61 Pm (145)	62 Sm 150.4	63 Eu 152.0	64 Gd 157.3	65 Tb 158.9	66 Dy 162.5	67 Ho 164.9	68 Er 167.3	69 Tm 168.9	70 Yb 173.0	71 Lu 175.0
†	90 Th 232.0	91 Pa (231)	92 U 238.0	93 Np (237)	94 Pu (244)	95 Am (243)	96 Cm (247)	97 Bk (247)	98 Cf (251)	99 Es (252)	100 Fm (257)	101 Md (258)	102 No (259)	103 Lr (260)

Biological & Biochemical Foundations of Living Systems
MCAT® Practice Test #2 – Answer Sheet

Passage 1

1 : A   B   C   D
2 : A   B   C   D
3 : A   B   C   D
4 : A   B   C   D
5 : A   B   C   D
6 : A   B   C   D
7 : A   B   C   D

Passage 2

8 :   A   B   C   D
9:    A   B   C   D
10:   A   B   C   D
11 : A   B   C   D
12 : A   B   C   D
13 : A   B   C   D

Independent questions

14 : A   B   C   D
15 : A   B   C   D
16 : A   B   C   D
17 : A   B   C   D

Passage 3

18 : A   B   C   D
19 : A   B   C   D
20 : A   B   C   D
21 : A   B   C   D
22 : A   B   C   D
23 : A   B   C   D

Passage 4

24 : A   B   C   D
25 : A   B   C   D
26 : A   B   C   D
27 : A   B   C   D
28 : A   B   C   D

Independent questions

29 : A   B   C   D
30 : A   B   C   D
31 : A   B   C   D
32 : A   B   C   D
33 : A   B   C   D

Passage 5

34 : A   B   C   D
35 : A   B   C   D
36 : A   B   C   D
37 : A   B   C   D
38 : A   B   C   D

Passage 6

39 : A   B   C   D
40 : A   B   C   D
41 : A   B   C   D
42 : A   B   C   D
43 : A   B   C   D

Independent questions

44 : A   B   C   D
45 : A   B   C   D
46 : A   B   C   D
47 : A   B   C   D

Passage 7

48 : A   B   C   D
49 : A   B   C   D
50:   A   B   C   D
51 : A   B   C   D
52 : A   B   C   D

Independent questions

53 : A   B   C   D
54 : A   B   C   D
55 : A   B   C   D
56 : A   B   C   D
57 : A   B   C   D
58 : A   B   C   D
59 : A   B   C   D

This page is intentionally left blank

Passage 1
(Questions 1–7)

Researchers are studying a eukaryotic organism that has a highly active mechanism for DNA replication, transcription and translation. The organism has both a haploid and a diploid state. In the haploid state, only one copy of each chromosome complement is present. In the diploid state, two copies of each chromosome complement, usually homozygous for most traits, are present. To investigate this organism, two mutations were induced and the resulting cell lines were labeled as mutants #1 and #2, and these mutants demonstrated unique phenotypes.

To elucidate the events of transcription and translation, a wild-type variant of the organism was exposed to standard mutagens, including intercalating agents such as ethidium bromide, which resulted in the creation of the two mutants. The researchers analyzed the exact sequence of events leading from DNA to RNA, and from RNA to protein products. Figure 1 illustrates this sequence of the wild-type and the sequences of the two mutant organisms.

Experiment A:

Mutant #1 was plated onto a Petri dish and grown with a nutrient broth. The mutant #1 organism showed growth and reproduction patterns similar to the wild type, including the generation of a haploid stage. Mutant #2 was similarly treated, and this organism also displayed stable growth and reproductive patterns.

Experiment B:

Mutants #1 and #2 were exposed to a virus to which the wild type is resistant. Mutant #1 was also found to be resistant, while the virus infected and destroyed mutant #2. The haploid form of mutant #2 was then fused with the haploid form of the wild type. The diploid fused organisms were protected against virus infection. The diploid forms of mutant #2 were not protected against virus infection.

1. Mutant #2 codon aberrations eventually result in a nonfunctioning and nonproductive polypeptide due to:

   A. termination of translation
   B. aberration of centriole reproduction
   C. initiation of DNA replication
   D. repression of RNA replication

2. If mutants #1 and #2 are separated within individual Petri dishes and subsequent mutations arise where the two mutant strains are no longer able to reproduce sexually with each other, the process can be described as:

   A. population control resulting from genetic variation
   B. population control resulting from random mating
   C. niche variability resulting in phenotypic variation
   D. speciation arising from geographic isolation

3. Consistent with Darwin's views about evolution, mutant #2 represents a less "fit" organism than mutant #1, because:

   A. mutant #1 and #2 produce protein products of variable length
   B. mutant #1 is immune against a naturally-occurring virus, while mutant #2 is susceptible
   C. mutant #1 is endogenous in humans, while mutant #2 is found in amphibians
   D. mutant #1 replicates at a different rate than mutant #2

4. In Experiment B, how many copies of mutant #2 were present in the surviving diploid?

A. 0
B. 1
C. 2
D. 4

5. From Figure 1, a biomedical researcher concluded that a single point mutation in DNA altered the size of the translated product. What observation supports this conclusion?

A. valine is encoded by two different codons
B. mutant #2 translated a longer polypeptide than mutant #1
C. DNA point mutations created a stop codon which terminated the growing polypeptide
D. point mutations within the DNA increased the length of the RNA molecule

6. In labeling the RNA in mutants #1 and #2, which of the following labeled radioactive molecules would be most useful to label the RNA?

A. thymine
B. uracil
C. D-glucose
D. phosphate

7. In Figure 1, the mutation in mutant #2 is caused by a defect in:

A. RNA transcription
B. protein translation
C. DNA replication
D. post-translational modification

This page is intentionally left blank

Passage 2
(Questions 8–13)

Phenols are compounds containing a hydroxyl group attached to a benzene ring. Derivatives of phenols, such as naphthols (II) and phenanthrols (III), have chemical properties similar to many substituted phenols. Like other alcohols, phenols have higher boiling points than hydrocarbons of similar molecular weight. Like carboxylic acids, phenols are more acidic than their alcohol counterparts. Phenols are highly reactive and undergo several reactions because of the hydroxyl groups and the presence of the benzene ring. Several chemical tests distinguish phenols from alcohols and from carboxylic acids.

Thymol (IUPAC name: 2-isopropyl-5-methylphenol) is a phenol naturally occurring from thyme oil and can also be synthesized from *m*-cresol in Reaction A. Reaction B illustrates how thymol can be converted into menthol, another naturally-occurring organic compound.

8. Which of the following is the sequence of decreasing acidity among the four compounds below?

I II III IV

A. IV, I, III, II
B. IV, III, II, I
C. II, I, IV, III
D. IV, II, III, I

9. Which of the following structures corresponds to Compound Y ($C_{10}H_{14}O$), which dissolves in aqueous sodium hydroxide but is insoluble in aqueous sodium bicarbonate. The proton nuclear magnetic resonance (NMR) spectrum of Compound Y is as follows:

chemical shift	integration #	spin-spin splitting
δ 1.4	(9H)	singlet
δ 4.9	(IH)	singlet
δ 7.3	(4H)	multiplet

10. Which of the following is the product of the reaction of phenol with dilute nitric acid?

A.

B.

C.

D.

11. Comparing the pK_a values for cyclohexanol ($pK_a = 16$) to phenol ($pK_a = 9.95$), phenol is more acidic than cyclohexanol. Which of the following explains the greater acidity of phenol compared to cyclohexanol?

I.   phenoxide delocalizes the negative charge on the oxygen atom over the benzene ring

II. phenol is capable of strong hydrogen bonding, which increases the ability of phenol to disassociate a proton, making it more acidic than cyclohexanol

III. phenoxide, the conjugate base of phenol, is stabilized by resonance more than for cyclohexanol

   A. I only   **B.** I and II only   **C.** I and III only   **D.** I, II and III

12. Reaction A is an example of:

   A. free radical substitution   **C.** electrophilic aromatic substitution
   B. electrophilic addition   **D.** nucleophilic aromatic substitution

13. Which chemical test could distinguish between the two following compounds?

   A. compound I is soluble in $NaHCO_3$
   B. compound I is soluble in NaOH
   C. compound II decolorizes a solution of Br_2
   D. compound II is soluble in $NaHCO_3$

> Questions 14 through 17 are not based on any
> descriptive passage and are independent of each other

14. In thin layer chromatography (TLC), a sheet of absorbent paper is partially immersed in a non-polar solvent. The solvent rises through the absorbent paper through capillary action. Which of the following compounds demonstrates the greatest migration when placed on the absorbent paper near the bottom and the solvent is allowed to pass?

    A. $CH_3CH_2CH_3$ **B.** CH_3Cl **C.** NH_3 **D.** R-COOH

15. During meiosis, in which phase of oogenesis development does anaphase I occur?

    A. 1
    B. 2
    C. 3
    D. 4

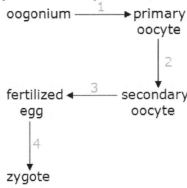

16. Why do acetoacetate and other ketone bodies form during low carbohydrate availability?

    A. Because acetyl-CoA is converted into glucose
    B. Because acetoacetate spontaneously decarboxylates into acetone
    C. Because citrate cannot be formed due to low level of oxaloacetate that binds to acetyl-CoA
    D. Because acetyl-CoA cannot combine with citrate because of a low level of citrate

17. In DiGeorge syndrome, caused by a deletion of a large portion of chromosome 22, there is defective embryonic development of the parathyroid glands. A patient with this syndrome would be expected to have:

    A. low serum calcium   **C.** low serum thyroid hormone
    B. high serum calcium   **D.** high serum PTH

Passage 3
(Questions 18–23)

The parathyroid glands are part of the endocrine system. The parathyroid glands are two small endocrine glands that detect low plasma calcium levels and respond by releasing parathyroid hormone (i.e. PTH). The parathyroid hormone affects bone, kidneys and intestine to regulate serum calcium levels.

PTH acts on the bone to release stored calcium into the bloodstream. Osteoclasts dissolve bone matrix by secreting acid and collagenase onto the bone surface to release calcium. In the presence of PTH and $1,25\text{-}(OH)_2 D$, the maturation of osteoclasts is accelerated, resulting in increased resorption and release of calcium from the bone mineral compartment.

In the kidneys, PTH acts within the nephron to increase calcium reabsorption in the thick ascending loop of Henle and in the distal tubule. These modifications to mechanisms within the kidneys recapture some calcium that was filtered by the kidney and reduce the amount of calcium excreted in the urine. PTH also upregulates the conversion of 25-hydroxyvitamin D (25-OH D) to 1,25-dihydroxyvitamin D ($1,25\text{-}OH_2 D$) in renal cells.

Additionally, Vitamin D stimulates calcium absorption within the intestine. $1,25$-dihydroxyvitamin D is the active form of vitamin D, which promotes the active transport of calcium through the mircovilli of intestinal epithelium. Thus, PTH works indirectly in the intestines, via $1,25\text{-}(OH)_2 D$ to maximize dietary calcium absorption.

18. Although converted from 25-hydroxyvitamin D to $1,25\text{-}(OH)_2 D$ in the kidneys, the sites of action of $1,25\text{-}(OH)_2 D$ include cells within the intestine and within peripheral bone. Based on this mode of action, $1,25\text{-}(OH)_2 D$ may be classified as:

   A. hormone
   B. neuropeptide
   C. coenzyme
   D. enzyme

19. Hormone secretion is often regulated by negative feedback inhibition. Which of the following signals is used to decrease PTH secretion for homeostasis?

   A. high serum PTH
   B. low bone density
   C. high serum calcium
   D. high serum phosphate

20. The precursor to 1,25-(OH)$_2$ D is 7-dehydrocholesterol. Cholesterol derivatives are also precursors of:

    A. epinephrine and norepinephrine
    B. cortisol and aldosterone
    C. adenine and guanine
    D. prolactin and oxytocin

21. Homeostasis regulation of serum calcium is necessary for the proper function of nervous system. Low blood Ca^{2+} levels may result in numbness and tingling in the hands and feet. Insufficient serum calcium would have the greatest effect on which of the following neuronal structures?

    A. axon
    B. dendrites
    C. axon terminal
    D. axon hillock

22. PTH most likely acts on target cells by:

    A. increasing Na$^+$ influx into the cell
    B. decreasing Na$^+$ influx into the cell
    C. increasing synthesis of the secondary messenger cAMP
    D. increasing 1,25-(OH)$_2$D transcription

23. McCune-Albright syndrome is a hereditary disease of precocious puberty and results in low serum calcium levels, despite elevated serum PTH levels. Which of the following is the most likely basis of the disorder?

    A. G$_s$-protein deficiency, which couples cAMP to the PTH receptor
    B. defective secretion of digestive enzymes by osteoclast
    C. absence of a nuclear receptor, which couples PTH to the parathyroid transcription factor
    D. osteoblast autostimulation

Passage 4
(Questions 24–28)

The kidneys regulate hydrogen ion (H^+) concentration in extracellular fluid primarily by controlling the concentration of bicarbonate ion (HCO_3^-). The process begins inside the epithelial cells of the proximal tubule, where the enzyme carbonic anhydrase catalyzes the formation of carbonic acid (H_2CO_3) from CO_2 and H_2O. The H_2CO_3 then dissociates into HCO_3^- and H^+. The HCO_3^- enters the extracellular fluid, while the H^+ is secreted into the tubule lumen via a Na^+/H^+ counter-transport mechanism that uses the Na^+ gradient established by the Na^+/K^+ pump.

Since the renal tubule is not very permeable to the HCO_3^- filtered into the glomerular filtrate, the reabsorption of HCO_3^- from the lumen into the tubular cells occurs indirectly. Carbonic anhydrase promotes the combination of HCO_3^- with the secreted H^+ to form H_2CO_3. The H_2CO_3 then dissociates into CO_2 and H_2O. The H_2O remains in the lumen while the CO_2 enters the tubular cells.

From Figure 1, inside the cells, every H^+ secreted into the lumen is countered by an HCO_3^- entering the extracellular fluid. Thus, the mechanism by which the kidneys regulate body fluid pH is by the titration of H^+ with HCO_3^-.

Figure 1.

The drug Diamox (i.e., acetazolamide) is a potent carbonic anhydrase inhibitor. Acetazolamide is available as a generic drug and is used as a diuretic, because it increases the rate of urine formation and thereby increases the excretion of water and other solutes from the body. Diuretics can be used to maintain adequate urine output or excrete excess fluid.

24. Spironolactone (an adrenocorticosteroid) is a competitive aldosterone antagonist and functions as a diuretic. Administering this drug to a patient would most likely result in:

    A. Na^+ plasma concentration increase and blood volume increase
    B. Na^+ plasma concentration increase and blood volume decrease
    C. Na^+ plasma concentration decrease and blood volume increase
    D. Na^+ plasma concentration decrease and blood volume decrease

25. Excretion of acidic urine by a patient results from:

    A. more H^+ being transported into the glomerular filtrate than HCO_3^- secreted into the tubular lumen
    B. more H^+ being secreted into the tubular lumen than HCO_3^- transported into the glomerular filtrate
    C. more HCO_3^- being secreted into the tubular lumen than H^+ transported into the glomerular filtrate
    D. more HCO_3^- being transported into the glomerular filtrate than H^+ secreted into the tubular lumen

26. What mechanism described in the passage is used to transport Na^+ into the tubular cells?

    A. endocytosis   **C.** facilitated diffusion
    B. exocytosis   **D.** active transport

27. Acetazolamide administration increases a patient's excretion of:

    I. H_2O II. H^+ III. HCO_3^- IV. Na^+

    A. III only   **C.** I, III and IV only
    B. III and IV only   **D.** I, II, III and IV

28. Which of the following hormones would affect the patient's blood volume to oppose the effect of administering acetazolamide?

    A. ADH
    B. somatostatin
    C. LH
    D. calcitonin

Questions 29 through 33 are not based on any
descriptive passage and are independent of each other

29. Which of the following functions describes the purpose of the lysosome membrane?

A. Creating a basic environment for hydrolytic enzymes of the lysosome within the cytoplasm
B. Creating an acidic environment for hydrolytic enzymes of the lysosome within the cytoplasm
C. Serving as an alternative site for peptide bond formation during protein synthesis
D. Being a continuation of the nuclear envelope

30. How many σ bonds and π bonds are there in ethene?

A. 1 σ and 2 π   C. 6 σ and 2 π
B. 1 σ and 5 π   D. 5 σ and 1 π

31. Why is PCC a better oxidant for the conversion of an alcohol into an aldehyde compared to other oxidizing agents?

A. PCC is a less powerful oxidant that doesn't oxidize an alcohol to a carboxylic acid
B. PCC is a less powerful oxidant that does not oxidize an aldehyde to an alcohol
C. PCC is a more powerful oxidant that oxidizes an alcohol to a carboxylic acid
D. PCC is a more powerful oxidant that oxidizes a carboxylic acid to an alcohol

32. Which of the following describes the reaction of acyl-CoA to enoyl-CoA conversion?

A. oxidation   C. hydrogenation
B. reduction   D. hydrolysis

33. For breeding, salmon travel from saltwater to freshwater. The salmon maintain solute balance by reversing their osmoregulatory mechanism when entering a different solute environment. Failure to reverse this mechanism results in:

A. No change, because movement between saltwater and freshwater does not affect osmotic pressure in salmon
B. Metabolic activity increase due to an increase in enzyme concentration
C. Death, because water influx causes cell lysis
D. Death, because cells become too concentrated for normal metabolism

This page is intentionally left blank

Passage 5
(Questions 34–38)

Simple acyclic alcohols are an important class of alcohols. Their general formula is $C_nH_{2n+1}OH$. An example of simple acyclic alcohols is ethanol (C_2H_5OH) – the type of alcohol found in alcoholic beverages.

The terpenoids (aka isoprenoids) are a large and diverse class of naturally occurring organic chemicals derived from five-carbon isoprene units. Plant terpenoids are commonly used for their aromatic qualities and play a role in traditional herbal remedies. They are also being studied for antibacterial, antineoplastic (i.e. a chemotherapeutic property that stops abnormal proliferation of cells) and other pharmaceutical applications. Terpenoids contribute to the scent of eucalyptus; menthol and camphor are well-known terpenoids.

Citronellol is an acyclic alcohol and natural acyclic monoterpenoid that is found in many plant oils, including (-)-citronellol in geraniums and rose. It is used in synthesis of perfumes, insect repellants and moth repellants for fabrics. Pulegone, a clear colorless oily liquid, is a related molecule found in plant oils and has a camphor and peppermint aroma.

Below is the synthesis of pulegone from citronellol.

Figure 1. Synthesis of pulegone from citronellol

34. Pulegone has the presence of the following functional groups:

A. aldehydes and an isopropyl alkene
B. ketone and isobutyl alkene
C. ketone and isopropyl alkene
D. hydroxyl and tert-butyl alkene

35. What is the absolute configuration of pulegone?

    A. *R*
    B. *S*
    C. *cis*
    D. *trans*

36. Which of the following structures is the most likely product when HBr is added to citronellol?

37. PCC promotes conversion of citrinellol to which molecule?

    A. citrinellone
    B. citrinellal
    C. citric acid
    D. no reaction

38. What is the relationship between citronellol and citronellal?

    A. enantiomers
    B. diastereomers
    C. geometric isomers
    D. none of the above

Passage 6
(Questions 39–43)

Beta-oxidation is the process when fatty acids are broken down in the mitochondria. Before fatty acids are oxidized, they are covalently binded to coenzyme A (CoA) on the mitochondrion's outer membrane. The sulfur atom of CoA attacks the carbonyl carbon of the fatty acid and H_2O dissociates. The hydrolysis of two high-energy phosphate bonds drives this reaction, producing acyl-CoA.

Special transport molecules shuttle the acyl-CoA across the inner membrane and into the mitochondria matrix. Further fatty acids beta-oxidation involves four recurring steps, whereby acyl-CoA is broken down by the sequential removal of two-carbon units in each cycle to form acetyl-CoA. Acetyl-CoA is the initial molecule that enters the Krebs cycle.

The beta-carbon of the fatty acyl-CoA is oxidized to a carbonyl that is attacked by the lone pair of electrons on the sulfur atom of another CoA. The CoA substrate molecule and the bound acetyl group dissociate. The acetyl-CoA, produced from fatty acid oxidation, enters the Krebs cycle and is further oxidized into CO_2. The Krebs cycle yields 3 NADH + 1 $FADH_2$ + 1 GTP, which is converted into ATP.

Figure 1. Beta-oxidation cycle

39. For an 18-carbon fatty acid to be completely oxidized, how many turns of the beta-oxidation cycle must be completed?

A. 1
B. 8
C. 9
D. 18

40. How many ATP would be produced if a 12-carbon fatty acid was completely oxidized to CO_2 and H_2O?

A. 5ATP
B. 51 ATP
C. 78 ATP
D. 80 ATP

41. Which of the following enzymes is involved in the conversion of acyl-CoA to enoyl-CoA?

A. reductase
B. ketothiolase
C. isomerase
D. dehydrogenase

42. The equation for one turn of the fatty acid degradation cycle is:

A. C_n-acyl-CoA + H_2O → acetyl-CoA
B. C_n-acyl-CoA → C_{n-2}-acyl-CoA + acetyl-CoA
C. C_n-acyl-CoA + NAD^+ + FAD + H_2O → C_{n-2}-acyl-CoA + NADH + $FADH_2$ + acetyl-CoA
D. C_n-acyl-CoA + NAD^+ + FAD + H_2O + CoA → C_{n-2}-acyl-CoA + NADH + $FADH_2$ + acetyl-CoA + H^+

43. Which of the following traits are shared by the reactions of beta-oxidation and fatty acid biosynthesis?

A. both biochemical pathways use or produce NADH
B. both biochemical pathways use or produce acetyl alcohol
C. both biochemical pathways occur in the mitochondrial matrix
D. both biochemical pathways use the same enzymes

Questions 44 through 47 are not based on any
descriptive passage and are independent of each other

44. The deletion of nucleotides occurs during DNA replication. For mutations involving the addition or deletion of three base pairs, the protein encoded for by the mutated gene is relatively normal. A reasonable explanation for this observation is that:

    A. cellular function is not affected by most DNA mutations
    B. the size of amino acid codons often varies
    C. the original reading frame is retained after removal of three nucleotide multiples
    D. non-mutated mRNA are translated successfully by ribosome one-third of the time

45. Which sequence is the correct cycle of spermatogenesis?

    A. spermatids → spermatogonia → spermatocytes → spermatozoa
    B. spermatids → spermatogonia → spermatozoa → spermatocytes
    C. spermatogonia → spermatids → spermatozoa → spermatocytes
    D. spermatogonia → spermatocytes → spermatids → spermatozoa

46. What is the IUPAC name for the molecule shown below?

    A. (S)-4,5 dimethyl-(Z)-2-hexene
    B. (S)-4,5 dimethyl-(E)-2-hexene
    C. (R)-4,5 dimethyl-(Z)-2-hexene
    D. (R)-4,5 dimethyl-(E)-2-hexene

47. Which of the following is the site for collagen polypeptide synthesis?

    A. lysosome
    B. mitochondrion
    C. smooth endoplasmic reticulum
    D. rough endoplasmic reticulum

This page is intentionally left blank

Passage 7
(Questions 48–52)

With the advent of recombinant biology, *gene therapy* is a technique used to insert foreign genes into cells. Researchers are now able to introduce DNA into cells to treat genetic defects. One technique for gene therapy uses a small bore pipette to microinject a gene into a target cell. This technique worked in many cases but is very time consuming and requires high technical skills. Another method is electroporation, whereby cells undergo electric shock to increase the permeability of the plasma membrane and DNA can enter cells. However, this procedure can destroy the cell. Alternative and highly effective gene therapy technique is when foreign genes are introduced into cells via a viral vector, where foreign genes enter the cell through the mechanism of normal viral infection.

Viral genomes consist of DNA or RNA, and the nucleic acid can be either single- or double-stranded. Simple RNA viruses use a mechanism where their genome is directly translated into mRNA (by the RNA *replicase* enzyme) without integration into host's DNA. On the other hand, when a DNA virus enters a cell, its DNA may be inserted into the host's genome via the lysogenic cycle. After integration into the host's genome, viral genes can be transcribed into mRNA and, subsequently, into proteins.

Retroviruses contain an RNA (either single- or double-stranded) genome and viral genome is transcribed into DNA by the enzyme *reverse transcriptase*. The newly synthesized DNA is then inserted into the host's genome, and viral genes can then be expressed to synthesize viral RNA and proteins. Retroviruses consist of a protein core that contains viral RNA and reverse transcriptase, and are surrounded by an outer protein envelope. The RNA of a retrovirus is made up of three coding regions – *gag, pol* and *env* – which encode for core proteins, reverse transcriptase and coat proteins, respectively.

Retroviruses present a more promising gene therapy technology than simple RNA viruses or DNA viruses. A retrovirus, carrying a specific gene, enters a target cell by receptor-mediated endocytosis. Its RNA gets transcribed into DNA, which then randomly integrates into the host's DNA, forming a provirus. The provirus would be copied along with the chromosomal DNA during the S phase of cell division. Retroviral vectors are constructed in a way that the therapeutic gene replaces *gag* or *env* coding region.

However, there are some practical problems associated with retroviral vector gene therapy because of the risk of random integration leading to the activation of *oncogenes*. Oncogenes arise when newly integrated fragments of nucleic acids stimulate the cell to divide and increase protein production beyond desirable levels. A major limitation is that due to the randomness of the virus vector integration into the host's genome, gene expression of desired genes can't be controlled. Future research is underway to target integration of the virus vector into specific regions of the host's genome; similar to transposons in maze described by Nobel laureate Barbara McClintock. Additionally, integration can take place only in the cells that can divide.

48. To successfully integrate a retrovirus into the cell's genome, which of the following events must take place?

A. New virions must be produced

B. The retroviral proteins encoded by *gag*, *pol* and *env* must be translated after integration

C. Reverse transcriptase must translate the retroviral genome

D. The retroviral protein envelope must bind to the cell's surface receptors

49. All of these cells would be good targets for retroviral gene therapy, EXCEPT:

A. hepatocytes

B. neuronal cells

C. bone marrow cells

D. epidermal cells

50. From in vitro gene therapy experiments, the retroviral delivery system is preferred over physical techniques (i.e. microinjection or electroporation) of introducing therapeutic genes into cells. Which of the following statements is the most likely explanation for this?

A. Retroviral gene delivery allows more control over the site of integration

B. Retroviral gene delivery results in more cells that integrate the new gene successfully

C. Retroviral gene delivery is less damaging to the cells and less labor-intensive

D. Retroviral gene delivery permits the insertion of therapeutic genes into all cell types

51. Simple RNA viruses are not suitable for gene therapy vectors because:

A. a therapeutic gene introduced within a viral RNA cannot be replicated

B. the RNA genome becomes unstable due to an insertion of a therapeutic gene

C. their genome size is not sufficient to carry a therapeutic gene

D. only specific cell types can be infected by simple RNA viruses

52. Following an integration of a therapeutic gene into a cell's DNA, the retroviral DNA:

A. causes nondisjunction to correct the genetic defect

B. is deemed "foreign" by the host's immune system and degraded

C. replicates and produces infectious virions

D. remains in the cell in a noninfectious form

> Questions 53 through 59 are not based on any
> descriptive passage and are independent of each other

53. Incomplete proteins lack one or more:

    A. essential amino acids   **C.** sulfur-containing amino acids
    B. nonpolar amino acids   **D.** polar amino acids

54. Which statement regarding the number of initiation and STOP codons is correct?

    A. There are multiple initiation codons, but a single STOP codon
    B. There are two STOP codons and four initiation codons
    C. There is a single STOP codon and single initiation codon
    D. There are multiple STOP codons, but a single initiation codon

55. How many carbon atoms are in a molecule of stearic acid?

    A. 12   **B.** 14   **C.** 16   **D.** 18

56. Fatty acids that mammals must obtain from nutrition are:

    A. essential   **C.** dietary
    B. saturated   **D.** esters

57. What type of amino acid is phenylalanine?

    A. basic   **C.** polar
    B. acidic   **D.** hydrophobic aromatic

58. The simplest lipids that can also be a part of or a source of many complex lipids are:

    A. terpenes   **C.** waxes
    B. sterols   **D.** triglycerols

59. What type of macromolecule is a saccharide?

    A. protein   **C.** carbohydrate
    B. nucleic acid   **D.** lipid

Biological & Biochemical Foundations of Living Systems

Practice Test #3

59 questions

For explanatory answers see pgs. 197-234

For CBT online format of this test that provides Diagnostics Report with performance statistics, difficulty rating of each question and other features visit:

www.MasterMCAT.com

Most questions in the Biological Sciences test are organized into groups, each containing a descriptive passage. After studying the passage select the one best answer to each question in the group. Some questions are not based on a descriptive passage and are also independent of each other. If you are not certain of an answer, eliminate the alternatives you know to be incorrect and then select an answer from the remaining alternatives. Indicate your selected answer by marking the corresponding answer on your answer sheet. A periodic table is provided for your use. You may consult it whenever you wish.

Periodic Table of the Elements

1 H 1.0																	2 He 4.0
3 Li 6.9	4 Be 9.0											5 B 10.8	6 C 12.0	7 N 14.0	8 O 16.0	9 F 19.0	10 Ne 20.2
11 Na 23.0	12 Mg 24.3											13 Al 27.0	14 Si 28.1	15 P 31.0	16 S 32.1	17 Cl 35.5	18 Ar 39.9
19 K 39.1	20 Ca 40.1	21 Sc 45.0	22 Ti 47.9	23 V 50.9	24 Cr 52.0	25 Mn 54.9	26 Fe 55.8	27 Co 58.9	28 Ni 58.7	29 Cu 63.5	30 Zn 65.4	31 Ga 69.7	32 Ge 72.6	33 As 74.9	34 Se 79.0	35 Br 79.9	36 Kr 83.8
37 Rb 85.5	38 Sr 87.6	39 Y 88.9	40 Zr 91.2	41 Nb 92.9	42 Mo 95.9	43 Tc (98)	44 Ru 101.1	45 Rh 102.9	46 Pd 106.4	47 Ag 107.9	48 Cd 112.4	49 In 114.8	50 Sn 118.7	51 Sb 121.8	52 Te 127.6	53 I 126.9	54 Xe 131.3
55 Cs 132.9	56 Ba 137.3	57 La* 138.9	72 Hf 178.5	73 Ta 180.9	74 W 183.9	75 Re 186.2	76 Os 190.2	77 Ir 192.2	78 Pt 195.1	79 Au 197.0	80 Hg 200.6	81 Tl 204.4	82 Pb 207.2	83 Bi 209.0	84 Po (209)	85 At (210)	86 Rn (222)
87 Fr (223)	88 Ra (226)	89 Ac† (227)	104 Rf (261)	105 Db (262)	106 Sg (266)	107 Bh (264)	108 Hs (277)	109 Mt (268)	110 Ds (281)	111 Uuu (272)	112 Uub (285)		114 Uuq (289)		116 Uuh (289)		

	58 Ce 140.1	59 Pr 140.9	60 Nd 144.2	61 Pm (145)	62 Sm 150.4	63 Eu 152.0	64 Gd 157.3	65 Tb 158.9	66 Dy 162.5	67 Ho 164.9	68 Er 167.3	69 Tm 168.9	70 Yb 173.0	71 Lu 175.0
†	90 Th 232.0	91 Pa (231)	92 U 238.0	93 Np (237)	94 Pu (244)	95 Am (243)	96 Cm (247)	97 Bk (247)	98 Cf (251)	99 Es (252)	100 Fm (257)	101 Md (258)	102 No (259)	103 Lr (260)

Biological & Biochemical Foundations of Living Systems
MCAT® Practice Test #3 – Answer Sheet

Passage 1

1 : A   B   C   D
2 : A   B   C   D
3 : A   B   C   D
4 : A   B   C   D
5 : A   B   C   D
6 : A   B   C   D

Passage 2

7 : A   B   C   D
8 : A   B   C   D
9 : A   B   C   D
10 : A   B   C   D
11 : A   B   C   D

Independent questions

12 : A   B   C   D
13 : A   B   C   D
14 : A   B   C   D
15 : A   B   C   D

Passage 3

16 : A   B   C   D
17 : A   B   C   D
18 : A   B   C   D
19 : A   B   C   D
20 : A   B   C   D
21 : A   B   C   D
22 : A   B   C   D

Passage 4

23 : A   B   C   D
24 : A   B   C   D
25 : A   B   C   D
26 : A   B   C   D
27 : A   B   C   D
28 : A   B   C   D

Independent questions

29 : A   B   C   D
30 : A   B   C   D
31 : A   B   C   D
32 : A   B   C   D
33 : A   B   C   D

Passage 5

34 : A   B   C   D
35 : A   B   C   D
36 : A   B   C   D
37 : A   B   C   D
38 : A   B   C   D
39 : A   B   C   D

Passage 6

40 : A   B   C   D
41 : A   B   C   D
42 : A   B   C   D
43 : A   B   C   D

Independent questions

44 : A   B   C   D
45 : A   B   C   D
46 : A   B   C   D
47 : A   B   C   D

Passage 7

48 : A   B   C   D
49 : A   B   C   D
50 : A   B   C   D
51 : A   B   C   D
52 : A   B   C   D

Independent questions

53 : A   B   C   D
54 : A   B   C   D
55 : A   B   C   D
56 : A   B   C   D
57 : A   B   C   D
58 : A   B   C   D
59 : A   B   C   D

This page is intentionally left blank

Passage 1
(Questions 1–6)

Aerobic respiration is the major process that provides cellular energy for oxygen requiring organisms. During cellular respiration, glucose is metabolized to generate chemical energy in the form of ATP:

$$C_6H_{12}O_6 + 6O_2 \rightarrow 6CO_2 + 6H_2O + 36 \text{ ATP}$$

Mitochondrion is the biochemical machinery within the cell utilized for cellular respiration. Mitochondria are present in the cytoplasm of most eukaryotic cells. The number of mitochondria per cell varies depending on tissue type and individual cell function.

Mitochondria have their own genome independent from the cell's genetic material. However, mitochondrial replication depends upon nuclear DNA to encode essential proteins required for replication of mitochondria. Mitochondria replicate randomly and independently of cell cycle.

The mitochondrial separate genome and the ribosomes of the protein synthesizing machinery became the foundation for the endosymbiotic theory. Endosymbiotic theory proposes that mitochondria originated as a separate prokaryotic organism that was engulfed by a larger anaerobic eukaryotic cell millions of years ago. The two cells formed a symbiotic relationship and eventually became dependent on each other. The eukaryotic cell sustained the bacterium, while the bacterium provided additional energy for the cell. Gradually, the two cells evolved into the present-day eukaryotic cell, with the mitochondrion retaining some of its own DNA. Mitochondrial DNA is inherited in a non-Mendelian fashion, because mitochondria, like other organelles, are inherited from the maternal gamete that supplies the cytoplasm to the fertilized egg. The study of individual mitochondria is used to investigate evolutionary relationships among different organisms.

1. Which of the following statements distinguishes the mitochondrial genome from the nuclear genome?

    A. Most mitochondrial DNA nucleotides encode for protein
    B. Specific mitochondrial DNA mutations are lethal
    C. Mitochondrial DNA is a double helix structure
    D. Some mitochondrial genes encode for tRNA

2. In which phase(s) of the eukaryotic cell cycle does mitochondrial DNA replicate?

I. G_1　　II. S　　III. G_2　　IV. M

A. I only
B. II only

C. II and IV only
D. I, II, III and IV

3. A wild-type strain of cyanobacteria (algae) is crossed with the opposite mating type of a mutant strain of cyanobacteria. All mitochondrial functions of the mutant strain are lost because of deletions within the mitochondrial genome. All progeny also lack mitochondrial functions. From the passage, which of the following best explains this observation?

A. The presence in mitochondria of genetic material distinct from nuclear DNA
B. Recombination of mitochondrial DNA during organelle replication
C. Non-Mendelian inheritance of mitochondrial DNA
D. The endosymbiotic hypothesis

4. Four human cell cultures (colon cells, epidermal cells, erythrocytes and skeletal muscle cells) were grown in a radioactive adenine medium. After several days of growth, centrifugation was used to isolate the mitochondria. The radioactivity level of the mitochondria was measured by a liquid scintillation counter. Which of the following cell types would have the highest level of radioactivity?

A. colon cells
B. epidermal cells

C. erythrocytes
D. skeletal muscle cells

5. Which of the following statement does NOT support the endosymbiotic theory?

A. Mitochondrial DNA is circular and not enclosed by a nuclear membrane
B. Mitochondrial DNA encodes for its own ribosomal RNA
C. Mitochondrial ribosomes resemble eukaryotic ribosomes more than prokaryotic ribosomes
D. Many present day bacteria live within eukaryotic cells and digest nutrients within the hosts

6. Experimental data shows that mitochondrial DNA of humans mutates at a relatively low frequency. Due to mitochondria having an important role in the cell, these mutations most likely are:

A. nondisjunctions
B. point mutations

C. frameshift mutations
D. lethal mutations

Passage 2
(Questions 7–11)

Protons adjacent to a carbonyl functional group are referred to as α and are significantly more acidic than protons adjacent to carbon atoms within the hydrocarbon chain. The increased acidity characteristic for α hydrogens results from the electron withdrawing effect of the neighboring carbon-oxygen double bond. In addition, the resulting anion is stabilized by the resonance shown below:

A reaction of the enolate anion with an alkyl halide or carbonyl compound forms a carbon-carbon bond at the α position. Condensation of an enolate with an aldehyde or ketone forms an unstable alcohol, which is a reaction intermediate and not an isolated product. The intermediate spontaneously reacts, via dehydration, to form an α,β-unsaturated compound.

7. Which of the following ketones would NOT react with the strong base LDA?

8. Which of the following compounds would be the intermediate alcohol from the condensation reactions shown below?

A.

B.

C.

D.

9. What is the order of decreasing basicity for the following reagents?

I. $H_3C—C\equiv C^-Na^+$ IV.

II. $CH_3O^-Na^+$

III. $NaHCO_3$

N^-Li^+

A. IV > I > II > III
B. II > I > IV > III

C. IV > II > III > I
D. III > IV > I > II

10. Which carbonyl compound has the most acidic proton?

A.

B.

C.

EtO   OEt

D.

11. Which set of the following reactants would result in the formation of ethyl-2-hexanoate?

A. step 1: propanol, ethyl acetate and LDA; step 2: H^+
B. step 1: butanal, ethyl acetate and LDA; step 2: H^+
C. step 1: pentanal, ethyl acetate and LDA; step 2: H^+
D. step 1: hexanal, ethyl acetate and LDA; step 2: H^+

> Questions 12 through 15 are not based on any
> descriptive passage and are independent of each other

12. In the graph shown, the solid line represents the reaction profile A + B → C + D in the absence of a catalyst. Which dotted line best represents the reaction profile in the presence of a catalyst?

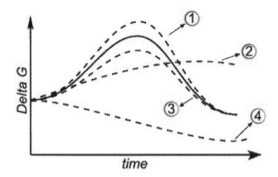

A. 1

B. 2

C. 3

D. 4

13. How would the beta-oxidation cycle be affected by depleting oxygen within the cell?

A. NADH and $FADH_2$ accumulate, and the cycle slows

B. Krebs cycle replaces beta-oxidation

C. CoA availability decreases

D. Beta-oxidation accelerates to satisfy energy needs

14. Which of the following is the correct ranking of C-O bond length from shortest to longest?

A. $CO < CO_2 < CO_3^{2-}$

B. $CO < CO_3^{2-} < CO_2$

C. $CO_3^{2-} < CO < CO_2$

D. $CO_3^{2-} < CO_2 < CO$

15. Which of the following properties distinguish fungal and animal cells from bacterial cells?

I. Presence of cell walls

II. Presence of ribosomes

III. Asexual reproduction

IV. Presence of membrane bound organelles

A. I and II only

B. III and IV only

C. IV only

D. I, II and IV only

This page is intentionally left blank

Passage 3
(Questions 16–22)

Viruses are classified into two major groups: DNA viruses and RNA viruses. Herpes simplex virus type 1 (HSV-1) infection, also known as Human Herpes Virus 1 (HHV-1) is almost universal among humans.

HSV-1 infects humans and hides in the nervous system via retrograde movement through afferent sensory nerve fibers. During latency period, the nervous system functions as a viral reservoir from which infection can recur, and this accounts for a virus's durability in a human body. Reactivation of the virus is usually expressed by watery blisters commonly known as cold sores or fever blisters. During this phase, viral replication and shedding occur as the most common way of herpes simplex transmission.

Following initial contact, production of the herpes virus growth mediators takes place. Viral growth factors bind axon terminal receptors and are related to tumor necrosis factors.

The structure of herpes viruses consists of a relatively large double-stranded, linear DNA genome encased within an icosahedral protein cage called the capsid, which is wrapped in a lipid bilayer called the envelope. The envelope is joined to the capsid by means of a tegument. This complete particle is known as the virion. Replication and assembly of the virus takes place via nuclear machinery.

HSV-1 infection is productive if the cell is permissive to the virus and allows viral replication and virion release. HSV-1 cell infection is often not productive due to a viral genome integration block that occurs upstream. However, stimulation of an infected cell will eliminate this block and allow for virion production. Abortive infection results when cells are non-permissive. In this case restrictive attacks occur when a few virion particles are produced. Viral production then ceases, but the genome integration persists.

Figure 1. Steps of HSV-1 infection

---

16. Where in the nervous system will the latent virus of herpes simplex be localized?

A. The neurotransmitter

B. The axon hillock

C. Lower motor neuron dendrites

D. The afferent nervous system ganglion

17. The spreading of HSV-1 virus occurs during shedding by direct contact with the lesion. Which of the following locations is the source for the virus to acquire its glycoprotein-covered envelope?

A. Nuclear membrane after transcription

B. Storage vacuoles during lysis

C. Outer cell wall during lysis

D. Rough ER during protein synthesis

18. Which infection type(s) result(s) in the integration of the viral genome into the host cell chromosome?

I.   restrictive   II. productive   III. abortive

A. I only   **B.** II only   **C.** I and II only   **D.** I, II and III

19. If the infectivity/particle ratio of picornaviruses is about 0.1%, what is the number of infectious particles present in a culture of 25,000 virions?

A. 5   **B.** 25   **C.** 250   **D.** 2500

20. Which of the following statements is NOT the cause of the abortive viral cycle?

A. Infected esophagus cells lack DNA replication machinery

B. Hepatitis C patients lack the majority of viral liver cell receptors

C. Host autoimmune antibodies bind to the viral antigen and prevent infection

D. Random mutations of influenza virus plasma membrane antigens causes genetic drift

21. Where will radioactive tegument dye be localized?

A. The protein-filled area between capsid and envelope

B. The protein-filled area between envelope and extracellular glycoprotein

C. The protein-filled area between DNA core and nucleosome

D. The protein-filled area between capsid and DNA core

22. From the information provided in the passage, which statement must be true for tumor necrosis factors (TNFs)?

A. TNFs are taken up by dendrites and transported toward the neuron cell body

B. TNFs are produced following a malignant cancerous spread through the basement membrane

C. TNF uptake and transport are inhibited, following an injury to the axon terminal

D. TNFs function with nerve growth factors to stimulate voltage gated Na^+ channels

Passage 4
(Questions 23–28)

Translation is a mechanism of protein synthesis. Proteins are synthesized on ribosomes that are either free in the cytoplasm or bound to the rough endoplasmic reticulum (rough ER). The *signal hypothesis* states that about 8 initial amino acids (known as a leader sequence) are joined initially to the growing polypeptide. In the absence of a leader sequence, the ribosomes remain free in the cytosol. If the leader sequence is present, translation of the nascent polypeptide pauses, and the ribosomes, along with the attached mRNA, migrate and attach to the ER.

Proteins that are used for transport to organelles, the plasma membrane, or to be secreted from the cell have *N-terminus signal peptide* of about 8 amino acids, which are responsible for the insertion of the nascent polypeptide through the membrane of the ER. After the leading end of the polypeptide is inserted into the lumen of the ER, the leader sequence (i.e. signal peptide) is cleaved by an enzyme within the ER lumen.

With the aid of chaperone proteins in the endoplasmic reticulum, proteins produced for the secretory pathway are folded into tertiary and quaternary structures. Those that are folded properly are packaged into transport vesicles that bud from the membrane of the ER via endocytosis. This packaging into a vesicle requires a region on the polypeptide that is recognized by a receptor of the Golgi membrane. The receptor-protein complex binds to the vesicle and then brings it to its destination, where it fuses to the cis face (closest to the ER) of the Golgi apparatus.

A pathway of vesicular transport from the Golgi involves lysosomal enzymes that carry a unique mannose-6-phosphate (M6P) marker that was added in the Golgi. The marker is recognized by specific M6P-receptor proteins that concentrate the polypeptide within a region of the Golgi membrane. These isolations of the M6P-receptor proteins facilitate their packaging into secretory vesicle, and after vesicle buds from the Golgi membrane, it moves to the lysosome and fuses with the lysosomal membrane. Because of the low pH of the lysosome, the M6P-receptor releases its bound protein. The lysosomal high H^+ concentration also produces the conformation change of the lysosomal enzymes.

23. The lumen of the endoplasmic reticulum most closely corresponds to the:

   A. cytoplasm
   B. ribosome
   C. intermembrane space of the mitochondria
   D. extracellular environment

24. If a protein destined to become a lysosomal enzyme was synthesized lacking a signal peptide, where in the cell is the enzyme targeted?

    A. Golgi apparatus
    B. lysosome
    C. cytosol
    D. plasma membrane

25. In a cell that failed to label proteins with the M6P marker, which of the following processes would be disrupted?

    A. Oxidative phosphorylation
    B. Intracellular digestion of macromolecules
    C. Lysosomal formation
    D. Protein synthesis

26. Within the cell, where is the M6P receptor transcribed?

    A. nucleolus
    B. smooth ER
    C. ribosome
    D. nucleus

27. Which of these enzymes functions in an acidic environment?

    A. pepsin
    B. endonuclease
    C. signal peptidase
    D. salivary amylase

28. Which of the following is required for the transport of proteins to the lysosome?

    A. Endocytosis
    B. Absence of a leader sequence
    C. Acidic pH of the Golgi
    D. Vesicular transport from the rough ER to the Golgi

> Questions 29 through 33 are not based on any
> descriptive passage and are independent of each other

29. Which of the following properties within a polypeptide chain determines the globular conformation of a protein?

    A. Number of individual amino acids
    B. Linear sequence of amino acids
    C. Relative concentration of amino acids
    D. Peptide optical activity measured in the polarimeter

30. In the Newman projection shown below, what does the circle represent?

    A. First carbon along the C_1–C_2 axis of the bond
    B. First carbon along the C_2–C_3 axis of the bond
    C. Second carbon along the C_2–C_3 axis of the bond
    D. Second carbon along the C_3–C_4 axis of the bond

31. What is the degree of unsaturation for a molecule with the molecular formula $C_{18}H_{20}$?

    A. 2
    B. 9
    C. 18
    D. 36

32. If distillation was used to separate hexanol from butanol, which product would distill first?

    A. hexanol
    B. butanol
    C. they distill simultaneously
    D. cannot be determined

33. All of the following are involved in energy production within the mitochondria, EXCEPT:

    A. glycolysis
    B. Krebs cycle
    C. electron transport chain
    D. oxidative phosphorylation

Passage 5
(Questions 34–39)

Acetylsalicylic acid (known by the brand name Aspirin) is one of the most commonly used drugs. It has analgesic (pain relieving), antipyretic (fever-reducing) and anti-inflammatory properties. The drug works by blocking the synthesis of *prostaglandins*. A prostaglandin is any member of a lipid compound group enzymatically derived from fatty acids. Every prostaglandin is a 20-carbon (including a 5-carbon ring) unsaturated carboxylic acid.

Prostaglandins are involved in a variety of physiological processes and have important functions in the body. They are mediators and have strong physiological effects (e.g. regulating the contraction and relaxation of smooth muscle). These *autocrine* or *paracrine* hormones (i.e. messenger molecules acting locally) are produced throughout the human body with target cells present in the immediate vicinity of the site of their secretion.

Acetylsalicylic acid is a white crystalline substance that is an acetyl derivative and is a weak acid with a melting point of 136 °C (277 °F) and a boiling point of 140 °C (284 °F). Acetylsalicylic acid can be produced through acetylation of salicylic acid by acetic anhydride in the presence of an acid catalyst, and is shown in the following reaction:

salicylic acid   acetic anhydride   acetylsalicylic acid   acetic acid

Reaction 1. Synthesis of acetylsalicylic acid

The acetylsalicylic acid synthesis is classified as an *esterification* reaction. Salicylic acid is treated with acetic anhydride, an acid derivative, which causes a chemical reaction that turns salicylic acid's hydroxyl group into an ester group (R-OH → R-OCOCH$_3$). This process yields acetylsalicylic acid and acetic acid, which for this reaction is considered a byproduct. Small amounts of sulfuric acid (and sometimes phosphoric acid) are almost always used as a catalyst.

Reaction 2. Mechanism of acetylsalicylic acid synthesis

In a college lab, this synthesis was carried out via the following procedure:

10 mL of acetic anhydride, 4 g of salicylic acid and 2 mL of concentrated sulfuric acid were mixed, and the resulting solution was heated for 10 minutes. Upon cooling the mix in an ice bath, a crude white product X precipitated. 100 mL of cold distilled water was added to complete the crystallization. By suction filtration, the product X was isolated and then washed with several aliquots of cold water.

Product X was dissolved in 50 mL of saturated sodium bicarbonate and the solution was filtered to remove an insoluble material. Then, 3 M of hydrochloric acid was added to the filtrate and product Y precipitated. It was collected by suction filtration and recrystallized in a mixture of petroleum ether (benzine) and common ether.

After analyzing product X, it showed the presence of acetylsalicylic acid, trace levels of salicylic acid and a contaminate of high molecular weight.

34. In the experiment described in the passage, salicylic acid primarily acts as an alcohol. What is the likely product when salicylic acid is reacted with an excess of methanol in the presence of sulfuric acid?

A. methyl salicylate **B.** benzoic acid **C.** phenol **D.** benzaldehyde

35. When acetylsalicylic acid is exposed to humid air, it acquires a vinegar-like smell, because:

    A. moist air reacts with residual salicylic acid to form citric acid

    B. it undergoes hydrolysis into salicylic and acetic acids

    C. it undergoes hydrolysis into salicylic acid and acetic anhydride

    D. it undergoes hydrolysis into acetic acid and citric acid

36. What is the purpose of dissolving product X in saturated $NaHCO_3$ in the experiment conducted in a college lab?

    A. To precipitate any side product contaminants as sodium salts

    B. To remove water from the reaction

    C. To form the water-soluble sodium salt of aspirin

    D. To neutralize any remaining salicylic acid

37. Phenyl salicylate is a molecule different from acetylsalicylic acid, but also possesses analgesic properties. Which of the following could be reacted with salicylic acid in the presence of sulfuric acid to produce phenyl salicylate?

    A. $PhCH_2OH$ **B.** $PhCO_2H$ **C.** PhOH   **D.** Benzene

38. For the synthesis of acetylsalicylic acid, what is the reaction mechanism?

    A. Nucleophilic addition   **C.** Nucleophilic aromatic substitution

    B. Nucleophilic acyl substitution   **D.** Electrophilic aromatic substitution

39. Which of the following is the likely structure of the high-molecular weight contaminant in product X?

Passage 6
(Questions 40–43)

A female at birth contains on average 300,000 follicles (with a range from 35,000 to 2.5 million). These follicles are immature (*primordial*), and each contains an immature primary oocyte. By the time of puberty, the number decreases to an average of 180,000 (the range is 25,000-1.5 million). Only about 400 follicles ever mature and produce an oocyte. During the process of *folliculogenesis* (i.e. maturation), a follicle develops from a *primary follicle* to a *secondary follicle*, then to a *vesicular* (Graafian) follicle. The whole process of folliculogenesis, from primordial to a preovulatory follicle, belongs to the stage of *ootidogenesis* of *oogenesis*. A secondary follicle contains a secondary oocyte with a reduced number of chromosomes. The release of a secondary oocyte from the ovary is called *ovulation*.

Unlike male *spermatogenesis*, which can last indefinitely, folliculogenesis ends when the remaining follicles in the ovaries are incapable of responding to the hormonal signals that previously prompted some follicles to mature. The depletion in follicle supply sets the beginning of menopause in women.

The ovarian cycle is controlled by the *gonadotropic hormones* released by the pituitary: follicle-stimulating hormone (FSH) and luteinizing-hormone (LH). Imbalances of these hormones may often cause infertility in females. For treatment of many female reproductive disorders, therapies that act similar to FSH and LH are often used successfully.

In a pharmaceutical laboratory, scientists test two of such drugs. Drug X binds to LH receptors, while drug Y binds to FSH receptors. The scientists separated 15 mice with fertility disorders into three experimental groups. The mice in Group I were administered drug Y, while the mice in Group II were administered drug X, and the mice in Group III received a placebo. After 1 month, the scientists performed an *ovariectomy* (i.e. surgical removal of ovaries in laboratory animals) and counted the number of developing follicles in the mice ovaries.

Note: a normal female mouse has on average 10-12 developing follicles at any point in the menstrual cycle.

Mice	Group I	Group II	Group III
#1	5	6	6
#2	11	4	5
#3	8	16	6
#4	11	11	4
#5	8	5	9

Table 1. Number of developing follicles per mouse

40. From the data, which of the following conditions most likely is the cause of infertility observed in mice #3 in all three groups, given that they all are affected by the same reproductive disorder?

    A. Inability of FSH to bind FSH receptors

    B. Benign tumor of the pituitary

    C. Elevated levels of LH

    D. Gene mutation LH hormone

41. Which of the following conditions is LEAST likely to result in female infertility?

    A. downregulation of LH receptors

    B. inflammation of oviducts

    C. release of multiple follicles

    D. FSH gene mutation

42. Overstimulation of follicular development during reproductive therapies increases the probability of multiple ovulations often resulting in multiple pregnancies. Which of the test subjects is the best example for this case?

    A. Mouse #2 of Group I

    B. Mouse #3 of Group II

    C. Mouse #4 of Group II

    D. Mouse #5 of Group III

43. Which treatment is most likely responsible for the number of maturing follicles observed in mouse #5 in Group III?

    A. Stimulation of the pituitary

    B. FSH receptor inhibition

    C. LH receptor stimulation

    D. No relationship to treatment

Questions 44 through 47 are not based on any
descriptive passage and are independent of each other

44. During DNA replication, individual dNTP nucleotides are joined by bond formation that releases phosphate. Which of the following describes the bond type between two dNTP nucleotides?

    A. covalent bond
    B. peptide bond
    C. van der Waals bond
    D. ionic bond

45. Which of the following is true about polar amino acids?

    A. Side chains project towards the exterior of the protein chain
    B. Side chains contain only hydrogen and carbon atoms
    C. Side chains are hydrophobic
    D. Side chains have neutral moieties

46. What is the net number of ATP produced per glucose in an obligate anaerobe?

    A. 2 ATP
    B. 4 ATP
    C. 36 ATP
    D. 38 ATP

47. All of the following hormones are released by the anterior pituitary gland, EXCEPT:

    A. luteinizing hormone
    B. prolactin
    C. thyroid stimulating hormone
    D. Vasopressin

This page is intentionally left blank

Passage 7
(Questions 48–52)

The genome of all cells of the human body, except germ line cells (i.e. gametes of either sperm or egg) and mature red blood cells (i.e. erythrocytes), contains identical DNA on chromosomes. Even with the same genetic material, cells of different tissue are diverse and specialized. This diversity of cellular function is due primarily to cell-specific variations in protein expression, which is regulated mostly at the transcriptional level. Different genes are expressed by transcriptional controls that determine cellular function and growth.

Specifically, gene transcription is controlled by upstream regulatory sequences that include regulatory genes and promoters. Regulators and promoters are controlled by extracellular signals (e.g. hormones) and intracellular signals (e.g. calcium or glucose). Regulators stimulate or inhibit gene transcription of a gene, while activated promoters only increase transcription.

A major cause of cancer is a cell's inability to regulate the cell cycle. Genetic mutations may occur at any level of the cell growth regulation system. There are two gene categories that, if mutated, often result in cancer: *oncogenes* and *tumor suppressor genes*. Oncogenes regulate cell growth and division and a mutation of the oncogene itself or its promoters can result in uncontrolled cell growth and division. Tumor suppressor genes regulate the cell cycle and may induce cell death when a cell has abnormal function. Mutations of tumor suppressor genes impair this regulatory ability and, without this control mechanism, the malfunctioning cells are able to proliferate.

When regulators or promoter sequences for genes involved in oncogenesis (also called carcinogenesis or tumorigenesis) are identified, it is possible to use drug treatments to regulate transcription of these genes. Certain drugs are effective at controlling the growth of cancerous cells, but have significant side effects that include diarrhea, significant hair loss, decreased immunity and kidney damage.

48. Given that oncogenes and tumor suppressor genes mutations usually arise during DNA replication, which phase of the cell cycle most likely is the phase for cancerous mutations?

A. S

C. cytokinesis

B. metaphase

D. G_0

49. What is the likely action mechanism of the cancer drugs mentioned in the passage?

A. Changes at the nucleotide level of an oncogene

B. Upregulation of the activator for an oncogene

C. Increased expression of a tumor suppressor gene

D. Blocking the promoter of a tumor suppressor gene from binding transcription factors

50. A new cancer drug with the brand name Colcrys acts to prevent cell division by inhibiting microtubule formation. In what stage of mitosis would this drug be most effective?

A. prophase

C. anaphase

B. metaphase

D. telophase

51. Along with its corresponding gene, a promoter sequence may be transcribed in one mRNA transcript. The mRNA sequence containing the transcribed promoter must be cleaved to make translation possible. Which cell region is most likely the site of this cleavage?

A. Golgi apparatus

C. cytoplasm

B. nucleus

D. nucleolus

52. A novel approach to cancer treatment employs modified tRNA molecules that carry inappropriate combinations of amino acids and anticodons. The tRNA molecule with the nucleotide triplets on one end is *charged* with mismatched amino acids on the other end. What is the likely mechanism of the anticancer action of these modified tRNA molecules?

A. Inhibition of cancer cells to translate protein

B. Inhibition of cancer cells to transcribe protein

C. Inhibition of ribosomes to bind to the mRNA

D. Change in the tertiary structure of the translated protein

> Questions 53 through 59 are not based on any
> descriptive passage and are independent of each other

53. How many carbon atoms are in a molecule of oleic acid?

    A. 14   **B.** 16   **C.** 18   **D.** 20

54. Amylose is different from amylopectin, because it:

    A. forms a helix with no branch points
    B. is highly branched, while amylopectin is linear
    C. has more glucose residues than amylopectin
    D. is composed of a different monomer than is amylopectin

55. What value is expressed by the slope in a Lineweaver-Burke plot?

    A. V_{max}/K_m **B.** K_m/V_{max} **C.** K_m **D.** $1/[S]$

56. Which statement about the initiation codon is correct?

    A. It is part of the TATA box
    B. It binds a protein complex that begins replication
    C. It specifies methionine
    D. It specifies uracil

57. Which tyrosine-derived molecule has the correct relationship?

    A. Norepinephrine – thyroid hormone
    B. Thyroxine – catecholamine
    C. Dopaquinone – precursor of melanin
    D. Dopamine – thyroid hormone

58. Which statement is correct about essential amino acids?

    A. They are not synthesized *de novo* by the body and must be part of the diet
    B. They are not synthesized by the body in sufficient amounts
    C. There are twelve essential amino acids
    D. They are plentiful in all animal protein

59. A term used for a carbohydrate polymer is:

    A. Multimer
    B. Oligosaccharide
    C. Glycan
    D. Polycarb

Biological & Biochemical Foundations of Living Systems

Practice Test #4

59 questions

For explanatory answers see pgs. 235-281

For CBT online format of this test that provides Diagnostics Report with performance statistics, difficulty rating of each question and other features visit:

www.MasterMCAT.com

Most questions in the Biological Sciences test are organized into groups, each containing a descriptive passage. After studying the passage select the one best answer to each question in the group. Some questions are not based on a descriptive passage and are also independent of each other. If you are not certain of an answer, eliminate the alternatives you know to be incorrect and then select an answer from the remaining alternatives. Indicate your selected answer by marking the corresponding answer on your answer sheet. A periodic table is provided for your use. You may consult it whenever you wish.

Periodic Table of the Elements

1 H 1.0																	2 He 4.0
3 Li 6.9	4 Be 9.0											5 B 10.8	6 C 12.0	7 N 14.0	8 O 16.0	9 F 19.0	10 Ne 20.2
11 Na 23.0	12 Mg 24.3											13 Al 27.0	14 Si 28.1	15 P 31.0	16 S 32.1	17 Cl 35.5	18 Ar 39.9
19 K 39.1	20 Ca 40.1	21 Sc 45.0	22 Ti 47.9	23 V 50.9	24 Cr 52.0	25 Mn 54.9	26 Fe 55.8	27 Co 58.9	28 Ni 58.7	29 Cu 63.5	30 Zn 65.4	31 Ga 69.7	32 Ge 72.6	33 As 74.9	34 Se 79.0	35 Br 79.9	36 Kr 83.8
37 Rb 85.5	38 Sr 87.6	39 Y 88.9	40 Zr 91.2	41 Nb 92.9	42 Mo 95.9	43 Tc (98)	44 Ru 101.1	45 Rh 102.9	46 Pd 106.4	47 Ag 107.9	48 Cd 112.4	49 In 114.8	50 Sn 118.7	51 Sb 121.8	52 Te 127.6	53 I 126.9	54 Xe 131.3
55 Cs 132.9	56 Ba 137.3	57 La* 138.9	72 Hf 178.5	73 Ta 180.9	74 W 183.9	75 Re 186.2	76 Os 190.2	77 Ir 192.2	78 Pt 195.1	79 Au 197.0	80 Hg 200.6	81 Tl 204.4	82 Pb 207.2	83 Bi 209.0	84 Po (209)	85 At (210)	86 Rn (222)
87 Fr (223)	88 Ra (226)	89 Ac† (227)	104 Rf (261)	105 Db (262)	106 Sg (266)	107 Bh (264)	108 Hs (277)	109 Mt (268)	110 Ds (281)	111 Uuu (272)	112 Uub (285)		114 Uuq (289)		116 Uuh (289)		

	58 Ce 140.1	59 Pr 140.9	60 Nd 144.2	61 Pm (145)	62 Sm 150.4	63 Eu 152.0	64 Gd 157.3	65 Tb 158.9	66 Dy 162.5	67 Ho 164.9	68 Er 167.3	69 Tm 168.9	70 Yb 173.0	71 Lu 175.0
†	90 Th 232.0	91 Pa (231)	92 U 238.0	93 Np (237)	94 Pu (244)	95 Am (243)	96 Cm (247)	97 Bk (247)	98 Cf (251)	99 Es (252)	100 Fm (257)	101 Md (258)	102 No (259)	103 Lr (260)

Biological & Biochemical Foundations of Living Systems
MCAT® Practice Test #4 – Answer Sheet

Passage 1

1 :   A   B   C   D
2 :   A   B   C   D
3 :   A   B   C   D
4 :   A   B   C   D
5 :   A   B   C   D
6 :   A   B   C   D
7 :   A   B   C   D

Passage 2

8 :   A   B   C   D
9 :   A   B   C   D
10 :   A   B   C   D
11 :   A   B   C   D
12 :   A   B   C   D

Independent questions

13 :   A   B   C   D
14 :   A   B   C   D
15 :   A   B   C   D
16 :   A   B   C   D

Passage 3

17 :   A   B   C   D
18 :   A   B   C   D
19 :   A   B   C   D
20 :   A   B   C   D
21 :   A   B   C   D

Passage 4

22 :   A   B   C   D
23 :   A   B   C   D
24 :   A   B   C   D
25 :   A   B   C   D
26 :   A   B   C   D

Independent questions

27 :   A   B   C   D
28 :   A   B   C   D
29 :   A   B   C   D
30 :   A   B   C   D

Passage 5

31 :   A   B   C   D
32 :   A   B   C   D
33 :   A   B   C   D
34 :   A   B   C   D
35 :   A   B   C   D

Passage 6

36 :   A   B   C   D
37 :   A   B   C   D
38 :   A   B   C   D
39 :   A   B   C   D
40 :   A   B   C   D
41 :   A   B   C   D

Independent questions

42 :   A   B   C   D
43 :   A   B   C   D
44 :   A   B   C   D
45 :   A   B   C   D
46 :   A   B   C   D

Passage 7

47 :   A   B   C   D
48 :   A   B   C   D
49 :   A   B   C   D
50 :   A   B   C   D
51 :   A   B   C   D
52 :   A   B   C   D

Independent questions

53 :   A   B   C   D
54 :   A   B   C   D
55 :   A   B   C   D
56 :   A   B   C   D
57 :   A   B   C   D
58 :   A   B   C   D
59 :   A   B   C   D

Passage 1
(Questions 1–7)

There are two proteins that are involved in transporting O_2 in vertebrates; hemoglobin (Hb) is found in red blood cells and myoglobin (Mb) is found in muscle cells. The hemoglobin protein accounts for about 97% of the dry weight of red blood cells. In erythrocytes, the hemoglobin carries O_2 from the lungs to the tissue undergoing cellular respiration. Hemoglobin has an oxygen binding capacity of 1.3 ml O_2 per gram of hemoglobin, which increases the total blood oxygen capacity over seventy-fold compared to dissolved oxygen in blood.

When a tissue's metabolic rate increases, carbon dioxide production also increases. In addition to O_2, Hb also transports CO_2. Of all the CO_2 transported in blood, 7-10% is dissolved in blood plasma, 70% is bicarbonate ions (HCO_3^-) and 20% is bound to the globin to Hb as carbaminohemoglobin.

CO_2 combines with water to form carbonic acid (H_2CO_3), which quickly dissociates. This reaction occurs primarily in red blood cells, where *carbonic anhydrase* reversibly and rapidly catalyzes the reaction:

$$CO_2 + H_2O \leftrightarrow H_2CO_3 \leftrightarrow H^+ + HCO_3^-$$

Hb of vertebrates has a quaternary structure comprised of four individual polypeptide chains: two α and two β protein polypeptides, each with a heme group bound as a prosthetic group. The four polypeptide chains are held together by hydrogen bonding.

Figure 1. Hemoglobin

The binding of O_2 to Hb depends on the cooperativity of the Hb subunits. Cooperativity means that the binding of O_2 at one heme group increases the binding of O_2 at another heme within the Hb molecule through conformational changes of the entire hemoglobin molecule. This shape (conformational) change means it is energetically favorable for subsequent binding of O_2. Conversely, the unloading of O_2 at one heme increases the unloading of O_2 at other heme groups by a similar conformational change of the molecule.

Oxygen's affinity for Hb varies among different species and within species depending on multiple factors like blood pH, developmental stage (i.e. fetal versus adult), and body size. For example, small animals dissociate O_2 at a given partial pressure more readily than large animals, because they have a higher metabolic rate and require more O_2 per gram of body mass.

Figure 2 represents the O_2-dissociation of Hb (this is represented by sigmoidal curves B, C and D) and myoglobin (hyperbolic curve A), where saturation is the percent of O_2-binding sites occupied at specific partial pressures of O_2.

The *utilization coefficient* is the fraction of O_2 diffusing from Hb to the tissue as blood passes through the capillary beds. A normal value for the *utilization coefficient* is about 0.25.

Figure 2.

In 1959, Max Perutz determined the molecular structure of myoglobin by x-ray crystallography, which led to his sharing of the 1962 Nobel prize with John Kendrew. Myoglobin is a single-chain globular protein (consisting of 154 amino acids) that transports and stores O_2 in muscle. Mb contains a heme (i.e. iron-containing porphyrin) prosthetic group with a molecular weight of 17.7 kd (kilodalton, 1 dalton is defined as 1/12 the mass of a neutral unbound carbon atom). As seen in Figure 2, Mb (curve A) has a greater affinity for O_2 than Hb. Unlike the blood-borne hemoglobin, myoglobin does not exhibit cooperative binding, because cooperativity is present only in quaternary proteins that undergo allosteric changes. A high concentration of myoglobin in muscle cells allows organisms to hold their breath for extended periods of time. Diving mammals, such as whales and seals, have muscles with abundant myoglobin levels.

1. The mountain goat has developed a type of hemoglobin adapted to unusually high altitudes. If curve C represents the O_2 dissociation curve for a cow's Hb, which curve most closely resembles the O_2 dissociation curve for a mountain goat's Hb?

    A. curve A   **B.** curve B   **C.** curve C   **D.** curve D

2. If curve C represents the O_2-dissociation curve for a hippopotamus' Hb, which curve would most closely correspond with the Hb of a squirrel?

    A. curve A   **B.** curve B   **C.** curve C   **D.** curve D

3. If curve C represents the O_2-dissociation curve for the Hb of an adult human, which of the following best explains why curve B most closely corresponds with the curve for fetal Hb?

    A. O_2 affinity of fetal Hb is lower than adult Hb
    B. O_2 affinity of fetal Hb is higher than adult Hb
    C. Metabolic rate of fetal tissue is lower than adult tissue
    D. Metabolic rate of fetal tissue is higher than adult tissue

4. Which of the following best explains the sigmoidal shape of the Hb O_2-dissociation curve?

    A. Conformational changes in the polypeptide subunits of the Hb molecule
    B. Heme groups within the Hb are being reduced and oxidized
    C. Changing $[H^+]$ in the blood
    D. Changing $[CO_2]$ transported by Hb in the blood

5. A sample of adult human Hb was placed in a $6M$ urea solution, which resulted in the disruption of nonconvalent bonds. After that, the Hb α chains were isolated. If curve C represents the O_2-dissociation curve for an adult human Hb *in vivo,* which curve most closely corresponds with the curve of the isolated α chains?

    A. curve A   **B.** curve B   **C.** curve C   **D.** curve D

6. In response to physiological changes, the utilization coefficient of an organism is constantly being adjusted. What value most closely represents the utilization coefficient for human adult Hb during strenuous exercise?

    A. 0.0675   **B.** 0.15   **C.** 0.25   **D.** 0.60

7. The Mb content in the muscle of a humpback whale is about 0.005 moles/kg. Approximately how much O_2 is bound to the Mb of a humpback that has 10,000 kg of muscle (assuming the Mb is saturated with O_2)?

    A. 12.5 moles   **B.** 50 moles   **C.** 200 moles   **D.** 2×10^7 moles

Passage 2
(Questions 8–13)

Corpus luteum (from the Latin "yellow body") is a temporary endocrine structure (yellow mass of cells) in female mammals. It is involved in the production of relatively high levels of progesterone and moderate levels of estradiol (predominant potent estrogen) and inhibin A. The estrogen it secretes inhibits the secretion of LH and FSH by the pituitary, which prevents multiple ovulations.

The corpus luteum is essential for establishing and maintaining pregnancy in females. It is typically very large relative to the size of the ovary (in humans, the size ranges from under 2 cm to 5 cm in diameter) and its color results from concentrating carotenoids from the diet.

The corpus luteum develops from an ovarian follicle during the luteal phase of the menstrual cycle or estrous cycle, following the release of a secondary oocyte from the follicle during ovulation. While the *oocyte* (subsequently the *zygote,* if fertilization occurs) traverses the *oviduct* (Fallopian tube) into the uterus, the corpus luteum remains in the ovary.

Progesterone secreted by the corpus luteum is a steroid hormone responsible for the development and maintenance of the endometrium – the thick lining of the uterus that provides an area rich in blood vessels in which the zygote(s) can develop. If the egg is fertilized and implantation occurs, by day 9 post-fertilization the cells of the blastocyst secrete the hormone called *human chorionic gonadotropin* (hCG), which signals the corpus luteum to continue progesterone secretion. From this point on, the corpus luteum is called the *corpus luteum graviditatis.* The presence of hCG in the urine is the indicator used by home pregnancy test kits.

If the egg is not fertilized, the corpus luteum stops secreting progesterone and decays after approximately 14 days in humans. If fertilization occurred, throughout the first trimester, the corpus luteum secretes hormones at steadily increasing levels. In the second trimester of pregnancy, the placenta (in placental animals, including humans) eventually takes over progesterone production, and the corpus luteum degrades without embryo/fetus loss.

8. Could high estrogen levels be used in home pregnancy tests to indicate possible pregnancy?

    A. No, because estrogen levels also rise prior to ovulation
    B. Yes, because estrogen is secreted at high levels during pregnancy
    C. No, because antibodies in the pregnancy test kit only recognize epitopes of proteins
    D. No, because estrogen is a steroid hormone and is not excreted into the urine by kidneys

9. All of these methods, if administered prior to ovulation, could theoretically be used as a method of female birth control, EXCEPT injecting:

    A. monoclonal antibodies for progesterone and estrogen
    B. antagonists of LH and FSH
    C. agonists that mimic the actions of estrogen and progesterone
    D. agonists that mimic the actions of LH and FSH

10. How would pregnancy be affected by the removal of the ovaries in the fifth month of gestation?

    A. Not affected, because LH secreted by the ovaries is not necessary in the fifth month of gestation
    B. Not affected, because progesterone secreted by the ovaries is not necessary in the fifth month of gestation
    C. Terminated, because LH secreted by the ovaries is necessary in the fifth month of gestation
    D. Terminated, because progesterone secreted by the ovaries is necessary in the fifth month of gestation

11. Very low levels of circulating progesterone and estrogen:

    A. inhibit the release of LH and FSH, thereby not inhibiting ovulation
    B. inhibit the release of LH and FSH, thereby inhibiting ovulation
    C. do not inhibit the release of LH and FSH, thereby not inhibiting ovulation
    D. do not inhibit the release of LH and FSH, thereby inhibiting ovulation

12. To confirm the pregnancy, which of these hormones must be present at high levels in a blood sample of a female patient who suspects to be 10 weeks pregnant?

    I.   Estrogen and progesterone
    II. FSH and LH
    III. hCG

    A. I only
    B. I and II only
    C. II and III only
    D. I and III only

> Questions 13 through 16 are not based on any
> descriptive passage and are independent of each other

13. Which of the following molecules is the site of NMR spin-spin coupling?

    A. CH_4
    B. FCH_2CH_2F
    C. $(CH_3)_3CCl$
    D. CH_3CH_2Br

14. Which of the following is correct about the hybridization of the three carbon atoms indicated by arrows in the following molecule?

    A. C_1 is *sp* hybridized, C_2 is sp^2 hybridized and C_3 is sp^3 hybridized
    B. C_1 is sp^2 hybridized, C_2 is sp^2 hybridized and C_3 is *sp* hybridized
    C. C_1 is *sp* hybridized, C_2 is sp^2 hybridized and C_3 is sp^2 hybridized
    D. C_1 is sp^2 hybridized, C_2 is sp^2 hybridized and C_3 is sp^2 hybridized

15. The extracellular fluid volume depends on the total sodium content in the body. The balance between Na^+ intake and Na^+ loss regulates Na^+ levels. Which of the following will occur following the administration of digoxin, a poison that blocks the Na^+/K^+ ATPase?

    A. Increased intracellular $[H_2O]$
    B. Increased intracellular $[Cl^-]$
    C. Increased extracellular $[Na^+]$
    D. Increased intracellular $[K^+]$

16. To selectively function on ingested proteins and avoid digestion of a body's proteins in the digestive system, pancreatic peptidases must be tightly regulated. Which mechanism activates pancreatic peptidases?

    A. osmolarity
    B. coenzyme binding
    C. carbohydrate moieties
    D. proteolytic cleavage

This page is intentionally left blank

Passage 3
(Questions 17–21)

In pharmacology, a natural product is a chemical compound or substance produced by a living organism found in nature that usually has a pharmacological or biological activity for pharmaceutical drug discovery and drug design. However, a natural product can be classified as such even if it can be prepared by laboratory synthesis. Not all natural products can be fully synthesized, because many have very complex structures, making it too difficult or expensive to synthesize on an industrial scale. These compounds can only be harvested from their natural source - a process which can be tedious, time consuming, expensive and wasteful on the natural resource.

Enediynes are a class of natural bacterial products characterized by either nine- or ten-membered rings containing two triple bonds separated by a double bond. Many enediyne compounds are extremely toxic to DNA. They are known to cleave DNA molecules and appear to be quite effective as selective agents for anticancer activity. Therefore, enediynes are being investigated as antitumor therapeutic agents.

Classes of enediynes target DNA by binding with DNA in the minor groove. Enediynes then abstract hydrogen atoms from the deoxyribose (sugar) backbone of DNA, which results in strand scission. These small molecules are active ingredients of the majority of FDA-approved agents and continue to be one of the major biomolecules for drug discovery. This enediyne molecule is proven to be a potent antitumor agent:

Figure 1. Neocarzinostatin

Neocarzinostatin is a chromoprotein enediyne antibiotic with anti-tumoral activity secreted by the bacteria *Streptomyces macromomyceticus*. It consists of two parts, a labile chromophore (bicyclic dienediyne structure shown) and a 113 amino acid apoprotein with the chromophores non-covalently bound with a high affinity. The *chromophore* is a very potent DNA-damaging agent, because it is very labile (easily broken down) and plays a role in protecting and releasing the cleaved target DNA. Opening of the epoxide under reductive conditions present in cells creates favorable conditions and leads to a diradical intermediate and subsequent double-stranded DNA cleavage.

17. Which functional group is NOT present in the molecule of neocarzinostatin?

A. thiol
B. hydroxyl
C. ester
D. epoxide

18. What is the hybridization of the two carbon atoms and the oxygen atom indicated by the arrows in Figure 1?

A. C_1 is sp^2, C_2 is sp^2 and O is sp^2 hybridized
B. C_1 is sp^2, C_2 is sp and O is sp hybridized
C. C_1 is sp, C_2 is sp^2 and O is sp^2 hybridized
D. C_1 is sp, C_2 is sp^3 and O is sp^3 hybridized

19. How many chiral carbons are in the molecule of neocarzinostatin?

A. 4
B. 8
C. 10
D. 12

20. How many π bonds are in the molecule of neocarzinostatin?

A. 7
B. 9
C. 11
D. 13

21. Which of the following is correct about the absolute configuration of the carbon atom indicated by (*)?

A. It has an *S* absolute configuration
B. It has an *R* absolute configuration
C. It is not chiral
D. Absolute configuration cannot be determined

Passage 4
(Questions 22–26)

The human digestive system functions by a highly coordinated chain of mechanisms consisting of ingestion, digestion and nutrient absorption. Digestion is a progressive process that begins with ingestion into the mouth, continues with digestion in the stomach and then with digestion and absorption in the three sections of the small intestine.

Digestion involves macromolecules being broken down by enzymes into their component molecules before absorption through the villi of the small intestine. Nutrients from digested food, such as vitamins, minerals and subunits of macromolecules (e.g. monosaccharides, amino acids, di– or tripeptides, glycerol and fatty acids) are absorbed via either diffusion or transport (facilitated or active) mechanisms. These transport mechanisms may occur with or without mineral co-transport.

Digestive enzymes at the intestinal brush border work with digestive enzymes secreted by salivary glands and the pancreas to facilitate nutrient absorption. Digestion of complex carbohydrates into simple sugars is an example of this process. Pancreatic α-amylase hydrolyzes the 1,4–glycosidic bonds in complex starches to oligosaccharides in the lumen of the small intestine. The membrane-bound intestinal α-glucosidases hydrolyze oligosaccharides, trisaccharides and disaccharides to glucose and other monosaccharides in the small intestine.

Acarbose is a starch blocker used as an anti-diabetic drug to treat type-2 diabetes mellitus. Acarbose is an inhibitor of α–1,4-glucosidase (an enteric brush-border enzyme) and pancreatic α-amylase, which release glucose from complex starches. The inhibition of these enzyme systems reduces the rate of digestion of complex carbohydrates, resulting in less glucose being absorbed, because the carbohydrates are not broken down into glucose molecules. For diabetic patients, the short-term effect of such drug therapy is decreased current blood glucose levels and the long-term effect is a reduction of the HbA1C levels.

Figure 1. Acarbose molecule

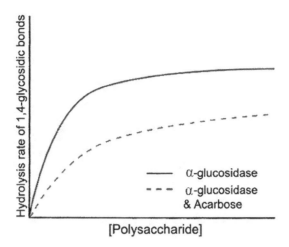

Figure 2. The kinetics of α-glucosidase in the presence/absence of acarbose.

22. According to the graph (Figure 2), how are α-1,4-glucosidase enzyme kinetics affected by acarbose?

   A. The concentration of available enzyme is reduced

   B. Enzyme specificity for the substrate is changed

   C. The K_{eq} binding of the ligand-enzyme complex is changed

   D. Covalent bonds that irreversibly inactivate the enzyme's active site are formed

23. Which type of α-1,4–glucosidase inhibition is most closely demonstrated by acarbose?

       I. competitive   II. noncompetitive   III. allosteric

   A. I only   **B.** II only   **C.** II and III only   **D.** I and III only

24. Which condition most closely resembles the symptoms resulting from α-1,4-glucosidase inhibition by acarbose?

   A. Infection by *V. cholera*   **C.** Deficiency of lactase

   B. Deficiency of intrinsic factor   **D.** Deficiency of bile acid

25. Which molecule does NOT require micelle formation for intestinal absorption?

   A. vitamin A   **B.** triglycerides   **C.** cholesterol   **D.** bile acid

26. Glucosidase is best characterized as a:

   A. hydrolase   **B.** isomerase   **C.** ligase   **D.** phosphatase

Questions 27 through 30 are not based on any
descriptive passage and are independent of each other

27. Which of the following is/are required for the proper function of the DNA-dependent
DNA polymerase?

      I. DNA template strand
     II. primase (RNA primer)
     III. 4 different nucleotides
     IV. RNA polymerase

  A. I and II only
  B. I and III only
  C. I, II and III only
  D. I, II, III and IV

28. Given that the availability of the carbon source determines energy yield, catabolism
of which molecule will result in the highest energy yield?

  A. Short-chain unsaturated fatty acid
  B. Short-chain saturated fatty acid
  C. Long-chain conjugated fatty acid
  D. Long-chain saturated fatty acid

29. Which molecule has the closest to 3000-3500 cm^{-1} infrared (IR) stretch?

  A. $H_2C=CH_2CH_3$
  B. CH_3CH_2COOH
  C. CH_3CH_2OH
  D. $(CH_3CH_2)_2CO$

30. Which of these compounds has/have a dipole moment?

     I. CCl_4
     II. CH_3CH_2OH
     III. $CH_3CHBrCH_3$

  A. II only
  B. III only
  C. I and III only
  D. II and III only

Passage 5
(Questions 31–35)

Penicillins are one of the most successful classes of antibiotics derived from *Penicillium* fungi. They include penicillin G, penicillin V, procaine penicillin and benzathine penicillin. Penicillin antibiotics were the first drugs that treated serious diseases such as syphilis, staphylococci and streptococci. Penicillins are still widely used today, but many types of bacteria are now resistant to them. All penicillins are β-lactam antibiotics and are used in the treatment of bacterial infections caused by susceptible, usually Gram-positive, organisms.

The initial efforts to synthesize penicillin proved difficult with discrepancies in the structure being reported from different laboratories. In 1957, chemist John Sheehan at the Massachusetts Institute of Technology (MIT) completed the first chemical synthesis of penicillin. However, the synthesis developed by Sheehan was not appropriate for mass production of penicillins. One of the intermediate compounds was 6-aminopenicillanic acid (6-APA). Attaching different groups to the 6-APA allowed the synthesis of new forms of penicillin.

Figure 1. Penicillin biosynthesis

The structure of the penicillins includes a five-membered ring containing both sulfur and nitrogen (i.e. thioazolidine ring) joined to a four-membered ring containing a cyclic amide (i.e. β-lactam). These two rings are necessary for the biological activities of penicillin, and cleavage of either ring disrupts antibacterial activity.

Figure 2. Core structure of penicillins (beta-lactam ring highlighted)

A medical student performed three experiments as shown in Table 1 to elucidate how penicillin resulted in the death of bacterial cell.

	Method	Experimental results
Experiment 1	Two bacterial species were cultured and grown on agar plates. Both species had normal peptidoglycan cell walls. One population was exposed to penicillin, while the other was not exposed to penicillin.	About 93% of the bacteria treated with penicillin underwent cytolysis and did not survive, while the bacteria that were not exposed to penicillin were unaffected.
Experiment 2	Two bacterial species were cultured and grown on agar plates. One species had an intact peptidoglycan cell wall, while the other species had an incomplete cell wall. Both groups were exposed to penicillin on the agar plates.	The bacteria with incomplete cell walls survived, while 93% of those with intact peptidoglycan cell walls did not survive.
Experiment 3	The 7% who survived the treatment of penicillin in Experiment 2 were cultured and grown on agar plates. These colonies were repeatedly inoculated with penicillin.	The colonies grew continuously with no apparent effect from the antibiotic.

Table 1.

31. It is reasonable to hypothesize that penicillin causes bacterial death likely by:

    A. blocking the colonies' access to nutrients
    B. disrupting the integrity of the bacterial cell wall
    C. establishing excessive rigidity in the bacterial cell wall
    D. inducing mutations in bacteria from Gram-negative to Gram-positive strains

32. Knowing that penicillin G is rapidly hydrolyzed under acidic conditions, which limitation applies to its use?

    A. It is not active in the range of plasma pH
    B. It must be administered intravenously
    C. It must be taken 30 to 60 minutes before eating
    D. It should be avoided by young children and elderly patients

33. From the experiments, which bacterial species are most resistant to penicillin?

    A. Species unable to transcribe DNA to RNA
    B. Species with complete peptidoglycan cell walls
    C. Species with incomplete cross-linked cell walls
    D. Species with the greatest intracellular osmotic pressure

34. What causes the bacterial cells to undergo cytolysis upon the weakening of their cell wall?

    A. Water enters the cells due to osmotic pressure
    B. Proteins are not able to exit the cell through vesicles
    C. Solutes are forced out of the cells through active transport mechanisms
    D. Facilitated diffusion causes lipid-insoluble substances to cross the cell membrane

35. It is a reasonable hypothesis that 7% of the cell-walled bacteria treated with penicillin in Experiments 1 and 2 survived due to:

    A. the bacterial cell wall's impermeability to penicillin
    B. agar on the growth plates that hydrolyzed and degraded penicillin
    C. plasmids that synthesized penicillinase
    D. the limitation of diffusion, which resulted in select colonies not being exposed to penicillin

Passage 6
(Questions 36–41)

Adipose tissue is loose connective tissue composed of adipocytes and stores free fatty acids as triglycerides. A fatty acid is a carboxylic acid with a long aliphatic tail (often with even numbers of carbons between 4 and 28) that is either saturated or unsaturated. Saturated refers to the aliphatic chain which lacks double bonds, while unsaturated chains contain one or more double bonds.

Glycerol, a three-carbon molecule, contains three hydroxyl groups with a single OH on each of the three carbons. Glycerol is the backbone for triglycerides, and each hydroxyl group is the attachment point for a free fatty acid. The hydroxyl on the glycerol attacks the carboxylic acid group of the free fatty acid to form an ester linkage bond.

Figure 1. Glycerol

Figure 2. Fatty acid

Figure 3. Triglyceride

Triglycerides are released from adipose tissue into the circulatory system during high demands for energy by peripheral muscle tissue. The release of free fatty acids is controlled by a complex series of reactions tightly modulated by *hormone-sensitive lipase* (HSL). HSL hydrolyzes the first fatty acid from a triglyceride, freeing a fatty acid and a diglyceride. HSL is activated when the body needs to mobilize energy stores and responds positively to catecholamines and adrenocorticotropic hormone (ACTH), but is inhibited by insulin. Lipase activators bind receptors that are coupled to adenylate cyclase, which increases cAMP for activation of an appropriate *kinase* (PKA) that then activates HSL.

Free fatty acids targeted for breakdown are transported, bound to *albumin,* through the circulation. However, fatty acids targeted for adipose storage sites in adipocytes are transported in large lipid-protein micelle particles termed *lipoproteins* (i.e. LDL). During high rates of mitochondrial fatty acid oxidation, acetyl CoA is produced in large amounts. If the generation of acetyl CoA from glycolysis exceeds utilization by the Krebs cycle, an alternative pathway is ketone body synthesis. During the onset of starvation, skeletal and cardiac muscles preferentially metabolize ketone bodies, which preserve endogenous glucose for the brain.

36. Albumin is the most abundant protein distributed throughout the circulatory system and accounts for about 50% of plasma proteins. By which bond, and for what reason, does albumin bind to the free fatty acids?

    A. Hydrogen bonding to albumin stabilizes fatty acid absolute configuration
    B. Covalent bonding to albumin increases lipid solubility
    C. Ionic bonding to albumin stabilizes free fatty acid structure
    D. Van der Waals binding to albumin increases lipid solubility

37. A person suffering untreated diabetes can experience ketoacidosis due to a reduced supply of glucose. Which of the following correlates with diabetic ketoacidosis?

    A. High plasma insulin levels
    B. Increase in fatty acid oxidation
    C. Ketone bodies increase plasma alkalinity to clinically dangerous levels
    D. Decreased levels of acetyl CoA lead to increased production of ketone bodies

38. Which of the following is the site of the breakdown for β-oxidation?

    A. mitochondria   **B.** lysosomes   **C.** the cytoplasm of the cell   **D.** the nucleolus

39. The main regulation point for fatty acid catabolism is *lipolysis*. All of the following are direct products of adipose tissue breakdown, EXCEPT:

    A. acetyl CoA   **B.** glycerol   **C.** free fatty acids   **D.** ketone bodies

40. Which organ is the last to use ketone bodies as an energy source?

    A. kidneys   **B.** brain   **C.** cardiac tissue   **D.** skeletal muscle

41. Which of the following bonds between glycerol and the free fatty acids is cleaved by phosphorylated *hormone-sensitive lipase* via hydrolysis?

    A. hydrogen bond   **C.** ionic bond
    B. ester bond   **D.** disulfide bond

> Questions 42 through 46 are not based on any
> descriptive passage and are independent of each other

42. What is the correct sequence of organelles passed by the proteins targeted for the secretory pathway?

    A. ER → vesicle → Golgi → vesicle → plasma membrane
    B. ER → vesicle → Golgi → cytoplasm → plasma membrane
    C. Golgi → ER → vesicle → cytoplasm → proteosome
    D. cytoplasm → vesicle → Golgi → ER → vesicle → plasma membrane

43. During replication, which molecule do single stranded binding proteins (SSBP) attach to in order to maintain the uncoiled configuration of the nucleotide strands of the double helix uncoiled by the helicase enzyme?

    A. dsDNA   **B.** ssDNA   **C.** dsRNA   **D.** ssRNA

44. A biochemist hypothesized that the glucose transport protein is located only on the outer surface of the cell membrane. Is such hypothesis correct?

    A. Yes, because transport proteins are located only on the outer surface of the lipid bilayer
    B. Yes, because transport proteins are located only on the inner surface of the lipid bilayer
    C. No, because transport proteins are transmembrane and span the entire lipid bilayer
    D. No, because the hydrophilic heads of the lipid bilayer attract polar residues of the protein

45. Beta-oxidation occurs in the same location as:

    I. glycolysis   II. the Krebs cycle   III. pyruvate decarboxylation into acetyl-CoA

    A. I only   **B.** I and II only   **C.** II and III only   **D.** I, II and III

46. Which molecule has an infrared stretch closest to 1700 cm^{-1}?

    A. $CH_3CH_2CH_2CPh_3$ **C.** $CH_3CH_2CH_2CH_2CHO$
    B. $CH_3CH_2CH_2CH_2OH$ **D.** $CH_3CHClCH_2CH_2OCH_2CH_3$

This page is intentionally left blank

Passage 7

(Questions 47–52)

Esters are compounds consisting of a carbonyl adjacent to an ether linkage. They are derived by reacting a carboxylic acid (or its derivate) with a hydroxyl of an alcohol or phenol. Esters are often formed by condensing *via* dehydration (removal of water) of an alcohol acid with an acid.

Figure 1. Ester functional group (R and R' represent alkyl chains)

Esters are ubiquitous in biological molecules. Most naturally occurring fats and oils are the fatty acid esters of glycerol, while phosphoesters form the backbone of nucleic acids (e.g. DNA and RNA molecules), as shown in Figure 2. Esters with low molecular weight are commonly used as fragrances and are found in essential oils and pheromones.

Acid-catalyzed esterification is a mechanism of nucleophilic attack by the oxygen of the alcohol on the carboxylic acid (Figure 3). The isotope of oxygen, labeled in the alcohol as $R'^{18}OH$, was used to elucidate the reaction mechanism. The ester product was separated from unused reactants and side reaction contaminants in the reaction mixture. The water from the reaction mixture was collected as a separate fraction via distillation.

Figure 2. Two phosphodiester bonds are formed by connecting the phosphate group (PO_4^{3-}) between three nucleotides.

Figure 3. Esterification reaction mechanism

47. Which of these carboxylic acids has the lowest pK_a?

A. $ClCH_2CH_2CH_2COOH$

C. $Cl_3CCH_2CH_2COOH$

B. $CH_3CH_2CH_2COOH$

D. $CH_3CH_2CHClCOOH$

48. Given that esterification may occur between parts of the same molecule, which compound would most easily undergo intramolecular esterification to form a cyclic ester?

A. $HOOCCH_2CH_2OH$

C. $HOOCCH_2CH_2CH_2CH_2OH$

B. $HOOCCH_2CH_2CH_2OH$

D. $HOOCCH_2CH_2CH_2CH_2CH_2CH_2OH$

49. An alternative method for forming esters is:

$$CH_3CH_2COO^- + RX \rightarrow CH_3CH_2COOR + X^-$$

The reason that this reaction occurs is because:

A. carboxylates are good nucleophiles

C. halide acts as a good electrophile

B. carboxylates are good electrophiles

D. halide is a poor conjugate base

50. The rate of the reaction is negligible without the acid catalyst. The catalyst is attacked by the:

A. carbonyl carbon and facilitates the attack of the carbonyl nucleophile

B. carbonyl carbon and facilitates the carbonyl oxygen electrophile

C. carbonyl oxygen and facilitates the attack of the alcohol nucleophile

D. carbonyl oxygen and facilitates the carbonyl carbon electrophile

51. Which alkyl halide most readily forms an ester with sodium pentanoate $(CH_3CH_2CH_2CH_2COO^-Na^+)$?

A. CH_3Br

C. $CH_3(CH_2)_6CH_2Br$

B. $(CH_3)_2CHBr$

D. $CH_3CH_2CH_2CH_2Br$

52. Which statement is correct, assuming that only the forward reaction occurs (Figure 3)?

A. Ester fraction does not contain labeled oxygen, while the water fraction does

B. Water fraction does not contain labeled oxygen while the ester does

C. Neither the ester fraction nor the water fraction contains labeled oxygen

D. Both the ester fraction and the water fraction contain labeled oxygen

Questions 53 through 59 are not based on any
descriptive passage and are independent of each other

53. Which of the following amino acids is an essential amino acid in the diets of children, but not adults?

    A. Asparate   **B.** Glycine   **C.** Arginine   **D.** Lysine

54. At room temperature, triglycerols containing only saturated long chain fatty acids remain:

    A. oils   **B.** solid   **C.** liquid   **D.** unsaturated

55. Which of the following is an inactive precursor of protease enzymes synthesized in the pancreas?

    A. ribozyme   **C.** zymogen
    B. isozyme   **D.** allosteric enzyme

56. The most common naturally occurring fatty acids have:

    A. 12-20 carbon atoms with an odd number of carbon atoms
    B. 12-20 carbon atoms with an even number of carbon atoms
    C. 20-50 carbon atoms with an odd number of carbon atoms
    D. 20-50 carbon atoms with an even number of carbon atoms

57. The anticodon is located on the:

    A. DNA   **B.** tRNA   **C.** mRNA   **D.** rRNA

58. Which disaccharide, when present in large excess over glucose, can be metabolized by *E. coli* through use of the operon?

    A. galactose   **B.** lactose   **C.** sucrose   **D.** cellobiose

59. Which mechanism is used to interconvert anomers?

    A. Isotopic exchange reaction
    B. Mutarotation
    C. Conformational change around carbon-carbon bonds
    D. Anomers cannot be interconverted

Explanatory Answers

Biological & Biochemical Foundations of Living Systems
MCAT® Practice Test #1 – Answer Key

Passage 1
1 : B
2 : C
3 : A
4 : D
5 : D

Passage 2
6 : B
7 : D
8 : C
9 : D
10 : A

Independent questions
11 : A
12 : B
13 : D
14 : C

Passage 3
15 : A
16 : B
17 : A
18 : A
19 : C
20 : D

Passage 4
21 : D
22 : B
23 : D
24 : C
25 : B
26 : A

Independent questions
27 : C
28 : C
29 : D

Passage 5
30 : A
31 : B
32 : D
33 : C
34 : B
35 : D

Passage 6
36 : B
37 : B
38 : B
39 : B
40 : A

Independent questions
41 : A
42 : A
43 : C
44 : D
45 : D
46 : C

Passage 7
47 : C
48 : C
49 : B
50 : D
51 : A
52 : B

Independent questions
53 : B
54 : C
55 : D
56 : D
57 : B
58 : A
59 : C

Passage 1
(Questions 1–5)

An antibiotic is a soluble substance derived from a mold or a bacterium, and inhibits the growth of other microorganisms. Despite the absence of the bacterial beta-lactamase gene that typically confers penicillin resistance, there is a strain of penicillin-resistant pneumococci bacteria. Additionally, some of the cells in this strain are unable to metabolize the disaccharides of sucrose and lactose. A microbiologist studying this strain discovered that all of the cells in this strain were infected with two different types of bacteriophage: phage A and phage B. Both phages insert their DNA into the bacterial chromosome. The researcher infected wildtype pneumococci with the two phages to determine if the bacteriophage infection could give rise to this new bacterial strain.

Experiment 1
Two separate 25 ml nutrient broth solutions containing actively growing wild-type pneumococci were mixed with 15 μl of phage A and 15 μl of phage B. In addition, another 25 ml broth solution containing only wild-type pneumococci was used as a control. After 30 minutes of room temperature incubation, the microbiologist diluted 1 μl of the broth solutions in separate 1 ml aliquots of sterile water. These dilutions were plated on three different agar plates containing glucose, sucrose and lactose, respectively. The plates were incubated at 37 °C for 12 hours, and the results are summarized in Table 1.

Plates	phage A infected cells	phage B infected cells	wild-type cells
glucose	+	+	+
sucrose	+	–	+
lactose	+	–	–

(+) plates show bacterial growth; (–) plates show no growth

Table 1

Experiment 2
10 μl of each of the broth solutions from Experiment 1 were again diluted in separate 5 ml aliquots of sterile water. These dilutions were plated on three different agar plates containing tetracyne, ampicillin and no antibiotic, respectively. The plates were incubated at 37 °C for 12 hours, and the results are summarized in Table 2.

Plates	phage A infected cells	phage B infected cells	wild-type cells
Tetracyne	–	–	–
Ampicillin	+	+	–
No antibiotic	+	+	+

(+) plates show bacterial growth; (–) plates show no growth

Table 2

1. Which of the following best account(s) for the results of Experiment 2?

    I. **Wild-type bacteria have no natural resistance to either ampicillin or tetracyne**

    II. **Phage A DNA and phage B DNA encode for beta-lactamase**

    III. Phage A and phage B disrupted the wild-type bacteria's ability to resist ampicillin

    IV. Phage A DNA and phage B DNA encode for enzymes that inhibit tetracyne's harmful effects

    A. II only

    B. **I and II only**

    C. III and IV only

    D. I, II and IV only

B is correct.

In Table 2, the control (i.e. wild type) bacteria were unable to grow in the presence of either tetracyne or ampicillin. Therefore, the wild-type bacteria do not have any natural resistance to these two antibiotics, and so Roman numeral I is correct.

Eliminate all answer choices containing Roman numeral III, because the wild-type bacteria have no natural resistance to ampicillin.

From Table 2, bacteria infected with either phage A or phage B are able to grow in the presence of ampicillin, but not in the presence of tetracyne. Both phage A DNA and phage B DNA must contain the gene that encodes for beta-lactamase, because this is the enzyme that confers ampicillin resistance.

MCAT Tip: do not focus on very specific details of the experimental protocol because this can slow the reading and none of the questions actually require you to refer back to the protocol. Focus your attention on the rationale of the experiments. Do not focus on the minutiae because the passage is available to refer to at any time.

2. Plaques are transparent areas within a bacterial lawn caused by bacterial cell death. In which of the following cycles must phage A be able to produce plaques?

    A. S phase

    B. translocation

    C. **lytic**

    D. lysogenic

C is correct.

The lysis (lytic cycle) of the bacterial cell produces plaques that are transparent areas within a bacterial lawn caused by bacterial cell death. The lysis of the bacterial cells results from the eruption of infectious viral particles.

The question asks about the cycle of viral infection when bacteriophages assemble new viral particles and lyse (rupture) the host cell. This passage relates to strains of phage that began their infection in a lysogenic stage, because the passage states that the phage DNA was integrated (i.e. inserted) into the bacterial genome.

When certain phages (i.e. viruses) infect bacteria, one of two events may occur. The viral DNA may enter the cell and initiate a lytic cycle infection, whereby new viral particles are assembled and the bacterium lyses.

Alternatively, the viral DNA may become integrated into the bacterial chromosome. Once integrated into the bacterial chromosome, the viral DNA replicates with the host chromosome and passes (during cell division of the host cells) to daughter cells. The virus is dormant within the cell, and this is the lysogenic cycle. Periodically, an integrated virus (i.e. prophage) becomes activated, the virus DNA is excised from the host genome and the lytic cycle begins.

A common example of this alternation between the lytic and lysogenic cycle in humans is the herpes virus, whereby it can alternate between the dormant (i.e. lysogenic cycle) phase and active replication phase of the lytic cycle.

The eukaryotic cell cycle (interphase and mitosis) is not related to a viral infection. Mitosis (PMAT: stages of prophase, metaphase, anaphase and telophase) is the nuclear division of eukaryotic somatic (i.e. body) cells, characterized by chromosome replication and formation of two identical daughter cells, each with a complete copy of the chromosomes within the nuclei.

3. Which of the following best describes the appearance of pneumococci, a streptococcal bacterium, when stained and then viewed with a compound light microscope?

   A. spherical
   B. rod
   C. helical
   D. cuboidal

A is correct.
Bacteria are categorized on the basis of their shape. Pneumococci bacteria, when stained and viewed under a light microscope, are spherical in shape.

The three basic bacterial shapes are spherical, rod and helical (or spiral).

Spherical bacteria are known as cocci (i.e. berries).

Rod-shaped bacteria are known as bacilli.

Helical bacteria are known as spirochetes (or spirilla) and are the least common of the three groups.

Streptococcus pneumoniae (pneumococcus), a member of the genus Streptococcus, is a significant human pathogenic bacterium. *S. pneumoniae* was identified as a major cause of pneumonia in the 19th century. Aside from this, the organism causes many other types of pneumococcal infection, including acute sinusitis, otitis media, meningitis, bacteremia, sepsis, osteomyelitis, septic arthritis, endocarditis, peritonitis, pericarditis, cellulitis, and brain abscess.

Pneumococci are a part of respiratory tract natural flora, but (as with many natural flora) can become pathogenic under certain conditions, such as if the immune system of the host is weakened.

B: rod-shaped bacteria include the common bacteria, *Escherichia coli* (i.e. *E. coli*), named after the German pediatrician and bacteriologist (Escherich; 1857-1911). *E. coli* is a genus of aerobic, facultative anaerobic bacteria containing short, motile or nonmotile, Gram-negative rods. Motile cells are peritrichous, relating to cilia or other appendicular organs projecting from the periphery of a cell. Glucose and lactose are fermented with the production of acid and gas. These organisms are found in feces; some are pathogenic to humans, causing enteritis, peritonitis, cystitis, etc.

C: among the representatives of helical bacteria, there is *Treponema pallidum*, which cannot be seen on a Gram stained smear because this organism is very thin. This bacterium is known for causing syphilis and transmits via sexual contact or from mother to fetus across placenta.

D: bacteria are not classified as cuboidal. Cuboidal refers to the shape of tissue type.

4. Based on the results of the experiments, which statement is most likely true of phage A?

    A. Phage A reduced the ampicillin on the agar plates and therefore allowed bacterial growth
    B. Phage A inserted its DNA into the bacterial chromosome, rendering ampicillin ineffective against the bacterial cell wall
    C. Phage A inhibited the growth of the bacteria
    D. Phage A contained the viral gene that encoded for beta-lactamase

D is correct.

The correct answer is that phage A contained the viral gene that encoded for beta-lactamase. All answers refer to ampicillin resistance and phage A. A bacteriophage is a virus that infects bacteria.

From Table 2, the bacteria infected with phage A were able to grow on agar plates containing ampicillin. From the passage (and Table 2), the uninfected wild-type bacterial cells do not contain the gene that encodes for beta-lactamase. Beta-lactamase confers ampicillin resistance, because no bacterial growth was observed when the control dilution was incubated in the presence of ampicillin. Combining these two pieces of information, phage A must be responsible for the observed ampicillin resistance in Experiment 2.

Choice C should be eliminated because bacterial growth did occur in both Experiments 1 and 2, when the bacteria were infected with phage A.

The other choices are all possible ways in which the bacterial cells could have become resistant to ampicillin. So, decide between these three answers based on the experimental data.

The ampicillin resistance observed in the bacteria infected with phage A in Experiment 2 must have been conferred by the insertion of phage A DNA, which contained the gene that codes for beta-lactamase.

Beta-lactam is the core structure of ampicillins. The term penicillin refers to over 50 chemically related antibiotics. All penicillins (e.g. ampicillin) have a common core structure of a beta-lactam ring.

Penicillins prevent the cross-linking of the peptidoglycan and interfere with the final stage of the cell wall formation in bacteria. Penicillins do not destroy fully formed bacteria, but inhibit the formation of additional bacteria by inhibiting the synthesis of the cell wall.

The passage does not state the exact mechanism by which this gene functions, and therefore you are not expected to know this information. Perhaps beta-lactamase does function via the mechanisms proposed by affecting the bacterium cell wall or by reducing the penicillin on the agar plate. However, neither of these proposed mechanisms can be concluded from the experimental data.

The only conclusion is that ampicillin resistance is encoded for by the gene for beta-lactamase, because the only difference between these bacterial cells and the wild-type cells of the control group is the phage A infection.

5. Which of the following conclusions is consistent with the data in Table 1?

    A. Phage A inserted its DNA into the bacterial chromosome region that encodes for the enzymes of glycolysis

    B. Phage A prevented larger molecules, such as lactose and sucrose, from passing through the bacterial cell wall

    C. Phage B utilized all of the sucrose and lactose and starved out the bacteria

    D. Phage B inserted its DNA into the bacterial chromosome region that encodes for disaccharide digesting enzymes

D is correct.

Phage B inserted its DNA into the bacterial chromosome region that encodes for disaccharide digesting enzymes. According to Table 1, the bacteria infected with phage B were only able to grow on glucose and not in the presence of either sucrose or lactose (both are disaccharides). Therefore, phage B inhibits the bacteria's metabolism of disaccharides.

Since phage A has no deleterious effects on bacterial metabolism, as indicated by the ability to grow on all three plates, choices A and B can be eliminated. Therefore, if phage A DNA was incorporated into the bacterial chromosome region that encodes for the enzymes of glycolysis, the bacteria would have been unable to grow on glucose, since glycolysis provides the ATP required for growth. If phage A had prevented lactose and sucrose entrance into the cells, the bacteria would have been unable to grow on either of these sugars, because the cells would not have had access to metabolic fuel.

Since viruses are not autonomous life forms, they would be unable to utilize any sugar; viruses do not possess the metabolic machinery to metabolize nutrients.

Insertion of phage B DNA into the chromosome region that encodes for the enzymes that digest disaccharides (such as sucrose and lactose) would disrupt the metabolism of these nutrients. Therefore, no bacterial growth is expected when phage B-infected bacteria were incubated with either sucrose or lactose (as shown in Table 1).

Passage 2
(Questions 6–10)

Water is the most abundant compound in the human body and comprises about 60% of total body weight. The exact contribution of water to total body weight within a person varies with gender and also tends to decrease for men.

Total body water (TBW) is distributed between two fluid compartments. These compartments contain the intracellular fluid (ICF) and extracellular fluid (ECF). The sum of ICF and ECF volumes equals TBW:

$$\text{TBW volume} = \text{ECF volume} + \text{ICF volume}$$

There are approximately 100 trillion cells in the human body. Intracellular fluid is the fluid contained within the membrane of each cell. ICF accounts for about 65%, or about 2/3, of TBW. Extracellular fluid is the fluid surrounding the individual cells within the body. ECF, present outside of body cells, can be further divided into interstitial fluid (IF), lymph fluid and blood plasma. Interstitial fluid and lymph fluid together comprise about 27% of the TBW. Blood plasma accounts for another 8% of the TBW.

Other extracellular fluids are found in specialized compartments, such as the urinary tract, digestive tract, bone and synovial fluids that lubricate the joints and organs.

Total body water (TBW) can be measured with isotope dilution. After ingesting a trace dose of a known isotopic marker, saliva samples are collected from the patient over several hours. The measurements are compared between experimental and baseline data. The calculation of body mass before and after the experiment provides a ratio of TBW to total body mass. The data is analyzed using the following formula:

$$\text{Volume} = \text{Amount (g)} / \text{Concentration}$$

6. In periods of low water intake, the renin-angiotensin feedback mechanism is used to minimize the amount of water lost by the system. The kidney works in conjunction with which of the following organs to excrete acidic metabolites and regulate acid-base buffer stores?

   A. brain   **B. lungs**   **C.** heart   **D.** liver

B is correct.

The kidneys are bean-shaped organs (about 11 cm long, 5 cm wide and 3 cm thick) lying on either side of the vertebral column, posterior to the peritoneum, about opposite the twelfth thoracic and first three lumbar vertebrae. The nephron is the functional cell of the kidney that produces urine.

The kidneys work in conjunction with the lungs to excrete acidic (H^+) metabolites and regulate acid-base buffer stores. CO_2, which contributes to the acidity of blood, is expelled via the lungs. The lungs correct an abnormally high acid concentration by increasing expirations (i.e. hyperventilation), thereby increasing CO_2 expiration.

7. In isotope dilution technique, a dose of approximately 7 milligrams of O^{18} labeled water was used as a tracer. If 21.0 M/L was the estimated particle concentration, what is the estimate of TBW?

   A. 0.33   **B.** 33.3   **C.** 0.33×10^{-2} **D.** $\mathbf{33.3 \times 10^{-5}}$

D is correct.

According to the equation in the passage:
Volume = amount (g) / concentration
7 milligrams = 0.007 grams
Thus, 0.007 / 21.0 M/L = 3.33 x 10^{-4} or 33.3 x 10^{-5}

8. The movement of water into the cell from the interstitial space to the cytosol is an example of:

    I. facilitated transport   **III. osmosis**
    II. active transport   **IV. passive transport**

   A. I only   **B.** III only   **C. I, III and IV only**   **D.** I, II, III and IV

C is correct.

The plasma membrane consists of a fluid mosaic model. The phospholipids consist of a polar head (hydrophilic phosphate group) and the non-polar tails (hydrophobic fatty acid chains). Water and small uncharged molecules are able to pass freely through the bilayer of the plasma membrane. Movement of molecules down their concentration gradient is a spontaneous process (i.e. no energy needed) known as diffusion. Osmosis is a subset of diffusion and refers to the movement of water down its concentration gradient.

The plasma membranes of various plant and animal cells contain aquaporins through which water can flow more rapidly into the cell than by osmosis through the phospholipid bilayer. Aquaporins (i.e., water channels) are integral pore proteins within the plasma membrane that selectively conduct water molecules in and out of the cell, while preventing the passage of ions and other solutes.

Facilitated transport is the same process as passive transport (aka passive diffusion). This process requires a protein pore (or channel) through the membrane that provides a path for larger or charged molecules to move down their concentration gradient. Like diffusion and osmosis, movement of solutes down a concentration gradient does not require energy (e.g. ATP).

Active transport uses a protein pore or channel, but solutes (molecules dissolved in the solution) move up their concentration gradient. Because movement is up a concentration gradient (movement from a lower concentration to a higher concentration), energy is needed for active transport.

9. Edema is characterized by the presence of excess fluid forced out of circulation and into the extracellular space of tissue or serous cavities. Often, edema is due to circulatory or renal difficulty. Which of the following could be a direct cause of edema?

    A. Decreased permeability of capillary walls

    B. Increased osmotic pressure within a capillary

    C. Decreased hydrostatic pressure within a capillary

    D. Increased hydrostatic pressure within a capillary

D is correct.

An increase in hydrostatic pressure (e.g. a force generated by blood volume) within a capillary would create a stronger force of the fluid inside. This increased hydrostatic pressure would increase the amount of fluid that leaks out of the capillary and moves into the extracellular space. By definition, this accumulation of fluid in the interstitial tissue leads to edema.

A: decreasing capillary permeability would not cause edema, because the decreased permeability of the capillary would cause even less leakage of fluid into the extracellular space.

B: if osmotic pressure is increased within a capillary, this would only increase the reabsorption of fluid back into the capillary, and no edema would result.

C: decreasing hydrostatic pressure within a capillary bed would have the opposite effect. A decreased force on the fluid in the capillary leads to decreased leakage of fluid into the extracellular space.

10. An experiment is conducted to estimate total body water. According to the passage, which of the following must be true?

    A. ECF comprises 35% of TBW and is estimated at 1/3 of body water

    B. ECF comprises 65% of TBW and is estimated at 2/3 of body water

    C. ICF comprises 50% of TBW and is estimated at 1/2 of body water

    D. ICF comprises 35% of TBW and is estimated at 1/3 of body water

A is correct.

According to the passage, ICF comprises 65% of TBW and about 2/3 of total body water.

Because ICF + ECF = TBW, ECF = TBW – ICF and equals 35% TBW, which is about 1/3 of body water.

Total body water
Volume = 40 L
body weight - 60%

Extracellular fluid (ECF)
Volume = 15 L
body weight - 20%

Intracellular fluid (ICF)
Volume = 25 L
body weight - 40%

Interstitial fluid (IF)
Volume = 12 L
80% of ECF

Plasma
Volume = 3 L, 20% of ECF

The major fluid compartments of the body.
Values are for 70 kg (154 lbs) male.

Questions 11 through 14 are not based on any
descriptive passage and are independent of each other

11. Which of the following compounds would most likely produce color?

A.

B.

C.

D.

A is correct.

This molecule has four conjugated bonds and produces a brownish color. Conjugation means alternating double and single bonds and requires an sp^2 carbon (e.g. double bond, carbocation, radical or carbanion) for the delocalization of the electrons within the sp^2 carbon (double bonds).

B: has too few double bonds to produce color.

C: has three double bonds, but they are isolated and conjugated (in a set of two) and less likely to be colored.

D: has a large number of double bonds, but they are isolated (not conjugated), so its absorbance wavelength is below the visible range.

12. Which of the following molecules of digestion is NOT transported by a specific carrier in the intestinal cell wall?

   A. fructose   **B.** **sucrose**   **C.** alanine   **D.** tripeptides

B is correct.

Carbohydrates have a molecular formula of $C_nH_{2n}O_n$ are composed of sugars and end in ~ose. Sucrose must first be digested before absorption. Sucrose, unlike its component monosaccharides (glucose and fructose), is not absorbed via a carrier.

Proteins, unlike carbohydrates, do not have to be hydrolyzed to single subunits (e.g. monosaccharide for carbohydrates and amino acid for proteins) to be absorbed and transported into the small intestine. Single amino acids, dipeptides and tripeptides are all transported across intestinal cell membranes via carrier proteins. Alanine is one of twenty amino acids.

13. Which of the following molecules would be a major product in the reaction of the molecule shown with a chloride anion in carbon tetrachloride (CCl_4)?

D is correct.

In the aprotic solvent of carbon tetrachloride (CCl_4), the preferred mechanism is S_N2. S_N2 is a concerted mechanism that produces inversion of stereochemistry. S_N2 mechanisms prefer a solvent, such as CCl_4, that is a nonpolar aprotic (i.e. no protons dissociate and being released into the solution).

Tertiary substrates undergo the formation of a carbocation intermediate (S_N1 mechanism) and prefer a polar protic solvent (e.g. CH_3OH or H_2O). S_N1 mechanisms produce racemic mixtures with about equal probability of the two enantiomers (+) / (−) as measured with a polarimeter, because the carbocation intermediate is trigonal planar (i.e. flat) and the nucleophile is likely to attack from either face of the trigonal planar intermediate.

14. The nucleus of a tadpole myocardial cell is removed and transplanted into an enucleated frog zygote. After transplant, the frog zygote develops normally. The experimental results suggest that:

   A. the zygote cytoplasm contains RNA for normal adult development
   B. cell differentiation is controlled by irreversible gene repression
   C. **cell differentiation is controlled by selective gene repression**
   D. the ribosomes in the zygote nucleus are the same as in an adult frog

C is correct.

The nucleus of a zygote (fertilized egg) contains all the genetic information (e.g. genome) needed by all future cells of an adult organism. As the zygote divides and segments of the growing organism differentiate, each individual cell maintains a complete complement of genetic information. However, a differentiated cell does not express all the gene-encoded protein products, because some genes are selectively expressed, while others are repressed. Within individual cells, certain gene expression is selectively on or off, depending on the cell type. Selective activation is very important, because even though a myocardial (heart) cell contains the same genetic information as an osteoblast (bone cell), each cell in the body has a specialized function requiring selective gene expression. When certain genes that are normally turned off are aberrantly expressed, cancer (uncontrolled cell growth) may result.

This experiment involves transplantation of genetic material of a differentiated (myocardial) cell into an enucleated frog zygote, and the zygote develops normally. The results suggest that a differentiated (myocardial) nucleus contains the same genetic information (genome) as the nucleus within the non-differentiated zygote. A zygote is totipotent (or omnipotent) and can differentiate and develop into a complete organism. The fact that the nucleus was originally in a differentiated cell also suggests selective repression of DNA. If the myocardial nucleus lacked genetic material essential to a developing organism, the zygote would develop into a mass of myocardial cells and, with certain essential genes absent, the zygote would not develop normally.

A: the experiment did not specifically address this question, and the results do not support (or contradict) this conclusion. Another experiment, such as testing if an enucleated cell containing the RNA within the zygote would develop normally, needs to be conducted to support (or contradict) this theory.

B: the experiment proves that irreversible repression of genes is false. Inactivation of genes must be reversible, otherwise the transplanted nucleus would not direct the zygote to divide and develop into all the different cell types found in an adult frog.

D: this is not tested and the experiment does not support (or contradict) this choice. Eukaryotic ribosomes are the same in all cells and are located within the cytoplasm, not the nucleus, of the cell.

Passage 3
(Questions 15– 20)

The Earth's atmosphere absorbs the energy of most wavelengths of electromagnetic energy. However, significant amounts of radiation reach the Earth's surface through two regions of non-absorption. The first region transmits ultraviolet and visible light, as well as infrared light or heat. The second region transmits radio waves. Organisms living on earth have evolved a number of pigments that interact with light. Some pigments capture light energy, some provide protection from light-induced damage, some serve as camouflage and some serve signaling purposes.

Polyenes are poly-unsaturated organic compounds that contain one or more sets of conjugation. Conjugation is the alteration of double and single bonds, which results in an overall lower energy state of the molecule. Polyenes are important photoreceptors. Without conjugation, or conjugated with only one or two other carbon-carbon double bonds, the molecule normally has enough energy to absorb within the ultraviolet region of the spectrum. The energy state of polyenes with numerous conjugated double bonds can be lowered, so they enter the visible region of the spectrum. These compounds are often yellow or other colors.

Certain wavelengths of light (quanta) possess exactly the correct amount of energy to raise electrons within the molecule from their ground state to higher-energy orbitals. For most organic compounds, these wavelengths are in the UV range. However, conjugated double bond systems stabilize the electrons, so that they can be excited by lower-frequency photons with wavelengths in the visible spectrum. Such pigments are known as chromophores and transmit the complimentary color to the one absorbed. For example, carotene is a hydrocarbon compound with eleven conjugated double bonds that absorb blue light and transmit orange light. The absorbed wavelength generally increases with the number of conjugated bonds. The presence of rings and side-chains within the molecule also affects the wavelengths of energy that the molecule absorbs.

Nucleic acids are biological molecules affected by light. DNA absorbs ultraviolet light and is damaged by UVC (electromagnetic energy with wavelength less that 280 nm), UVB (280-315 nm) and UVA (315-400 nm). UVA also stimulates the melanin cells during sun exposure and there is increasing amount of evidence that UVA damages skin.

Wavelength	Color
390 - 460 nm	violet
460 - 490 nm	blue
490 - 580 nm	green
580 - 600 nm	yellow
620 - 790 nm	red

15. The color-producing property of conjugated polyenes is dependent upon:

A. resonance   **B.** polarity   **C.** optical activity   **D.** antibonding orbitals

A is correct.

Resonance is responsible for reducing the energy of electromagnetic radiation (light) needed to excite an electron by promoting an electron into a higher-energy (i.e. antibonding) orbital.

B: the polarity of molecules depends on electronegativity and the shape of the molecule, and it is a factor independent of color.

C: optical activity is the property of being able to rotate the plane-polarized light. The ability to rotate plane-polarized light (e.g. chiral molecules such as enantiomers, diastereomers and meso compounds) is not related to color.

D: almost any molecule can absorb light and have an electron raised to an antibonding orbital. This process does not normally produce color, because the frequency of the light involved is usually outside the visible range. Resonance reduces the amount of energy needed, bringing the frequency into the visible spectrum.

16. The four compounds represented by the electronic spectra below were evaluated as potential sunscreens. From strongest to weakest, what is the correct sequence of sunscreen effectiveness among these four absorption profiles?

A. I, II, III, IV   **B. II, III, IV, I**   **C.** II, IV, I, III   **D.** IV, I, II, III

B is correct.

Substance II is the best sunscreen because it absorbs over a broad spectrum of wavelengths, including all three types of ultraviolet light (e.g. UVA 315-400nm; UVB 280-315nm; UVC <280nm). The absorption spectrum of the pigment that protects human skin from sunlight (i.e. melanin) has a similar absorption profile.

Spectrum III, which absorbs UVB and UVC (the most dangerous wavelengths of ultraviolet light), would be the next best choice as an effective sunscreen.

Spectrum IV absorbs UVA, so it would reduce tanning, but it would also let through the dangerous UVB and UVC, and burn symptoms would develop.

Spectrum I would be of little value as a sunscreen, because it absorbs almost exclusively in the visible range (greater than 400 nm). Therefore, it is the weakest sunscreen among presented compounds.

17. A chromophore is the moiety of a molecule responsible for its color. Two pigments differ in the lengths of the conjugated polyene chains. The first pigment transmits yellow light and the second transmits red light. What can be said about the sizes of the chromophores?

    A. First chromophore is shorter
    B. Second chromophore is shorter
    C. One of the chromophores must be a dimer
    D. Comparative lengths of chromophores cannot be determined

A is correct.

When a molecule absorbs certain wavelengths of visible light and transmits or reflects others, the molecule has color. For each compound, transmitted light is complimentary in color to the light absorbed by the molecule. Thus, the first chromophore absorbs violet light (transmits yellow – intermediate wavelength), and the second absorbs green light (transmits red – longer wavelength). Violet light has a shorter wavelength than green and, thus, has a higher energy.

From the passage, longer chromophores generally absorb longer wavelength light than shorter chromophors. Therefore, the pigment that absorbs the green light (i.e. has a red color) must be longer. Even for longer pigments, there is no basis for concluding that it is a dimer (i.e. compound made of two identical subunits).

The chemical structure of retinol (vitamin A) is an example of a conjugated molecule containing six double bonds:

18. Many exoskeleton organisms produce a blue or green carotene-protein complex. What is the most likely cause of the color change from green to red when a lobster is boiled?

    A. The protein is separated from the carotenoid pigment
    B. Increase in temperature permits the prosthetic group to become partially hydrated
    C. Heat causes the prosthetic group to become oxidized
    D. The prosthetic group spontaneously disassociates

A is correct.

The color of a crustacean changes when it is boiled because the protein is separated from the carotenoid pigment. From the passage, the carotene by itself is orange. The green color comes from absorption of light by the entire carotene-protein complex. Boiled lobsters are red because of the presence of other pigments.

Upon cooking, the heat disrupts the intermolecular attractions that attach the carotene molecule (the protein's prosthetic group) to the protein itself. This change in the molecule (i.e. dissociation of the prosthetic group) causes a change in the wavelength of the light absorbed. The red color of the cooked lobster is the transmission color of the isolated carotenoid, with the conjugated bonds from the protein removed.

Cofactors can be divided into two broad groups: organic cofactors, such as flavin or heme (red blood cells use heme for binding the oxygen) and inorganic cofactors, such as the metal ions Mg^{2+}, Cu^+ and Mn^{2+}.

B: organic cofactors are sometimes further divided into coenzymes and prosthetic groups. Coenzymes refer specifically to enzymes and, as such, to the functional properties of a protein. A prosthetic group emphasizes the nature of the binding of a cofactor to a protein (tight or covalent) and, thus, refers to a structural property. An increase in temperature is only a physical change and would not change the absorption wavelength.

C: if carotene were hydrated or oxidized, it would break the chain of conjugation completely and produce a colorless compound.

D: a prosthetic group is a tightly or covalently bonded co-factor (i.e., non-protein chemical compound or metallic ion) which remains associated with the protein unless cleaved (e.g., heat or enzymatic activity).

19. Why is a solution of benzene colorless?

    A. Benzene does not absorb light
    B. Benzene is not conjugated
    C. Absorption energy is too high for a frequency to be visible
    D. Absorption energy is too low for a frequency to be visible

C is correct.

The greater the number of conjugated bonds in a molecule, the more strongly electrons in excited states will be stabilized. Thus, the more conjugated a molecule, the lower the frequency and the longer the wavelength that will excite it.

Benzene, with only three double bonds, requires absorption of relatively high energy light. This energy, as discussed in the passage, is higher than for the colored compounds. The light required to excite benzene electrons is in the ultraviolet range, so no color is produced when benzene absorbs light, and a solution of benzene is colorless.

20. The electrons that give color to a carotene molecule are found in:

A. *d* orbitals   **B.** *f* orbitals   **C.** *s* orbitals   **D. *p* orbitals**

D is correct.

Double bonds, like in carotene, are formed by the overlap of the *p* orbitals (of the sp^2 hybridized molecule). The double bond is formed by the overlap of perpendicular *p* orbitals. The pi bond of the double bond is stabilized by the conjugated polyene system. Conjugation refers to the alternating double and single bonds. Conjugation permits the pi electrons to be excited by lower frequencies of light.

The pi (i.e. π) electrons, which give conjugated bonds their stability, are in the p and not in the *s* orbitals. Carbon and hydrogen bonds, which are the major component of organic molecules like carotene, lack *d* or *f* orbitals.

The chemical structure of Beta-carotene (a precursor of vitamin A) is an example of a conjugated molecule containing eleven double bonds:

Passage 4
(Questions 21–26)

Adenosine triphosphate (ATP) is the energy source for many biochemical reactions within the cell, including many membrane transport processes. However, several membrane transport processes do not use the energy liberated from the hydrolysis of ATP. Instead, these transport processes are coupled to the flow of cations and/or anions down their electrochemical gradient. For example, glucose is transported into some animal cells by the simultaneous entry of Na^+. Sodium ions and glucose bind to a specific transport protein and, together, both molecules enter the cell. A symport is a protein responsible for the concerted movement (in the same direction) of two such molecules. An antiport protein carries two species in opposite directions. The rate and extent of the glucose transport depend on the Na^+ gradient across the plasma membrane. Na^+ entering the cell along with glucose, via symport transport, is pumped out again by the Na^+/K^+ ATPase pump.

A medical student investigated a type of bacteria that transports glucose across its cell membrane by use of a sodium-glucose cotransport mechanism. She performed two experiments in which bacterial cells were placed in glucose-containing media that differed with respect to relative ion concentration and ATP content. Glycolysis was inhibited in the cells during these experiments.

Experiment 1:

Bacterial cells with relatively low intracellular Na^+ concentration were placed in a glucose-rich medium. The medium had a relatively high Na^+ concentration, but lacked ATP. At regular time intervals, the glucose and sodium concentrations were analyzed from the medium (Figure 1).

Figure 1. Glucose and Na+ concentrations in ATP-deficient medium

Experiment 2:

Bacterial cells with relatively low intracellular Na^+ concentration were placed in a glucose-rich medium. The medium had relatively high concentrations of both Na^+ and ATP. At regular time intervals, the medium was analyzed for the concentration of glucose, Na^+ and ATP (Figure 2). Over time, if radiolabeled ATP is used for the experiment, the majority of the radiolabel will be inside the cells in the form of ADP.

Figure 2. Glucose, Na⁺ and ATP concentrations in medium

21. Experiments 1 and 2 provide evidence that the cells take up glucose:

   A. in exchange for Na^+, if the ATP concentration is zero
   B. in exchange for ATP, if the extracellular Na^+ concentration remains constant
   C. together with Na^+, if the extracellular ATP concentration gradient is increasing
   D. together with Na^+, if a favorable sodium concentration gradient is maintained

D is correct.

In Experiment 1, both [glucose] and [Na^+] decrease in the medium and therefore are increased inside the cells. This suggests that a [Na^+] gradient was driving the transport of glucose into the cells.

In Experiment 2, [Na^+] remains the same as glucose is transported, but ATP in the medium is decreasing. This observation suggests that the cells are importing ATP and using ATP hydrolysis to maintain the Na^+ gradient to drive glucose transport.

There is no evidence for the exchange of ATP for glucose or for the exchange of Na^+ for glucose. Both, ATP (Graph V, Figure 2) and Na^+ (Graph II, Figure 1), decrease in the medium at the same time that glucose is decreasing. This graphical data suggests that Na^+ is being transported in the same direction as glucose. Extracellular ATP does not increase in these experiments.

22. From Experiments 1 and 2, the student hypothesized that the cells being investigated ultimately depend on energy to operate the sodium-glucose cotransport mechanism. Is this hypothesis supported by the data?

   A. Yes, because Figures 1 and 2 show that glucose crosses the cell membrane in exchange for phosphate
   B. Yes, because Figure 1 shows that a Na^+ gradient drives glucose transport, and Figure 2 shows that ATP maintains the Na^+ gradient
   C. No, because Figure 2 shows that extracellular glucose and ATP concentrations are independent
   D. No, because Figure 1 shows that glucose crosses the cell membrane indefinitely in the absence of exogenous energy

B is correct.

As shown in Figures 1 and 2, both the Na^+ (Graph II) concentration gradient and ATP hydrolysis (Graph V) maintain their gradient and energy drives glucose transport.
All other statements are false, so they can be eliminated.

23. Based on the passage, the initial event in the transport of glucose and sodium into a cell is:

    A. direct hydrolysis of ATP in the cytoplasm by the sodium-glucose cotransporter
    B. direct hydrolysis of ATP on the extracellular surface by the sodium-glucose cotransporter
    C. binding of Na^+ to specific secreted proteins in the surrounding medium
    D. binding of Na^+ and glucose in the surrounding medium to specific membrane proteins

D is correct.

Binding of specific proteins in the membrane to Na^+ and glucose in the surrounding medium is the only possible answer. A membrane protein must bind Na^+ and glucose in the extracellular side of the membrane prior to transport.

A and B: ATP hydrolysis is not catalyzed by the Na^+/glucose cotransporter. ATPase pump produces the initial Na^+.

C: there are no secreted proteins involved in the transport process.

24. The result of Experiments 1 and 2 indicate that ATP promotes the cellular uptake of glucose by serving as a source of:

    A. monosaccharide   **C. metabolic energy**
    B. enzymes   **D.** inorganic phosphate

C is correct.

The driving force is the energy provided in the breaking (i.e. hydrolysis) of ATP into ADP + P_i. The hydrolysis of the "high energy bond" in ATP supplies energy to drive transport.

A and B: ATP (a nucleotide) is neither an enzyme (proteins are enzymes) nor a monosaccharide (i.e. sugar subunit of carbohydrate).

D: although ATP can be a source of P_i, inorganic phosphate does not drive transport.

25. Within animal cells, the transport of Na^+/K^+ via the ATPase pump involves:

    A. facilitated diffusion   **C.** osmosis
    B. active transport   **D.** passive transport

B is correct.

Because active transport moves the Na^+/K^+ ions from a low concentration region to a high concentration region, energy is required in the form of ATP hydrolysis. The Na^+/K^+ ATPase pump transports Na^+ out of the cell against a concentration gradient. Because the concentration is increasing, ATP supplies the needed energy to drive transport.

A and D: facilitated diffusion (i.e. passive transport) involves the movement of ions through a protein channel down the concentration gradient and requires no energy.

C: osmosis (diffusion of water) requires no hydrolysis of ATP, because the process involves the movement of ions down the concentration gradient and requires no energy.

26. According to Figure 1, as Na^+ concentration in the medium approaches the same concentration found in the cells, glucose concentration in the medium would:

   A. level off, because a sodium gradient is not available to drive cotransport
   B. remain at its original level, because sodium concentration does not affect glucose concentration
   C. approach zero, because glucose and sodium are transported together
   D. increase, because less glucose is transported into the bacterial cells

A is correct.

The Na^+ concentration gradient provides the energy to drive glucose transport. When the Na^+ concentration is the same inside and outside of the cell, there is no gradient and, thus, no energy gradient to drive glucose transport. Therefore, when Na^+ concentration levels are equal on both sides of the membrane, transport of glucose into the cell stops, and the extracellular and intracellular glucose concentrations become equal.

In Figure 1, the Na^+ in the medium decreases but levels off before reaching zero.

> Questions 27 through 29 are not based on any
> descriptive passage and are independent of each other

27. Which of the following structures is found in bacterial cells?

A. nucleolus	**C. ribosome**
B. mitochondria	**D.** smooth endoplasmic reticulum

C is correct.

Ribosomes are the assemblies of protein and rRNA and are not organelles. The ribosomes in prokaryotes and eukaryotes are different, but both cell types have ribosomes. The ribosomes of prokaryotes are 30S (small subunit) and 50S (large subunit), making a 70S complete ribosome with both subunits assembled. The ribosomes of the eukaryote are 40S (small subunit) and 60S (large subunit), making a 80S complete ribosome with both subunits assembled.

Bacteria are prokaryotes, and therefore lack all membrane-bound organelles, including mitochondria, the ER (both smooth and rough), the nucleus and nucleolus. The nucleolus is located within the nucleus in eukaryotes and is the site of rRNA synthesis.

28. Exocrine secretions of the pancreas:

A. lower blood serum glucose levels	**C. aid in protein and fat digestion**
B. raise blood serum glucose levels	**D.** regulate metabolic rate of anabolism and catabolism

C is correct.

The pancreas functions as both an exocrine gland and endocrine gland. The pancreas is an elongated lobular gland extending from the duodenum (first of the three regions of the small intestine). From its exocrine part, the gland secretes pancreatic juice that is discharged into the intestine. From its endocrine part, it secretes insulin and glucagon.

An exocrine gland excretes its products into ducts (i.e. tubes) that often empty into epithelial tissue. Endocrine glands release hormones directly into the bloodstream. Hormones are chemical substances formed in a tissue or organ and carried in the blood to stimulate or inhibit the growth or function of one or more other tissues or organs.

As an endocrine gland, the pancreas produces and secretes two hormones: insulin and glucagon. Insulin is secreted by the beta cells of the pancreas. It lowers blood glucose levels by stimulating the uptake of glucose by the cells. Glucagon is secreted by the alpha cells of the pancreas and elevates blood glucose levels by stimulating the release of hepatic (e.g. liver) glycogen. One of the disorders of glycogen storage is von Gierke's disease.

As an exocrine gland, the pancreas secretes many enzymes that are involved in protein, fat, and carbohydrate digestion. All of the exocrine products of the pancreas are secreted into the small intestine. Pancreatic amylase hydrolyzes starch to maltose. Trypsin hydrolyzes peptide bonds and catalyzes the conversion of chymotrypsinogen to chymotrypsin. Chymotrypsin and carboxypeptidase also hydrolyze peptide bonds. Pancreatic lipase is an enzyme that hydrolyzes lipids.

The thyroid gland secretes thyroid hormones and calcitonin. Thyroxine (T_4 thyroid hormone) promotes growth and development and increases the metabolic rate in cells. Calcitonin, a 32 amino acid peptide hormone, is secreted primarily by C cells of the thyroid gland, and to a lesser extent by parathyroid glands and thymus. Calcitonin works in opposition to the parathyroid hormone: it increases the deposition of calcium and phosphate in bones and lowers the level of calcium in the blood.

Parathyroid hormone is a peptide hormone produced by the parathyroid glands. It maintains serum calcium levels by promoting intestinal absorption and renal tubular reabsorption of calcium, as well as release of calcium from bone to extracellular fluid.

29. What type of protein structure describes a complex of two alpha and two beta peptide chains within hemoglobin?

   A. primary   **B.** secondary   **C.** tertiary   **D. quaternary**

D is correct.

Important MCAT fact: There are four levels of protein structure.

The primary ($1°$) protein structure refers to the linear sequence of amino acids.

The secondary ($2°$) protein structure refers to the local folding along amino acids that are within 12 amino acids. Common motifs of secondary structure are alpha helix and beta-pleated sheets within the protein.

The tertiary ($3°$) protein structure refers to the three-dimensional shape of the properly folded polypeptide of the functional protein.

The quaternary ($4°$) protein structure is defined as two (or more) polypeptide chains linked together via a number of weak non-covalent interactions (e.g., H-bonds, Van der Waals) and/or strong disulfide bonds (between cysteine). Cystine is formed by two –SH groups between single cysteine that become one –S–S– group.

According to the question stem, adult hemoglobin consists of four polypeptide chains and, therefore, is an example of $4°$ protein structure. Quaternary structure requires that the protein contain more than one polypeptide chain. The chains are not separated during denaturation of the protein.

Passage 5
(Questions 30– 35)

Thrombosis is the formation or presence of a blood clot, which may cause infarction of tissue supplied by the vessel. Although the coagulation factors that are necessary to initiate blood clotting are present in the blood, clot formation in the intact vascular system is prevented by three properties of the vascular walls. First, the endothelial lining, which is sensitive to vascular damage, is smooth enough to prevent activation of the clotting system. Second, the inner surface of the endothelium is covered with mucopolysaccharide (glycocalyx) that repels the clotting factors and platelets in the blood. Third, an endothelial surface protein known as thrombomodulin binds thrombin, the enzyme that converts fibrinogen into fibrin in the final stage of clotting. The binding of thrombin to thrombomodulin reduces the amount of thrombin that can participate in clotting. Also, the thrombin-thrombomodulin complex activates protein C, a plasma protein that hinders clot formation by acting as an anticoagulant.

If the endothelial surface of a vessel has been roughened by arteriosclerosis or infection, and the glycocalyx-thrombomodulin layer has been lost, the first step of the intrinsic blood clotting pathway (Figure 1) will be triggered. The Factor XII protein changes its shape to become "activated" Factor XII. This conformational change within the protein initiates a cascade of reactions that result in the formation of thrombin and the subsequent conversion of fibrinogen to fibrin. Simultaneously, platelets release platelet factor 3, a lipoprotein that helps to activate the coagulation factors. A thrombus is an abnormal blood clot that develops in blood vessels and may impede or obstruct vascular flow.

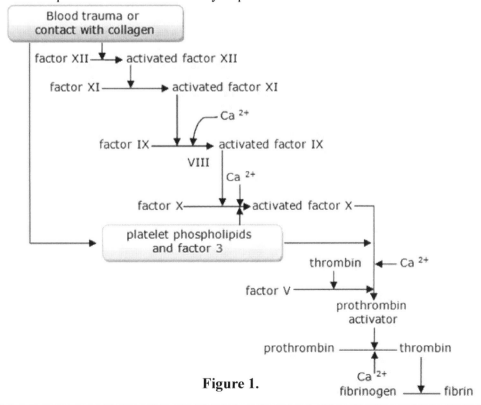

Figure 1.

An embolus is a thrombus that dislodges and travels in the bloodstream. Typically, an embolus will travel through the circulatory system until it becomes trapped at a narrow point, resulting in vessel blockage.

30. All of the following would cause prolonged clotting time in a human blood sample, EXCEPT:

A. addition of activated Factor X   C. addition of a calcium chelating agent
B. removal of platelets or fibrinogen   D. removal of Factor VIII

A is correct.

Prolonged clotting time results from an interference in the intrinsic pathway (Figure 1). The deficiency of any clotting factor (e.g. Factor VIII) or the deficiency of platelets (or platelet phospholipids) makes it more difficult for the blood to coagulate and for a clot to form.

Calcium ions are required for the promotion of all but the first two reactions in the pathway. Clotting would be slowed (or prevented) by reducing the calcium ion concentration in the blood (e.g. addition of a calcium chelating agent).

However, the addition of activated Factor X would not increase clotting time, because activated Factor X is one of the key components in the intrinsic pathway.

31. A physician injects small quantities of heparin in patients with pulmonary emboli histories to inhibit further thrombus formation. Heparin increases the activity of antithrombin III, the blood's primary inhibitor of thrombin. One possible adverse side effect of heparin administration is:

A. dizziness   C. degradation of existing emboli
B. minor bleeding   D. blood pressure increase

B is correct.

Heparin, a highly-sulfated glycosaminoglycan, is widely used as an injectable anticoagulant and has the highest negative charge density among all known biological molecules. It prevents the formation of abnormal blood clots by enhancing the activity of antithrombin III (the anticoagulant). Antithrombin III interferes with the intrinsic pathway, and blood clotting ability is significantly reduced by heparin injection. Minor damage to the patient's blood vessels will not be automatically repaired (as normal) and the patient may experience minor vascular bleeding as a result of heparin administration.

A: there is no indication that the oxygen-carrying capability of the blood, or the integrity of the blood vessels, would be compromised. Therefore, dizziness would be an unlikely result.

C: existing blood clots (e.g. emboli) are degraded by fibrinolytic enzymes. Interfering with the blood clotting pathway has no effect on existing clots.

D: a patient should not experience an increased blood pressure from interfering with the blood clotting function.

32. From the diagram in the passage, the function of Factor VIII in the activation of Factor X is that of a(n):

    A. zymogen   **B.** substrate   **C.** enzyme   **D. cofactor**

D is correct.

The intrinsic clotting pathway consists of a series of reactions in which proteins, such as Factor X, are converted from their inactive proenzyme form (zymogens, ending in -*ogen*) to the active form of the enzyme. Proenzymes (zymogens) are enzyme precursors that require some change (usually the hydrolysis of an inhibiting fragment that makes an active group) to render the enzyme active.

Examples of inactive enzymes include pepsinogen (in the stomach for digestion of proteins) and trypsinogen. Trypsin, pepsin and chymotrypsin are proteolytic digestive enzymes that cleave the peptide linkage of certain amino acids. Trypsin splits the peptide bond adjacent to lysine and arginine; pepsin cleaves peptide bonds adjacent to phenylalanine, tryptophan and tyrosine; chymotrypsin splits peptide bonds adjacent to tyrosine, phenylalanine, tryptophan and, to a lesser degree, methionine and leucine.

Factor X is the proenzyme that undergoes a transformation into the active form. Factor X serves as the substrate for the activated Factor IX (enzyme), which catalyzes the conversion of Factor X to its active form.

Factor VIII, Ca^{2+} and platelet phospholipids all serve as cofactors for the reaction, because they accelerate the conversion of Factor X into its active form.

33. The initial formation of thrombin in the intrinsic clotting pathway:

    A. deactivates the blood factors
    B. increases conversion of Factor XII to activated Factor XII
    C. has a positive feedback effect on thrombin formation
    D. causes a platelet reduction within plasma

C is correct.

When the cascade begins, Factor V and Factor VIII are initially inactive because no thrombin is present. Once clotting begins, thrombin is formed, activating Factors V and VIII. Factors V and VIII serve as cofactors in the reactions that activate Factor X and prothrombin activator. Thus, thrombin accelerates its own synthesis and the initial formation of thrombin has a positive feedback effect that supports accelerated thrombin formation.

A: thrombin is responsible for activation of several factors involved in the clotting cascade.

B: blood trauma (or contact with collagen) enhances the activation of Factor XII.

D: thrombin has no effect on the number of circulating platelets.

34. Based on information in the passage, which of the following is the most likely mechanism of action of protein C?

    A. Activation of Factors XII and X
    B. Deactivation of activated Factors V and VIII
    C. Acceleration of prothrombin formation
    D. Negative feedback effect of thrombomodulin

B is correct.

According to the passage, protein C is an anticoagulant that prevents clotting.

All other choices are mechanisms of coagulation and are incorrect, because protein C is an anticoagulant.

A and C: the promotion of the formation of prothrombin and activation of Factors X and XII would increase clotting (see Figure 1). Deactivation of activated Factors V and VIII, however, would prevent thrombin from having a positive feedback effect on its own formation, which is essential for clot formation. Deactivation of these factors (the actual mechanism of protein C function), renders protein C an effective anticoagulant.

D: a negative feedback regulation of thrombomodulin facilitates clotting, because thrombomodulin acts to slow the process.

35. Which of the following is most likely the origin of a pulmonary embolus that blocks the pulmonary artery?

    A. Left side of the heart   **C.** Pulmonary veins
    B. The aorta   **D. Veins within the lower extremities**

D is correct.

A pulmonary embolus is an abnormal blood clot that has been dislodged from its point of origin and carried through the circulatory system to the lungs. Within the lungs, the embolus blocks the pulmonary artery (or its branch). The movement of an embolus is impeded when it reaches a narrow point in the circulatory system. Therefore, there is a limited number of possible locations from which a pulmonary embolism could originate.

A: the embolus could not originate from the left side of the heart, because the passage through the systemic circulation to the right side of the heart and then to the pulmonary arteries would be virtually impossible for the embolus to make. The embolism would most likely lodge in some systemic vessel.

B and C: an embolus coming from the aorta, or the pulmonary veins, would also likely become lodged somewhere in a systemic vessel, such as the upper limbs, the lower extremities, or the brain.

Most pulmonary emboli originate in the veins of the lower legs. From the veins in the lower extremities, the embolism flows freely with venous blood up into the right side of the heart (right atrium and then right ventricle), and then into the pulmonary arteries (toward the lungs), where the embolism typically lodges.

Passage 6
(Questions 36–40)

Fermentation is an anaerobic process that results in the conversion of high-energy substrates into various waste products. Fermentation harvests only a small amount of the energy stored in glucose. There are two common types: alcoholic fermentation and lactic acid fermentation.

Alcoholic fermentation (also called ethanol fermentation) is a biological process, whereby sugars (e.g. glucose, fructose and sucrose) are converted into cellular energy and produce ethanol and carbon dioxide as metabolic waste products. Because yeasts perform this conversion in the absence of oxygen, alcoholic fermentation is considered an anaerobic process. Anaerobic respiration is a form of respiration that uses electron acceptors other than oxygen.

Lactic acid fermentation is a biological metabolic process that converts glucose, fructose and sucrose into cellular energy and the metabolite lactate. It is also an anaerobic fermentation that occurs in some bacteria and animal cells (e.g. muscle cells). In homolactic fermentation, one molecule of glucose is converted into two molecules of lactic acid. By contrast, heterolactic fermentation yields carbon dioxide and ethanol in addition to lactic acid via a process called the phosphoketolase pathway.

In alcoholic fermentation, the conversion of pyruvic acid to ethanol is a two-step process. In heterolactic acid fermentation, the conversion of pyruvic acid into lactic acid is a one-step process.

Figure 1. Alcoholic fermentation and lactic acid fermentation pathways.

36. Lactic acid accumulates in muscles and is transported by the blood to the liver. What is the effect of lactic acid on respiratory rate?

    A. It decreases respiratory rate
    B. It increases respiratory rate
    C. It has no effect on respiratory rate
    D. Respiratory rate initially decreases and then quickly levels off

B is correct.

Lactic acid decreases the pH of blood plasma. Carbon dioxide dissolved in blood plasma also decreases the pH through conversion to carbonic acid.

The respiratory rate increases when the blood plasma becomes acidic, because the person needs to exhale more CO_2. An increased respiratory rate achieves homeostasis by making the blood plasma slightly alkaline. Normally, blood plasma is slightly alkaline at about 7.35 pH level.

37. In lactic acid fermentation, pyruvate functions as an:

    A. electron acceptor for the reduction of NAD^+
    B. electron acceptor for the oxidation of NADH
    C. electron donor for the reduction of NAD^+
    D. electron donor for the oxidation of NADH

B is correct.

Pyruvate is reduced by gaining electrons. NADH is oxidized by loss of electrons.

Other choices are incorrect because in fermentation, NADH is oxidized to NAD^+. Fermentation occurs under anaerobic conditions, where the organism has a deficiency of O_2, and pyruvate cannot enter the Krebs cycle due to the deficiency of O_2. Pyruvate is shunted to the lactic acid cycle for the purpose of regenerating NAD^+, because glycolysis (aerobic and anaerobic) requires NAD^+ for the reduction to NADH, which is needed for glycolysis to yield a total of 4 ATP (net of 2 ATP) from glycolysis.

"LEO the lion says GER" is a common mnemonic. LEO: Loss of Electrons is Oxidation. GER: Gain of Electrons is Reduction.

In organic chemistry, oxidation is an increase of the number of bonds to oxygen (or electronegative atoms) or, conversely, the loss of bonds to hydrogen (and the accompanying gain of electrons to electronegative atoms/oxygen).

38. Fermentation differs from glycolysis, because in fermentation:

    A. glucose is oxidized   **C.** high-energy electrons are transferred to NAD^+
    B. NAD$^+$ is regenerated   **D.** ATP is produced

B is correct.

Fermentation occurs during anaerobic cellular respiration due to an oxygen debt, whereby the demand for ATP exceeds the capacity of the lungs and blood to transport O_2 to the tissue where O_2 is needed for the electron transport chain.

In fermentation, NAD^+ is regenerated. Glycolysis requires the availability of NAD^+. Glycolysis converts NAD^+ by reduction (gain of electrons) to NADH. Under anaerobic conditions, NADH is oxidized to regenerate NAD^+, concurrently reducing pyruvate to lactic acid. This is similar to metabolism in facultative anaerobes, which are able to use either fermentation or oxidative phosphorylation, depending on the availability of oxygen.

Muscle cells can use lactic-acid fermentation (without oxygen) during periods of strenuous physical activity.

Muscle cells preferentially use aerobic respiration except during strenuous exercise. Strenuous exercise uses oxygen faster than it can be supplied.

ATP, CTP, GTP, TTP and UTP are nucleotides. GTP is produced in the Krebs cycle of cellular respiration. During cellular respiration, ATP is produced during glycolysis (gross production is 4 ATP less 2 invested = net of 2 ATP) by substrate level phosphorylation (not requiring O_2).

During the ETC (electron transport chain), 32 ATP are produced via oxidation of NADH $\rightarrow NAD^+$ and $FADH_2 \rightarrow FADH$.

NADH produces three H^+, and $FADH_2$ produces two H^+. H^+ is pumped into the intermembrane space of the mitochondrion, and each H^+ produces 1 ATP by oxidative phosphorylation as the H^+ passes through the ATP synthase (i.e. ATPase), a protein embedded in the inner membrane of the mitochondria.

39. During alcoholic fermentation, pyruvic acid and acetaldehyde are, respectively:

   A. decarboxylated and oxidized   **C.** reduced and decarboxylated

   B. decarboxylated and reduced   **D.** decarboxylated and phosphorylated

B is correct.

Pyruvate is decarboxylated (loses a CO_2) to become lactic acid, while acetaldehyde is reduced by NADH, which is then oxidized to NAD^+.

40. During fermentation, the final electron acceptor from NADH is:

   A. an organic molecule   **B.** alcohol   **C.** NAD^+ **D.** ½ O_2

A is correct.

Fermentation is anaerobic cellular respiration. During fermentation, the final electron acceptor (from NADH to regenerate NAD^+) is the organic molecule of lactate (lactic acid).

Oxidative phosphorylation is aerobic cellular respiration. The final electron acceptor from NADH (high energy intermediate similar to $FADH_2$) during the electron transport chain (ETC) is O_2. Molecular oxygen ($\frac{1}{2} O_2$) is often referred to as the ultimate electron acceptor because of its role (accepting electrons and two H^+ to form H_2O) during the last stage of cellular respiration, the electron transport chain.

> Questions 41 through 46 are not based on any descriptive passage and are independent of each other

41. Which two atomic orbitals interact to form the D—D bond in D_2?

   A. *s* and *s*   **B.** *p* and *p*   **C.** *sp* and *sp*   **D.** sp^3 and sp^3

A is correct.

Deuterium is an isotope of hydrogen. Like hydrogen, deuterium has a single valence electron, and therefore has one *s* orbital. The single *s* orbital is not hybridized.

The D–D bond is formed by the internuclear σ (sigma) bond overlap of an *s* orbital from each deuterium, where σ bond refers to a single bond.

Carbon is the atom that undergoes hybridization of the 4 orbitals of $s + p + p + p$ (*s* is lower in energy than the p orbitals) to form 4 equal energy sp^3 orbitals pointing to the corners of a tetrahedron (shape) with a bond angle of 109.5°.

42. During skeletal muscle contraction, which bands of the sarcomere shorten?

   A. I and H bands   **C.** I bands and Z discs
   B. A and H bands   **D.** Z discs

A is correct.

The overlap between thick and thin filaments increases during contraction. The nonoverlapping regions decrease in length. During contraction, I bands (actin thin filaments only) and H bands (myosin thick filaments only) shorten.

B: the A bands are the length of myosin (thick filaments) and include the overlapping portion of the actin (thin filaments). The lengths of the A (actin and myosin overlap) bands do not change during contraction.

C and D: the Z discs are the connection points for the I band (actin) connection and demarcate the ends of the sarcomeres.

43. Human muscle cells behave in a manner similar to:

A. anaerobes

B. obligate aerobes

C. facultative anaerobes

D. strict aerobes

C is correct.

Muscle cells generate ATP through aerobic respiration. Aerobic respiration links glycolysis to the Krebs cycle and then to the ETC for oxidative phosphorylation.

Under anaerobic conditions, muscle cells can produce ATP through fermentation, using NADH to reduce pyruvate to lactic acid and regenerate NAD^+. Anaerobic respiration is similar to metabolism in facultative anaerobes, which are able to use either fermentation or oxidative phosphorylation, depending on the availability of oxygen.

A: muscle cells will preferentially use aerobic respiration, except during strenuous exercise, which depletes oxygen faster than it can be supplied to the tissue.

B and D: muscle cells can use lactic acid fermentation (anaerobic respiration) to survive without using oxygen during periods of strenuous physical activity.

44. During the production of urine, the nephron controls the composition of urine by all of the following physiological processes, EXCEPT:

A. reabsorption of H_2O

B. counter current exchange with blood

C. secretion of solutes into urine

D. filtration for Na^+ to remain in blood

D is correct.

The answer choice of filtration for Na^+ to remain in the blood is a false statement, and therefore the correct answer.

Only large solutes like proteins are filtered at the glomerulus and do not pass into the nephron. Ions such as Na^+ pass freely into the filtrate and must be reabsorbed in the proximal tubule (active transport), ascending loop of Henle (passive transport) and distal tubule (active transport) during the processing of filtrate to make urine.

45. Which of the following molecules is NOT transported via Na^+ dependent transport?

A. bile acids   **B.** galactose   **C.** proteins   **D. fatty acids**

D is correct.

The MCAT requires understanding of the absorption mechanisms for dietary nutrients such as carbohydrates, proteins and lipids.

Lipids are enclosed, absorbed and transported in the circulatory system as micelles (membrane enclosed vesicles). Lipids (dietary fat) are composed of glycerol and fatty acids.

A: bile is stored in the gall bladder. Bile acts as an emulsifier of dietary lipids to increase their surface area, because bile is amphipathic (hydrophobic and hydrophilic portion). The hydrophobic portion of the bile becomes embedded within the hydrophobic core of the lipid, while the hydrophilic portion of the lipid remains in contact with the hydrophilic chyme (dietary contents of the stomach and small intestine). Bile acids are reabsorbed via Na^+ dependent transport.

B and C: galactose (i.e. not fructose) and proteins (single amino acids, dipeptides and tripeptides) are transported across the small intestine membrane via Na^+ dependent cotransport.

46. Which of the following characteristics of water make it the most important solvent on earth?

I.   Water is non-polar   **III. Water is a Bronsted-Lowry acid**
II.   Water is a Bronsted-Lowry base   **IV. Water forms hydrogen bonds**

A. I and II only   **C. II, III and IV only**
B. II and III only   **D.** I, II, III and IV

C is correct.

Important MCAT topic: Water can act as both an acid (H_2O dissociates into $H^+ + OH^-$) and a base (H_2O abstracts $H^+ \rightarrow H_3O^+$).

Water is a polar compound, therefore statement I is false. Additionally, water makes hydrogen bonds to other water molecules. Hydrogen bonds occur when H is bonded directly to an electronegative atom, such as F, O, N or Cl. Note, many textbooks exclude Cl from the examples of hydrogen bond when hydrogen is directly bonded to either F (electronegativity: 3.98), O (3.44) or N (3.04). Due to its electronegativity of 3.16, Cl does form hydrogen bonds. However, these hydrogen bonds are weaker than predicted by electronegativity alone. Because of the larger orbital size of chlorine, the electron density is lower than necessary for strong hydrogen bonding (i.e. strong dipole-dipole attractions).

Hydrogen bonding between water molecules contributes to water having surface tension, capillary tension, high specific heat and so on; therefore, statement IV is correct.

A Bronsted-Lowry acid is any molecule that donates protons (H^+). A Bronsted-Lowry base is any molecule or ion that combines with a proton; ^-OH, ^-CN, NH_3. This definition replaces the older and more limited definition of bases. The Bronsted-Lowry acid is a substance (i.e. charged ions or uncharged molecules) that liberates hydrogen ions in solution. A Bronsted-Lowry base is a substance that removes H^+ from solution. This Bronsted-Lowry concept is useful for weak electrolytes (i.e. substances that dissociate into ions within the solution) and for buffers (i.e. solutions that resist changes in pH). Therefore, statement II and III apply to water and are correct.

Passage 7
(Questions 47–52)

The reaction between alkyl bromide and chloride anion may proceed via any one of four possible reaction mechanisms. The observed pathway is a function of the solvent polarity. Although all four reactions involve substitution, each mechanism produces a distinct product.

Researchers calculated the free energies of activation (ΔG) in kcal mol^{-1} for the different mechanisms in two different solvents.

Figure 1.

The experiments demonstrated that the preferred pathway for the molecules in non-polar organic solvents is S_N2. However, as the solvent polarity increases, the difference in energy between the pathways narrows. In water, the preferred pathway, with a lower energy of activation, is S_N1.

(Z)-1-bromo-2-butene

(E)-1-chloro-2-butene   1-chloro-3-methyl-2-butene

Figure 2.

47. Which of the following is true regarding the reaction of (Z)-1-bromo-2-butene with the chloride anion in carbon tetrachloride?

A. Reaction is unimolecular

C. Reaction is a concerted mechanism

B. Reaction produces a racemic mixture

D. Reaction rate is independent of [Cl⁻]

C is correct.

In CCl_4, the reaction undergoes the profile of an S_N2 mechanism. S_N2 reaction rates are dependent on the concentration of substrates and nucleophile (i.e. second order kinetics). S_N2 occurs in a concerted mechanism within one step, whereby the nucleophile attacks the carbon and displaces the leaving group. The concerted (single step) mechanism accounts for the inversion of stereochemistry and the fact that a stereospecific (e.g. R vs. S) single product is produced (i.e. not a racemic mixture). Racemic mixtures result from the S_N1 reaction involving a planar intermediate (carbocation) and the nucleophile attacking the trigonal planar (flat) intermediate to produce a mixture (racemate) of the stereospecific (R and S) products.

48. Which of the following molecules forms the most stable carbocation following the dissociation of the halide ion?

A. (E)-1-chloro-2-butene

C. 1-chloro-3-methyl-2-butene

B. (Z)-1-bromo-2-butene

D. no difference is expected

C is correct.

1-chloro-3-methyl-2-butene has an additional electron donating group (methyl) to help stabilize the positively charged carbocation. After the halide dissociates, the 1-chloro-3-methyl-2-butene resonances to form a tertiary cation.

A and B: both molecules can resonate, but form a less stable secondary carbocation.

49. Regarding the reaction of 1-chloro-3-methyl-2-butene with Cl⁻ in water, which of the following statements is supported by the passage?

A. A strong nucleophile is required for the reaction to proceed

B. A carbocation is formed

C. The reaction occurs with the inversion of stereochemistry

D. The reaction occurs with a single ΔG in the reaction profile

B is correct.

The mechanism is an S_N1 pathway with the formation of a carbocation.

All other answers are accurate for the concerted mechanism of an S_N2 pathway.

50. Which hypothesis explains the difference in the mechanism pathway (Figure 1) when the solvent is changed from CCl_4 to H_2O?

    A. Hydrogen bonding of the H_2O solvent stabilizes the transition state of the S_N2 pathway

    B. Hydrogen bonding of the H_2O solvent stabilizes the intermediate of the S_N2 pathway

    C. Hydrogen bonding of the H_2O solvent stabilizes the nucleophile of the S_N2 pathway

    D. Hydrogen bonding of the H_2O solvent stabilizes the carbocation intermediate of the S_N1 pathway

D is correct.

Hydrogen bonding in water stabilizes the carbocation formed in the S_N1 pathway, because the charged intermediate is stabilized to decrease the activation energy.

S_N2 mechanisms are favored in non-polar aprotic solvents, such as CCl_4, because the aprotic solvent does not liberate H^+, which would solvate (shield) the strong nucleophile (often charged species). Strong nucleophiles favor the concerted reaction mechanisms of the S_N2 and initiate the reaction prior to the formation of a carbocation. The substrate is important for determining if the reaction proceeds by S_N1 or S_N2. S_N1 favors tertiary ($3°$) substrates that can support a stable carbocation, while S_N2 favors the less sterically hindered primary ($1°$) substrate that does not form a stable carbocation.

51. Which of the following reagents must be reacted with (E)-1-chloro-2-butene for a saturated alkyl halide to be formed?

    A. H_2, Pd   **C.** 1) $Hg(OAc)_2$, H_2O 2) $NaBH_4$

    B. 1) BH_3, THF 2) H_2O_2, ⁻OH   **D.** concentrated H_2SO_4

A is correct.

The conversion of an alkene (double bond) to an alkane (single bond) is a reduction. Hydrogenation (adding H_2 with metal catalyst) is the only reducing reagent among the choices listed.

B: BH_3, THF / H_2O_2, ⁻OH (Hydroboration to alkenes) adds an –OH group at the non-Markovnikov (less substituted carbon) along the double bond.

C: $Hg(OAc)_2$, H_2O / $NaBH_4$ (Oxymercuration to alkenes) adds an –OH group at the Markovnikov (more substituted carbon) along the double bond.

D: concentrated H_2SO_4 is used for reduction of an alcohol to form an alkene.

52. Which of the following reagents, when reacted with 1-chloro-3-methyl-2-butene, will produce an alcohol with the hydroxyl group on C2?

    A. Lindlar   **C.** $Hg(OAc)_2$, H_2O / $NaBH_4$

    B. BH_3, THF / H_2O_2, ⁻OH   **D.** Grignard

B is correct.

Hydroboration (BH_3, THF followed by H_2O_2, ⁻OH) yields a non-Markovnikov orientation with hydroxyl group at the less substituted carbon (carbon 2) on 1-chloro-3-methyl-2-butene.

A: Lindlar is the reagent that converts an alkyne (triple bond) to a cis alkene. Another reaction, Li / NH_3 is the reagent that converts an alkyne (triple bond) to a trans alkene.

C: $Hg(OAc)_2$, H_2O / $NaBH_4$ (Oxymercuration to alkenes) adds an –OH group at the Markovnikov (more substituted carbon) along the double bond. This is the opposite regiospecificity desired from the question.

D: Grignard (Mg^{2+} inserted between the carbon-halide bond) is a common method for generation of carbanion (C with a pair of electrons – negative charged species). Grignard is used for extending the carbon-carbon chain length by attacking (oftentimes) an alkyl halide and displacing the leaving group during the new carbon-carbon bond formation. Note: the solution cannot contain a source of H^+ (protons such as from a protic solvent of water or alcohols), because the highly reactive (basic) Grignard will abstract the H^+ and the reaction will be quenched with the resulting alkane (undesired product) formation.

> Questions 53 through 59 are not based on any
> descriptive passage and are independent of each other

53. How many amino acids are essential to the human diet?

   A. 4   **B.** 9   **C.** 11   **D.** 12

B is correct.

Essential amino acids cannot be synthesized *de novo* (i.e. made new) within the human body, and therefore must be supplied in the diet. The nine amino acids humans cannot synthesize endogenously are histidine, isoleucine, leucine, lysine, methionine, phenylalanine, threonine, tryptophan and valine. A mnemonic for essential amino acids is: *PVT TIM HaLL*

Six amino acids are conditionally essential for humans, meaning their endogenous synthesis can be limited under special pathophysiological conditions (e.g. for infants or persons under severe catabolic distress). These six amino acids are arginine, cysteine, glutamine, glycine, proline and tyrosine. Five amino acids are neither essential nor conditionally essential in humans, because they can be synthesized in the body: alanine, asparagine, aspartic acid, glutamic acid and serine.

54. In eukaryotic cells, most of the ribosomal RNA are transcribed by RNA polymerase [ ], major structural genes are transcribed by RNA polymerase [ ], and tRNAs are transcribed by RNA polymerase [ ].

   A. II; I; III   **B.** II; III; I   **C.** I; II; III   **D.** I; III; II

C is correct.

55. Cellulose is not highly branched, because it does not have:

   A. β(1→4) glycosidic bonds   **C.** a polysaccharide backbone
   B. α(1→4) glycosidic bonds   **D.** α(1→6) glycosidic bonds

D is correct.

Cellulose linked by β(1→4) glycosidic bonds

56. Which formula represents palmitic acid?

A. $CH_3(CH_2)_8COOH$ 　　　　C. $CH_3(CH_2)_{16}COOH$

B. $CH_3(CH_2)_{18}COOH$ 　　　　**D. $CH_3(CH_2)_{14}COOH$**

D is correct.

Palmitic acid is the most common saturated fatty acid (IUPAC: hexadecanoic acid) found in animals, plants and microorganisms with the molecular formula $CH_3(CH_2)_{14}COOH$. Per its name, it is a major component of the oil from palm trees (e.g. palm oil), but can also be found in meats, cheeses, butter and dairy products. Palmitate refers to the salts and esters of palmitic acid.

57. Lipids can be either:

A. hydrophobic or hydrophilic 　　　　C. amphipathic or hydrophilic

B. hydrophobic or amphipathic 　　　　D. amphipathic or amphoteric

B is correct.

An amphipathic substance contains both a hydrophilic and hydrophobic region.
An amphoteric substance can act as an acid or a base, depending on pH (e.g. water).

58. Given that K_M measures the affinity of an enzyme and its substrate, without presence of inhibitors, for the reaction rate to increase:

A. k_{cat} is must decrease 　　　　C. k_1 must decrease

B. k_{cat} must increase 　　　　D. k_{-1} must increase

A is correct.

Michaelis-Menten equation for enzymes:

$$E + S \underset{k_{-1}}{\overset{k_1}{\rightleftharpoons}} ES \xrightarrow{k_{cat}} E + P$$

k_{cat} is the turnover rate (i.e., the maximum number of chemical conversions of substrate molecules per sec). k_{cat} the rate constant for $ES \rightarrow E + P$ (product formation). For single-step reactions, $k_{cat} = k_2$; for multi-step reactions, k_{cat} is the rate-limiting step.

K_M (the Michaelis constant) is the substrate concentration at 1/2 the maximum velocity. For efficient enzymes, the K_M is lower.

$$K_M = (k_{-1} + k_{cat}) / k_1$$

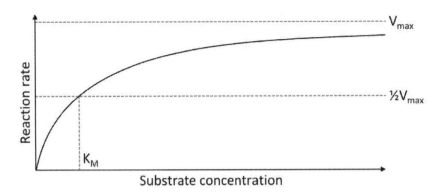

K_M measures the strength of the enzyme-substrate complex, where higher K_M indicates weak binding (slower reaction) and lower K_M indicates strong binding (faster reaction).

59. Which amino acid-derived molecule transports amino acids across the cell membrane?

    A. S-adenosylmethionine   **C. glutathione**
    B. insulin   **D.** γ-aminobutyric acid

C is correct.

In addition to transporting amino acids across the cell membrane, glutathione has multiple functions, such as being a major antioxidant produced by the cells, regulating the nitric oxide cycle, participating in metabolic and biochemical reactions of DNA synthesis and repair, protein synthesis, prostaglandin synthesis and enzyme activation, as well as playing a vital role in iron metabolism.

Biological & Biochemical Foundations of Living Systems
MCAT® Practice Test #2 – Answer Key

Passage 1
1 : A
2 : D
3 : B
4 : B
5 : C
6 : B
7 : C

Passage 2
8 : B
9 : A
10: C
11 : C
12 : C
13 : B

Independent questions
14 : A
15 : B
16 : C
17 : A

Passage 3
18 : A
19 : C
20 : B
21 : C
22 : C
23 : A

Passage 4
24 : D
25 : B
26 : C
27 : C
28 : A

Independent questions
29 : B
30 : D
31 : A
32 : A
33 : C

Passage 5
34 : C
35 : B
36 : B
37 : B
38 : D

Passage 6
39 : B
40 : C
41 : D
42 : D
43 : B

Independent questions
44 : C
45 : D
46 : A
47 : D

Passage 7
48 : D
49 : B
50: C
51 : A
52 : D

Independent questions
53 : A
54 : D
55 : D
56 : A
57 : D
58 : A
59 : C

Passage 1
(Questions 1–7)

Researchers are studying a eukaryotic organism that has a highly active mechanism for DNA replication, transcription and translation. The organism has both a haploid and a diploid state. In the haploid state, only one copy of each chromosome complement is present. In the diploid state, two copies of each chromosome complement, usually homozygous for most traits, are present. To investigate this organism, two mutations were induced and the resulting cell lines were labeled as mutants #1 and #2, and these mutants demonstrated unique phenotypes.

To elucidate the events of transcription and translation, a wild-type variant of the organism was exposed to standard mutagens, including intercalating agents such as ethidium bromide, which resulted in the creation of the two mutants. The researchers analyzed the exact sequence of events leading from DNA to RNA, and from RNA to protein products. Figure 1 illustrates this sequence of the wild-type and the sequences of the two mutant organisms.

Experiment A:

Mutant #1 was plated onto a Petri dish and grown with a nutrient broth. The mutant #1 organism showed growth and reproduction patterns similar to the wild type, including the generation of a haploid stage. Mutant #2 was similarly treated, and this organism also displayed stable growth and reproductive patterns.

Experiment B:

Mutants #1 and #2 were exposed to a virus to which the wild type is resistant. Mutant #1 was also found to be resistant, while the virus infected and destroyed mutant #2. The haploid form of mutant #2 was then fused with the haploid form of the wild type. The diploid fused organisms were protected against virus infection. The diploid forms of mutant #2 were not protected against virus infection.

1. Mutant #2 codon aberrations eventually result in a nonfunctioning and nonproductive polypeptide due to:

A. termination of translation	**C.** initiation of DNA replication
B. aberration of centriole reproduction	**D.** repression of RNA replication

A is correct.

Translation is the conversion of the mRNA into proteins (i.e. from language of nucleotides to amino acids). During translation of mRNA, stop codons cause translation to cease and the nascent polypeptide to be released from the ribosome. Mutant #2 caused translation to terminate earlier compared to the normal polypeptide. This termination event creates a shorter and potentially nonfunctional protein.

Mistakes can occur during translation (RNA into protein). A nonsense mutation involves a premature stop codon. A missense mutation results from a change in a nucleotide (within the codon) and causes a different amino acid to be incorporated into the growing polypeptide.

A central dogma of molecular biology is the flow of genetic information from DNA to RNA to protein. For RNA viruses (obligate parasites), the general premise is the same, but the retrovirus (RNA virus) uses its enzyme of reverse transcriptase on the host cell's machinery to convert genetic material of the virus (RNA) into the DNA genetic material of the infected host.

2. If mutants #1 and #2 are separated within individual Petri dishes and subsequent mutations arise where the two mutant strains are no longer able to reproduce sexually with each other, the process can be described as:

A. population control resulting from genetic variation

B. population control resulting from random mating

C. niche variability resulting in phenotypic variation

D. speciation arising from geographic isolation

D is correct.

Speciation refers to a barrier to reproduction between organisms. When populations (e.g. groups of organisms) are in contact with other populations and interbreeding (mating) occurs, barriers to reproduction are less likely to arise, and speciation will most likely not occur. However, geographic isolation allows a population to change its allelic (gene) frequency from other population. Additionally, reproductive isolation can arise and the two populations will no longer be able to mate and produce fertile offspring – thus, speciation has occurred.

3. Consistent with Darwin's views about evolution, mutant #2 represents a less "fit" organism than mutant #, 1 because:

   A. mutant #1 and #2 produce protein products of variable length
   B. **mutant #1 is immune against a naturally-occurring virus, while mutant #2 is susceptible**
   C. mutant #1 is endogenous in humans, while mutant #2 is found in amphibians
   D. mutant #1 replicates at a different rate than mutant #2

B is correct.

Fitness is measured by the number of future offspring that inherits the alleles (i.e. alternative forms of the gene) of the organisms.

If the mutants reproduce at different rates, it would indicate different fitness, but the passage states that the growth rate is the same.

Since mutant #1 is immune to the virus and mutant #2 is susceptible to the viral infection, mutant #2 would be expected to produce fewer offspring (in the population) and, therefore, has a lower fitness.

Fitness cannot be compared between two different species because of factors such as gestation periods, inherent survival rates, life cycle etc. The protein length is not related to the fitness of an organism as a whole.

4. In Experiment B, how many copies of mutant #2 were present in the surviving diploid?

   A. 0   **B. 1**   **C.** 2   **D.** 4

B is correct.

The diploid cell in Experiment B which survived was formed by the fusion of two haploid cells (fusion of wild-type and mutant #2). Haploid (gametes: egg and sperm) cells contain a single copy (1n), while diploid (somatic) cells contain 2 copies (2n) of the genetic material. Ploidy number refers to n (1n or 2n in humans). Thus, the surviving diploid (2n) cell contained a single copy of the wild-type and a single copy of the genome from mutant #2.

5. From Figure 1, a biomedical researcher concluded that a single point mutation in DNA altered the size of the translated product. What observation supports this conclusion?

    A. valine is encoded by two different codons

    B. mutant #2 translated a longer polypeptide than mutant #1

    C. DNA point mutations created a stop codon which terminated the growing polypeptide

    D. point mutations within the DNA increased the length of the RNA molecule

C is correct.

A nonsense mutation terminates protein translation by prematurely introducing a stop codon into the mRNA.

The genetic code converts the language of nucleotides – DNA and RNA – into the language of amino acids – proteins. The genetic code is redundant, which means that a single amino acid can be encoded for by more than a single codon (sequence of three nucleotides). The third base is more permissive, and this interchange of nucleotides for the same amino acid is referred to as wobble. Often, changing the third nucleotide does not change the amino acid. The genetic code has information (triplet code) that would include the possibility for 64 codes. There are 20 naturally occurring amino acids, 1 start codon (AUG for the amino acid methionine) and three stop (termination) codons.

6. In labeling the RNA in mutants #1 and #2, which of the following labeled radioactive molecules would be most useful to label the RNA?

    A. thymine   **B. uracil**   **C.** D-glucose   **D.** phosphate

B is correct.

Both DNA and RNA are nucleotides that contain a sugar-phosphate backbone of deoxyribose (DNA) and ribose (RNA) sugars.

Only DNA contains the thymine base, and only RNA contains the uracil base.

Ribose sugar is unique to RNA, while deoxyribose sugar is unique to DNA.

Deoxyribonucleotides (DNA) are synthesized from deoxyribose sugars and consist of the deoxyribose sugar, bases (A, C, G, T) and phosphate.

Labeled ribose becomes incorporated into the RNA as ribonucleotides. The nucleotide of RNA consists of ribose sugar, bases (A, C, G, U) and phosphate.

7. In Figure 1, the mutation in mutant #2 is caused by a defect in:

    A. RNA transcription
    B. protein translation
    C. DNA replication
    D. post-translational modification

C is correct.

Replication occurs in the S (synthesis) phase of interphase within the cell cycle. Replication is the duplication of DNA into two newly synthesized DNA daughter strands. DNA replication occurs via semiconservative replication with one new DNA strand and one original DNA (template) strand in the daughter DNA helix. For the mutation in Figure 1, changes (mutations) within the DNA nucleotides (genome) must occur during DNA replication.

A: RNA transcription is the synthesis of an mRNA molecule with bases complimentary to the DNA nucleotides.

B: protein translation is the assembly of amino acids from the information (sequence) of the mRNA molecule.

Passage 2
(Questions 8–13)

Phenols are compounds containing a hydroxyl group attached to a benzene ring. Derivatives of phenols, such as naphthols (II) and phenanthrols (III), have chemical properties similar to many substituted phenols. Like other alcohols, phenols have higher boiling points than hydrocarbons of similar molecular weight. Like carboxylic acids, phenols are more acidic than their alcohol counterparts. Phenols are highly reactive and undergo several reactions because of the hydroxyl groups and the presence of the benzene ring. Several chemical tests distinguish phenols from alcohols and from carboxylic acids.

Thymol (IUPAC name: 2-isopropyl-5-methylphenol) is a phenol naturally occurring from thyme oil and can also be synthesized from *m*-cresol in Reaction A. Reaction B illustrates how thymol can be converted into menthol, another naturally-occurring organic compound.

8. Which of the following is the sequence of decreasing acidity among the four compounds below?

A. IV, I, III, II   **B. IV, III, II, I**   **C.** II, I, IV, III   **D.** IV, II, III, I

B is correct.

Consider the characteristics of a substituted phenol towards increasing acidity of the hydroxyl group on the molecule. More electron-withdrawing groups attached to the phenol increase the dispersion and stabilization of the negative charge on phenoxide ($\sim O^-$) resulting from deprotonation of the alcohol.

Since resonance (delocalization of electron density) stabilizes the phenoxide ion, an increased number of valid resonance structures stabilizes the phenol and makes the molecule more acidic because the anion has lower energy.

Comparing the four phenols, three molecules have nitro (strong electron-withdrawing) groups and the fourth molecule has a methyl group (electron-donating via hyperconjugation). The trinitrophenol (IV) has the most nitro groups and is the most acidic. This resonance stability is followed by dinitrophenol (III), then *para*-nitrophenol (II) and then *para*-cresol (I), where methyl group replaces the nitro group.

9. Which of the following structures corresponds to Compound Y ($C_{10}H_{14}O$), which dissolves in aqueous sodium hydroxide but is insoluble in aqueous sodium bicarbonate. The proton nuclear magnetic resonance (NMR) spectrum of Compound Y is as follows:

chemical shift	integration #	spin-spin splitting
δ 1.4	(9H)	singlet
δ 4.9	(1H)	singlet
δ 7.3	(4H)	multiplet

A. H₃C

H₃C— —OH

H₃C

B. H₃C

H₃C— —O—⟨benzene⟩

H₃C

C.

H₃C Br

H₃C— —OH

H₃C Br

D.

H₃C

—COOH

H₃C

A is correct.

All four answer choices are aromatic compounds, so Compound Y must be aromatic. The chemical formula for this compound consists of carbons, hydrogens and oxygen. Eliminate choice C, because the molecule contains bromine atoms absent from the molecular formula of the question.

From the question, Compound Y is soluble in aqueous sodium hydroxide but not in aqueous sodium bicarbonate. Eliminate substituted benzoic acid (D), which would dissolve in sodium bicarbonate (weak base). The ability to dissolve in aqueous sodium hydroxide (strong base), but not in aqueous sodium bicarbonate, is characteristic of highly acidic phenols. This suggests that Compound Y is a phenol (-OH attached to benzene) and not a phenyl ether (B) because phenyl ethers (R-O- attached to benzene) are not acidic.

The NMR spectrum has three separate peaks. The multiplet with an integration number (i.e. hydrogens producing the area under the peak) of four has a chemical shift of δ 7.3 (higher numbers: downfield from deshielding) and represents the aromatic ring. Additionally, the spin-spin splitting (coupling) is consistent with four aromatic hydrogens. The singlet at a chemical shift of δ 1.4, with an integration number of 9, indicates a chemical shift of carbon-hydrogen single bonds. The second singlet peak at a chemical shift of δ 4.9 has an integration number of one.

The fact that the single hydrogen is shifted further downfield (δ **4.9**) indicates that the proton is deshielded, suggesting that the hydrogen is attached to a more electronegative element than carbon. This magnitude of shift (δ 4–5) is characteristic of the hydrogen of a phenol and data agrees with the conclusion that Compound Y is choice A.

10. Which of the following is the product of the reaction of phenol with dilute nitric acid?

C is correct.

The hydroxyl (~OH) groups have two lone pairs of electrons on the oxygen and therefore the hydroxyl is electron-donating. Electron-donating groups activate aromatic rings towards electrophilic aromatic substitution (EAS). Like all electron-donating groups (via the resonance of the lone pair electrons), hydroxyl groups are *ortho*-directors and *para*-directors. The nitro group adds to phenol to form two products of *ortho*-nitrophenol (minor product due to steric hindrance) and *para*-nitrophenol (major product due to less steric hindrance).

Compound A is incomplete because only the *para*-nitrophenol is shown. The *meta*-nitrophenol (D) is not formed, because the *meta*-substituted product involves intermediates with an anion on less stable atoms (compared to the stable intermediates) resulting from *ortho*- and *para*-substituents.

11. Comparing the pK$_a$ values for cyclohexanol (pK$_a$ = 16) to phenol (pK$_a$ = 9.95), phenol is more acidic than cyclohexanol. Which of the following explains the greater acidity of phenol compared to cyclohexanol?

I. phenoxide delocalizes the negative charge on the oxygen atom over the benzene ring
II. phenol is capable of strong hydrogen bonding, which increases the ability of phenol to disassociate a proton, making it more acidic than cyclohexanol
III. phenoxide, the conjugate base of phenol, is stabilized by resonance more than for cyclohexanol

   A. I only   **B.** I and II only   **C. I and III only**   **D.** I, II and III

C is correct.

Resonance stabilization is important to support the observation that phenols are more acidic than aliphatic alcohols (e.g. cyclohexanol). In the phenoxide ion (i.e. deprotonated phenol), the negative charge on the oxygen is dispersed, via resonance, throughout the benzene ring. These resonance structures stabilize the anion by distributing electron density. This delocalizing charge effect stabilizes the phenoxide ion (Statement III), which is included in the correct answer. Therefore, eliminate answer choices that do not include Statement III.

Similarly, the phenoxide ion (from phenol) has more possible resonance structures than the alkoxide (from hydroxyl) and supported by Statement I. Statements I and III draw the same conclusion and both imply that resonance (delocalization of electrons through a pi system of bonds) contributes to the stability of the anion.

Statement II is true fact, because phenols can hydrogen-bond more strongly than aliphatic alcohols, as supported by the higher boiling points mentioned in the passage. Hydrogen bonding is a consequence (not the reason) for the greater anion stability of phenol (compared to cyclohexanol), but hydrogen bonding does not account for the acidity of phenol. Therefore, statement II cannot be included in the correct answer choice.

12. Reaction A is an example of:

A. free radical substitution	**C. electrophilic aromatic substitution**
B. electrophilic addition	**D.** nucleophilic aromatic substitution

C is correct.

Like benzene, Reaction A is an electrophilic aromatic substitution (EAS) reaction where *meta*-cresol is converted to thymol. In *meta*-cresol, both the hydroxyl and methyl substituents are *ortho-para* directing (i.e. relative position) and activators (i.e. higher rate of reaction compared to benzene). Consider the direction of the substitution. The hydroxyl substituent is a more powerful activator (compared to a methyl substituent) and the electrophilic aromatic substitution occurs in the *ortho* position (one carbon away) relative to the hydroxyl group.

Analyze the reaction mechanism. Initially, the pi electrons of the propene abstract an H^+ (proton) from the sulfuric acid (i.e. Lewis acid), creating a secondary carbocation on the propene. This carbocation then acts as an electrophile and adds to the electron rich benzene ring at the *ortho* position (relative to hydroxyl). Addition of the propene carbocation forms an arenium (i.e. benzene) ion. The aromaticity of the benzene is restored by the loss of a proton to produce thymol. Therefore, this mechanism is an electrophilic aromatic substitution.

Although the carbocation adds to the ring, a proton is lost in order to restore aromaticity of the ring. The derivatives of benzene do not undergo addition (this would result in the loss of aromaticity). The derivatives of benzene undergo EAS to restore the aromatic ring in the final product. Therefore, Reaction A is an example of substitution (not addition). The carbocation, which adds to the ring, is an electrophile (not a nucleophile) because benzene is electron-rich and the substituents on *meta*-cresol enhance the electron density of the ring.

The sulfuric acid (Lewis acid) will not induce radical formation. In general, radical formation (e.g. unpaired electron) involves starting material of either a dihalide (Br_2 or Cl_2; and light/heat or alkyl halides) or other molecules such as BH_3 or HBr (in presence of peroxides: RO-OR, H_2O_2 or R_2O_2).

13. Which chemical test could distinguish between the two following compounds?

A. compound I is soluble in $NaHCO_3$

B. compound I is soluble in NaOH

C. compound II decolorizes a solution of Br_2

D. compound II is soluble in $NaHCO_3$

B is correct.

Compound I is *para*-cresol (or *para*-methylphenol) and Compound II is benzyl alcohol. Benzyl alcohol (with the OH not attached directly to benzene) behaves more like an aliphatic alcohol than phenol, and this difference can be used to distinguish the two compounds. The main distinction of these molecules is their solubility and this can be used to separate them from a mixture.

Phenols are acidic and are quite soluble in aqueous NaOH (sodium hydroxide is a strong base). Aliphatic alcohols (including benzyl alcohol here) are not acidic, and therefore not soluble in aqueous sodium hydroxide. An exception to solubility is observed for very short chain alcohols (with fewer than five carbons) that are water-soluble, because short chain alcohols can dissolve in aqueous solution.

However, benzyl alcohol is not a short chain molecule and therefore is not water-soluble. Benzyl alcohol is not soluble in sodium hydroxide solution. The solubility of *para*-cresol (I) in aqueous sodium hydroxide would provide an effective test to distinguish between the two compounds.

A mixture of these two compounds could be separated by dissolving them in an organic solvent, and then extracting the solution in a separatory funnel with aqueous sodium hydroxide. The benzyl alcohol would remain in the organic layer (not soluble in an aqueous solution) and the *para*-cresol (soluble in aqueous solution) would move into the aqueous layer. Compound I would not react with a bromine solution and decolorize it. Both compounds will react under stronger conditions (presence of a Lewis acid), but bromine in solution is too mild of a reagent to react with the stable aromatic ring. Therefore, both compounds I and II would not decolorize a bromine solution.

Neither of the two compounds is soluble in $NaHCO_3$ (sodium bicarbonate is a weak base). Since phenols are fairly weak acids, it requires a fairly strong base (NaOH) to cause deprotonation (abstraction of the acidic proton) of the phenol. Thus, *para*-cresol is not soluble in sodium bicarbonate. The benzyl alcohol is a weaker acid (than *para*-cresol) and would not dissolve in sodium bicarbonate.

Since neither compound I nor II will be soluble in sodium bicarbonate, sodium bicarbonate cannot be used to distinguish between them.

> Questions 14 through 17 are not based on any
> descriptive passage and are independent of each other

14. In thin layer chromatography (TLC), a sheet of absorbent paper is partially immersed in a non-polar solvent. The solvent rises through the absorbent paper through capillary action. Which of the following compounds demonstrates the greatest migration when placed on the absorbent paper near the bottom and the solvent is allowed to pass?

   A. $CH_3CH_2CH_3$ **B.** CH_3Cl **C.** NH_3 **D.** R-COOH

A is correct.

In thin layer paper chromatography, the non-polar compounds dissolve into the migrating non-polar solvent and non-polar compounds are carried with the solvent front.

Propane ($CH_3CH_2CH_3$) is the only non-polar compound listed. Propane will interact less strongly with the polar cellulose of the TLC paper and the propane dissolves into and moves with the mobile non-polar solvent. Thus, non-polar compounds move farther than more polar compounds, because polar molecules bond more strongly to the polar chromatography paper.

All other compounds are polar and thus will interact via bonds to the TLC paper and therefore these polar compounds migrate less than the non-polar propane.

15. During meiosis, in which phase of oogenesis development does anaphase I occur?

   A. 1
   B. 2
   C. 3
   D. 4

oogonium ――1――▶ primary oocyte

↓ 2

fertilized ◀――3―― secondary
egg   oocyte

↓ 4

zygote

B is correct.

Stage 2, the progression from primary to secondary oocytes includes anaphase I.

Meiosis refers to the cell cycle that occurs for gamete formation. Gametes are sperm (males) and eggs (females). For meiosis, there are two sequential rounds of cell division referred to as meiosis I and meiosis II. During embryonic development of females, oogenesis (formation of eggs) proceeds up to the formation of primary oocytes (diploid female gamete).

The primary oocytes (within the ovaries) are arrested in meiotic prophase I. The primary oocytes remain suspended at this stage until ovulation, and then the primary oocytes complete meiosis I. Meiosis I continues through anaphase I to form secondary oocytes, which are ovulated.

16. Why do acetoacetate and other ketone bodies form during low carbohydrate availability?

  A. Because acetyl-CoA is converted into glucose
  B. Because acetoacetate spontaneously decarboxylates into acetone
  C. Because citrate cannot be formed due to low level of oxaloacetate that binds to acetyl-CoA
  D. Because acetyl-CoA cannot combine with citrate because of a low level of citrate

C is correct.

Oxaloacetate combines with acetyl-CoA to form citrate at the initiation of the Krebs cycle. During low carbohydrate availability (e.g. fasting), oxaloacetate is used for gluconeogenesis (synthesis of glucose from non-carbohydrate sources), and its availability to the Krebs cycle is reduced. Lack of oxaloacetate inhibits acetyl-CoA from forming citrate.

Excess acetyl-CoA is converted to acetoacetate and other ketone bodies, which can be used by heart and skeletal muscle to produce energy. The brain, which usually depends on glucose as a sole energy source, can also use ketone bodies during a long fasting period.

A: a small amount of glucose is necessary to provide oxaloacetate needed for the Krebs cycle, but acetyl-CoA cannot be converted into glucose.

B: is true, but doesn't answer the question.

D: citrate is formed when oxaloacetate combines with acetyl-CoA in the Krebs cycle.

17. In DiGeorge syndrome, caused by a deletion of a large portion of chromosome 22, there is defective embryonic development of the parathyroid glands. A patient with this syndrome would be expected to have:

   A. low serum calcium
   B. high serum calcium
   C. low serum thyroid hormone
   D. high serum PTH

A is correct.

The parathyroid glands must develop normally to be able to secrete PTH. A deficiency in the ability to synthesize PTH permits the serum calcium levels in the patient to remain low. In the absence of PTH, calcium is not reabsorbed by the kidney (i.e. ascending loop and distal tubule) or released (i.e. osteoclast activity) by bone.

B: high serum calcium level is the negative feedback stimulus to inhibit PTH secretion. The negative feedback mechanism involves the antagonistic hormone calcitonin. Calcitonin is synthesized in the thyroids and released into the blood from high serum Ca^{2+}.

Passage 3
(Questions 18–23)

The parathyroid glands are part of the endocrine system. The parathyroid glands are two small endocrine glands that detect low plasma calcium levels and respond by releasing parathyroid hormone (i.e. PTH). The parathyroid hormone affects bone, kidneys and intestine to regulate serum calcium levels.

PTH acts on the bone to release stored calcium into the bloodstream. Osteoclasts dissolve bone matrix by secreting acid and collagenase onto the bone surface to release calcium. In the presence of PTH and $1,25\text{-}(OH)_2\,D$, the maturation of osteoclasts is accelerated, resulting in increased resorption and release of calcium from the bone mineral compartment.

In the kidneys, PTH acts within the nephron to increase calcium reabsorption in the thick ascending loop of Henle and in the distal tubule. These modifications to mechanisms within the kidneys recapture some calcium that was filtered by the kidney and reduce the amount of calcium excreted in the urine. PTH also upregulates the conversion of 25-hydroxyvitamin D (25-OH D) to 1,25-dihydroxyvitamin D ($1,25\text{-}OH_2\,D$) in renal cells.

Additionally, Vitamin D stimulates calcium absorption within the intestine. 1,25-dihydroxyvitamin D is the active form of vitamin D, which promotes the active transport of calcium through the mircovilli of intestinal epithelium. Thus, PTH works indirectly in the intestines, via $1,25\text{-}(OH)_2\,D$ to maximize dietary calcium absorption.

18. Although converted from 25-hydroxyvitamin D to $1,25\text{-}(OH)_2\,D$ in the kidneys, the sites of action of $1,25\text{-}(OH)_2\,D$ include cells within the intestine and within peripheral bone. Based on this mode of action, $1,25\text{-}(OH)_2\,D$ may be classified as:

A. hormone **B.** neuropeptide **C.** coenzyme **D.** enzyme

A is correct.

Hormones are substances released into the bloodstream, enabling them to exert effects on distant tissues. Hormones can be classified into two broad categories: steroid hormones and peptide hormones.

B: the activity of a neuropeptide (e.g. neurotransmitter) is confined to the synapse. The synapse is the space between adjacent neurons (nerve cells) or between neurons and muscle cells (e.g. neuromuscular junction).

C and D: enzymes and coenzymes affect the rate of the reaction by binding to the substrate (molecule being acted upon) and lowering the energy of activation (barrier from reactant to product formation). Note: enzymes have no effect on the relative stability of the reactants or products (ΔG of the reaction). Equilibrium is the rate of the forward reaction equal to the rate of the reverse reaction; enzymes have no effect on equilibrium.

19. Hormone secretion is often regulated by negative feedback inhibition. Which of the following signals is used to decrease PTH secretion for homeostasis?

    A. high serum PTH
    B. low bone density

    C. high serum calcium
    D. high serum phosphate

C is correct.

Parathyroid hormone (PTH) increases concentration of calcium level in the blood. A hormone is a molecule that is released into the blood and acts on a distant target organ or tissue. The antagonistic actions of calcitonin (from thyroid glands) and parathyroid hormone (from parathyroid glands) maintain the blood calcium levels within normal limits (i.e. homeostasis).

A and B: increased serum calcium levels exert a negative feedback inhibition on PTH secretion. Parathyroid glands are only sensitive to serum calcium levels, not bone density. PTH does not inhibit itself, because it does not function as an autocrine. An autocrine is a cell that releases a molecule and the molecule acts upon the cell that released it. Autocrines are common during embryogenesis. A paracrine is a cell that releases a molecule which acts on a cell nearby to the cell that released this molecule.

D: the choice high serum phosphate (HPO_4^{2-}) is an electrolyte imbalance and high level of serum phosphate (indirectly) stimulates PTH secretion. Phosphate was not mentioned in the passage, but parathyroid hormone causes the blood phosphate level to decrease (and increase the level of calcium in the blood).

20. The precursor to 1,25-$(OH)_2$ D is 7-dehydrocholesterol. Cholesterol derivatives are also precursors of:

    A. epinephrine and norepinephrine
    B. cortisol and aldosterone

    C. adenine and guanine
    D. prolactin and oxytocin

B is correct.

Cortisol (i.e. glucocorticoids) and aldosterone (i.e. mineralcorticoids) are steroid hormones synthesized by the adrenal cortex. Glucocorticoid denotes the type of biological activity. Glucocorticoids are steroid-like compounds capable of promoting hepatic glycogen deposition and of exerting a clinically useful anti-inflammatory effect. Cortisol is the most potent of the naturally occurring glucocorticoids. Mineralcorticoids are one of the steroids of the adrenal cortex that influence salt (e.g. sodium and potassium) metabolism.
A: epinephrine and norepinephrine are derived from the tyrosine amino acid. These modified amino acid proteins are synthesized by the adrenal medulla.

C: adenine and guanine are purine bases of nucleic acids (i.e. DNA and RNA).

D: prolactin (from anterior pituitary) and oxytocin (from posterior pituitary) are peptide (short amino acid chain) hormones that participate in lactogenesis.

21. Homeostasis regulation of serum calcium is necessary for the proper function of nervous system. Low blood Ca^{2+} levels may result in numbness and tingling in the hands and feet. Insufficient serum calcium would have the greatest effect on which of the following neuronal structures?

   A. axon   **B.** dendrites   **C. axon terminal**   **D.** axon hillock

C is correct.

When the action potential reaches the axon terminal, voltage-gated Ca^{2+} channels open and Ca^{2+} enters the cell. The Ca^{2+} influx causes vesicles containing neurotransmitters to fuse to the presynaptic membrane, releasing their contents into the synapse. Thus, a decrease in Ca^{2+} levels would decrease neurotransmitter release from the axon terminal.

A: the axon is the elongated portion of a neuron that conducts nerve impulses (e.g. action potential), typically from the cell body to the synapse.

B: the dendrite is the process extending from the relatively short cell body of a neuron and is typically branched to receive signals from axons of other neurons.

D: the axon hillock is located within the cell body of the neuron. The axon hillock aggregates depolarization stimuli and transmits the summation of depolarization to the neuron process for the action potential propagation, if threshold stimulation is achieved.

22. PTH most likely acts on target cells by:

   A. increasing Na^+ influx into the cell
   B. decreasing Na^+ influx into the cell
   C. increasing synthesis of the secondary messenger cAMP
   D. increasing 1,25-$(OH)_2D$ transcription

C is correct.

Hormones can be classified as steroid hormones, peptide hormones or amine hormones. PTH is a peptide hormone (i.e. consisting of a small chain of amino acids) and therefore utilizes secondary messengers (secondary messenger for PTH is cAMP).

A and B: PTH does not affect Na^+ transport across the cell membrane.

In review, only steroid hormones are able to pass through the plasma membrane, bind with a receptor in the cytoplasm and then, bound together, pass into the nucleus to act at the transcription level.

D: 1,25-$(OH)_2$ D is a vitamin, not a gene product, and thus cannot be transcribed. Additionally, the passage states that PTH catalyzes the conversion of vitamin D, not transcription.

23. McCune-Albright syndrome is a hereditary disease of precocious puberty and results in low serum calcium levels, despite elevated serum PTH levels. Which of the following is the most likely basis of the disorder?

    A. G_s-protein deficiency, which couples cAMP to the PTH receptor
    B. defective secretion of digestive enzymes by osteoclast
    C. absence of a nuclear receptor, which couples PTH to the parathyroid transcription factor
    D. osteoblast autostimulation

A is correct.

The chronic low serum calcium in the presence of elevated PTH suggests the target organ resistance to PTH. Since PTH is a peptide hormone, G protein dysfunction is a reasonable hypothesis. The correct choice is deficiency of the G_s-protein, which couples the PTH receptor to adenylate cyclase. The syndrome is affected by a mutation in the guanine nucleotide-binding protein gene (GNAS1) on 20q. This mutation prevents downregulation of cAMP signaling.

B: for nonfunctional osteoclast cells, PTH and 1,25-$(OH)_2$D would still be able to elevate serum calcium levels through their actions on the kidney and on the intestine.

C: peptide hormones (which PTH belongs to) do not enter the cell or bind to receptors within the cell. Steroid hormones migrate as a hormone/receptor complex and move into the nucleus.

D: the passage does not mention autostimulation of osteoblast bone cells.

Passage 4
(Questions 24–28)

The kidneys regulate hydrogen ion (H^+) concentration in extracellular fluid primarily by controlling the concentration of bicarbonate ion (HCO_3^-). The process begins inside the epithelial cells of the proximal tubule, where the enzyme carbonic anhydrase catalyzes the formation of carbonic acid (H_2CO_3) from CO_2 and H_2O. The H_2CO_3 then dissociates into HCO_3^- and H^+. The HCO_3^- enters the extracellular fluid, while the H^+ is secreted into the tubule lumen via a Na^+/H^+ counter-transport mechanism that uses the Na^+ gradient established by the Na^+/K^+ pump.

Since the renal tubule is not very permeable to the HCO_3^- filtered into the glomerular filtrate, the reabsorption of HCO_3^- from the lumen into the tubular cells occurs indirectly. Carbonic anhydrase promotes the combination of HCO_3^- with the secreted H^+ to form H_2CO_3. The H_2CO_3 then dissociates into CO_2 and H_2O. The H_2O remains in the lumen while the CO_2 enters the tubular cells.

From Figure 1, inside the cells, every H^+ secreted into the lumen is countered by an HCO_3^- entering the extracellular fluid. Thus, the mechanism by which the kidneys regulate body fluid pH is by the titration of H^+ with HCO_3^-.

Figure 1

The drug Diamox (i.e., acetazolamide) is a potent carbonic anhydrase inhibitor. Acetazolamide is available as a generic drug and is used as a diuretic, because it increases the rate of urine formation and thereby increases the excretion of water and other solutes from the body. Diuretics can be used to maintain adequate urine output or excrete excess fluid.

24. Spironolactone (an adrenocorticosteroid) is a competitive aldosterone antagonist and functions as a diuretic. Administering this drug to a patient would most likely result in:

- **A.** Na^+ plasma concentration increase and blood volume increase
- **B.** Na^+ plasma concentration increase and blood volume decrease
- **C.** Na^+ plasma concentration decrease and blood volume increase
- **D.** **Na^+ plasma concentration decrease and blood volume decrease**

D is correct.

According to the question, spironolactone is a diuretic that inhibits aldosterone. Aldosterone is the hormone that increases in the re-absorption of sodium ions from the nephron lumen and increases the potassium ions secretion into the nephron lumen.

Aldosterone increases the Na^+ plasma concentration. A medication that inhibits aldosterone will inhibit the re-absorption of Na^+ and decrease the Na^+ plasma concentration. Therefore, eliminate choices A and B.

Comparing choices C and D, aldosterone affects blood volume. Osmolarity is the number of solute particles per volume of liquid. In two compartments divided by a water permeable membrane, water diffuses from the area of lower concentration (lower osmolarity) to the area of higher concentration (higher osmolarity). Sodium is re-absorbed from the tubular filtrate into the tubular cells and eventually enters the bloodstream. Movement of sodium from the tubular lumen to the cells (and to the blood) increases the osmolarity of these regions, resulting in a corresponding movement of water from the filtrate, because water follows the movement of Na^+ and blood volume increases.

Inhibiting aldosterone reduces both the re-absorption of Na^+ and the movement of water, which results in decreased blood volume.

The question states that spironolactone is a diuretic, and the passage states that diuretics increase the excretion of water and other solutes. Therefore, administration of a diuretic results in a decrease concentration of solutes in plasma followed by a decrease of blood volume due to high urine excretion.

25. Excretion of acidic urine by a patient results from:

- **A.** more H^+ being transported into the glomerular filtrate than HCO_3^- secreted into the tubular lumen
- **B.** **more H^+ being secreted into the tubular lumen than HCO_3^- transported into the glomerular filtrate**
- **C.** more HCO_3^- being secreted into the tubular lumen than H^+ transported into the glomerular filtrate
- **D.** more HCO_3^- being transported into the glomerular filtrate than H^+ secreted into the tubular lumen

B is correct.

From the passage, the H^+ secretion into the lumen is balanced by HCO_3^-, transport from the glomerular filtrate into the extracellular fluid. This mechanism results in the regulation of body fluid pH by the kidneys. Acidity depends on H^+ concentration. Therefore, acidic urine has a higher concentration of H^+ compared to the concentration of HCO_3^-.

Acidic urine is produced when the lumen fluid (filtrate) has a high H^+ concentration relative to the HCO_3^- because more H^+ is secreted into the tubular lumen than HCO_3^- is transported into the glomerular filtrate.

26. What mechanism described in the passage is used to transport Na^+ into the tubular cells?

A. endocytosis   **B.** exocytosis   **C. facilitated diffusion**   **D.** active transport

C is correct.

From Figure 1 and the passage, H^+ is secreted into the lumen using the mechanism of Na^+/H^+ countertransport. Carbonic anhydrase catalyzes the formation of carbonic acid inside the tubular cell, which spontaneously degrades into bicarbonate ion and H^+, resulting in an H^+ increase within the cell. The H^+ is secreted into the lumen in exchange for Na^+. The Na^+ binds to a carrier protein on the luminal side of the cell membrane, while concurrently an H^+ binds to the opposite side of the same carrier protein. Because of the greater concentration of Na^+ outside the cell (compared to inside), Na^+ moves down its concentration gradient into the cell. This movement supplies the energy for transporting H^+ into the tubular lumen. As Na^+ moves into the cell via facilitated diffusion, no energy is required because movement is down its concentration gradient.

A: endocytosis is the uptake of extracellular material via invagination of the plasma membrane. In this question, one ion is being transported in exchange for another ion.

B: exocytosis is the release of intracellular material via budding of the plasma membrane.

D: active transport requires both a protein carrier and energy (e.g. ATP).

27. Acetazolamide administration increases a patient's excretion of:

I. H_2O   II. H^+ **III. HCO_3^-**   **IV. Na^+**

A. III only   **B.** III and IV only   **C. I, III and IV only**   **D.** I, II, III and IV

C is correct.

Figure 1 shows that carbonic anhydrase is both within the lumen and in the kidney tubular cells. H^+ and HCO_3^- (bicarbonate ions) are converted into H_2CO_3 (carbonic acid) in the lumen. Carbonic anhydrase catalyzes the further disassociation of H_2CO_3 into CO_2 (carbon dioxide) and H_2O. CO_2 is transported into the cells, while H_2O remains in the lumen.

Inside cells, carbonic anhydrase catalyzes the production of H_2CO_3 from H_2O and CO_2.

Carbon dioxide dissolved in water is in equilibrium with carbonic acid:

$$CO_2 + H_2O \overset{\text{carbonic anhydrase}}{\rightleftharpoons} H_2CO_3$$

Carbonic acid

H_2CO_3 dissociates into HCO_3^- and H^+ ions. The HCO_3^- exits the cell and enters the extracellular fluid, while the H^+ is secreted into the lumen in exchange for Na^+. Since acetazolamide is a carbonic anhydrase inhibitor, administering this drug to a patient would inhibit reactions catalyzed by the carbonic anhydrase enzyme. The Na^+ / H^+ countertransport and the reabsorption of HCO_3^- from the lumen into the tubular cells would be inhibited. Since the lumen filtrate is excreted as urine, acetozolamide lowers the H^+ concentration while increasing HCO_3^- and Na^+ concentrations in urine. The increase in urinary osmolarity draws water into the lumen to counter the increase of lumen osmolarity. Thus, Na^+, HCO_3^- and H_2O increase in the urine while H^+ decreases.

28. Which of the following hormones would affect the patient's blood volume to oppose the effect of administering acetazolamide?

    A. ADH   **B.** somatostatin   **C.** LH   **D.** calcitonin

A is correct.

Acetazolamide is a carbonic anhydrase inhibitor that reduces excretion of H^+ into the lumen and re-absorption of HCO_3^-. The excretion of H^+ into the lumen is necessary to provide means for Na^+ transport into tubular cells. If carbonic anhydrase is inhibited and no H^+ is produced in the tubular cell, Na^+ will remain in the lumen and increase the filtrate osmolarity. With increased filtrate osmolarity, water diffuses into the lumen, causing the urine volume to increase. Diuretics use this mechanism to excrete excess body fluids.

The hormone with the effect opposite to diuretics would decrease water excretion by increasing water reabsorption. ADH (antidiuretic hormone) is such a hormone that increases water reabsorption in the kidneys.

B: somatostatin is a hormone secreted by the hypothalamus which acts as a potent inhibitor of many other hormones such as: growth hormone, TRH (thyroid-releasing hormone), ACTH, insulin, glucagon, gastrin, renin and some others.

C: LH (luteinizing hormone) is a hormone produced by the anterior pituitary gland and it plays an important role in male and female reproductive cycles.

D: calcitonin is a 32-amino acid peptide hormone that reduces blood calcium. Calcitonin is secreted by the thyroid gland in response to high plasma calcium ion concentration. Calcitonin is an antagonist of parathyroid hormone (PTH) function. PTH increases blood calcium levels by stimulating osteoclasts to degrade mineralized bone.

Questions 29 through 33 are not based on any descriptive passage and are independent of each other

29. Which of the following functions describes the purpose of the lysosome membrane?
   A. Creating a basic environment for hydrolytic enzymes of the lysosome within the cytoplasm
   B. Creating an acidic environment for hydrolytic enzymes of the lysosome within the cytoplasm
   C. Serving as an alternative site for peptide bond formation during protein synthesis
   D. Being a continuation of the nuclear envelope

B is correct.

Lysosomes are membrane-bound sacs containing hydrolytic enzymes involved in intracellular digestion. Lysosomes fuse with intracellular vesicles and digest the macromolecules of proteins, polysaccharides, fats and nucleic acids. These macromolecules are degraded into their monomers and the subunits are reused by cells. Lysosomes also play a role in the recycling of cell organelles by engulfing and digesting depleted organelles and releasing their component molecules into the cytosol for reuse. These hydrolytic enzymes are contained within the lysosome and are optimally functional at acidic pH 5. Similar to the stomach (pH of 2 for pepsin), the lysosome pumps H^+ from the cytosol for an internal pH of 5. The lysosomal enzymes would not function properly in the neutral pH of the cytosol. The lysosome membrane enables the lysosome to maintain its acidic environment.

C: the lysosomes are not an alternate site for protein synthesis, because ribosomes are the site of protein synthesis. The ribosomes are free in the cytosol (proteins remaining in the cell) or attached to endoplasmic reticulum (rough ER) for production of proteins exported from the cell, or for the plasma membrane proteins, or for lysosome proteins. Lysosomes are involved in protein degradation, not the synthesis of proteins.

D: lysosome membranes are not in physical contact with the nuclear envelope (membrane). Lysosomes, like other membrane-bound organelles, are part of the cell's endomembrane system (a system of membranes linked through direct contact or communication via vesicles). The endoplasmic reticulum is continuous with the nuclear membrane at certain points.

30. How many σ bonds and π bonds are there in ethene?

   A. 1 σ and 2 π   B. 1 σ and 5 π   C. 6 σ and 2 π   **D. 5 σ and 1 π**

D is correct.

Ethene ($CH_2 = CH_2$) is a two carbon alkene.
Each C–H bond is a σ (sigma) single bond and there are four C–H bonds. Ethene also has one C–C σ bond and a C-C π (pi) double bond. Therefore, there are five σ (single) bonds and one π (double) bond in ethene.

31. Why is PCC a better oxidant for the conversion of an alcohol into an aldehyde compared to other oxidizing agents?

   A. PCC is a less powerful oxidant that doesn't oxidize an alcohol to a carboxylic acid
   B. PCC is a less powerful oxidant that does not oxidize an aldehyde to an alcohol
   C. PCC is a more powerful oxidant that oxidizes an alcohol to a carboxylic acid
   D. PCC is a more powerful oxidant that oxidizes a carboxylic acid to an alcohol

A is correct.

A primary alcohol is oxidized to an aldehyde by PCC (pyridinium chlorochromate) or a carboxylic acid with a stronger oxidizing agent (e.g. $KMnO_4$ or CrO_3). To stop oxidation at the aldehyde, a weaker oxidant (e.g. PCC) is needed. PCC oxidizes the primary alcohol to the aldehyde because it is a weaker oxidizing agent and will not fully oxidize the primary alcohol to the carboxylic acid as $KMnO_4$ (potassium permanganate) or Jones reagent (CrO_3).

32. Which of the following describes the reaction of acyl-CoA to enoyl-CoA conversion?

   A. oxidation   **B.** reduction   **C.** hydrogenation   **D.** hydrolysis

A is correct.

The conversion of acyl-CoA into enoyl-CoA involves the removal of two C-H bonds to generate a C=C double bond. Creating a double bond from a single bond is an oxidation. Oxidation-reduction is coupled; FAD is reduced as acyl-CoA is oxidized.

An enoyl consists of a carbonyl group plus a double bond between α (adjacent) carbon and β (two carbons away) carbon.

FAD is reduced (gains electrons) to $FADH_2$, consistent with the oxidation of acyl-CoA into enoyl-CoA. Oxidations are always accompanied by reductions (and vice versa).

33. For breeding, salmon travel from saltwater to freshwater. The salmon maintain solute balance by reversing their osmoregulatory mechanism when entering a different solute environment. Failure to reverse this mechanism results in:

   A. no change, because movement between saltwater and freshwater does not affect osmotic pressure in salmon
   B. metabolic activity increase due to an increase in enzyme concentration
   C. death, because water influx causes cell lysis
   D. death, because cells become too concentrated for normal metabolism

C is correct.

Freshwater is hypotonic relative to saltwater. In freshwater, the cells of the salmon have higher osmotic pressure than the surrounding environment. If salmon were unable to reverse their osmoregulatory mechanism, water would flow into the cells, causing them to swell and eventually lyse (burst).

Tonicity: A hypertonic solution contains a greater concentration of the impermeable solutes than cytosol. The resulting osmotic pressure causes a net movement of water out of the cell.

A hypotonic solution contains a lower concentration of impermeable solutes than cytosol. The resulting osmotic pressure causes a net movement of water into the cell.

Passage 5
(Questions 34–38)

Simple acyclic alcohols are an important class of alcohols. Their general formula is $C_nH_{2n+1}OH$. An example of simple acyclic alcohols is ethanol (C_2H_5OH) – the type of alcohol found in alcoholic beverages.

The terpenoids (aka isoprenoids) are a large and diverse class of naturally occurring organic chemicals derived from five-carbon isoprene units. Plant terpenoids are commonly used for their aromatic qualities and play a role in traditional herbal remedies. They are also being studied for antibacterial, antineoplastic (i.e. a chemotherapeutic property that stops abnormal proliferation of cells) and other pharmaceutical applications. Terpenoids contribute to the scent of eucalyptus; menthol and camphor are well-known terpenoids.

Citronellol is an acyclic alcohol and natural acyclic monoterpenoid that is found in many plant oils, including (-)-citronellol in geraniums and rose. It is used in synthesis of perfumes, insect repellants and moth repellants for fabrics. Pulegone, a clear colorless oily liquid, is a related molecule found in plant oils and has a camphor and peppermint aroma.

Below is the synthesis of pulegone from citronellol.

Figure 1. Synthesis of pulegone from citronellol

34. Pulegone has the presence of the following functional groups:

A. aldehydes and an isopropyl alkene

B. ketone and isobutyl alkene

C. ketone and isopropyl alkene

D. hydroxyl and tert-butyl alkene

C is correct.

Ketones end in ~one, alcohols (hydroxyl) ends in ~ol and aldehydes end in ~al. The carbon double bond oxygen within the carbon chain (as opposed to the terminal aldehyde) describes the ketone. The presence of a double bond within the hydrocarbon describes an alkene. Isopropyl refers to a three carbon chain with attachment to the C2 (middle) carbon.

35. What is the absolute configuration of pulegone?

A. *R*   **B.** *S*   **C.** *cis*   **D.** *trans*

B is correct.

There is a single stereogenic center at the methyl substituent within the ring. The hydrogen (not shown) points into the page. The Cahn-Inglold-Prelog (CIP) priorities around the stereogenic center are the carbonyl (#1), cyclic portion of the ring towards the alkene (#2) and the methyl (#3). The priorities are arranged counterclockwise and thus are (S).

Carbon 1, according to IUPAC, is the carbon with the most oxidized atom (e.g. ketone). The groups are then prioritized according to Cahn-Ingold-Prelog rules (i.e. atomic number of the atom at the point of attachment – and not the aggregation of atoms - to determine priorities). Note the counterclockwise arrangement (lowest priority points into page).

Clockwise rotation denotes an R, while counterclockwise rotation denotes an S configuration.

36. Which of the following structures is the most likely product when HBr is added to citronellol?

A.

B.

C.

D.

B is correct.

HBr results in the addition of H and Br across the double bond. The intermediate is a carbocation upon addition of H^+ with the most stable carbocation formation. Br then adds to the carbocation with the Markovnikov regiospecificity.

In general, ^-OH does not dissociate as a leaving group, because hydroxyl is a strong base (i.e. unstable) and therefore a poor leaving group, and Br will not replace the OH on the molecule. Hydroxyl groups can be converted to alkyl halides with special reagents such as $SOCl_2$ (substitution of Cl) or PBr_3 and PBr_5 (substitution of Br).

37. PCC promotes conversion of citrinellol to which molecule?

    A. citrinellone   **B. citrinellal**   **C.** citric acid   **D.** no reaction

B is correct.

PCC, discovered in 1975, is formed by the reaction of pyridine with chromium trioxide.

PCC in pyridine

Pyridinium chlorochromate (PCC) is a reddish orange solid reagent used to oxide primary alcohols (citrinellol) into aldehydes (~al ending) such as citrinellal, and secondary alcohols into ketones (~one ending).

PCC is a weaker oxidizing agent and will not fully oxidize the primary alcohol to the carboxylic acid as the Jones reagent (CrO_3) does. Jones reagent (CrO_3) oxidizes a primary alcohol – past aldehydes – to a carboxylic acid; a secondary alcohol is oxidized to a ketone. Therefore, PCC is the choice for an oxidizing agent that converts the primary alcohol to the aldehydes (and not to the completed oxidation of carboxylic acid).

Primary alcohol into COOH

Primary alcohol into aldehyde

Secondary alcohol into ketone

Secondary alcohol into ketone

38. What is the relationship between citronellol and citronellal?

    A. enantiomers   **C.** geometric isomers
    B. diastereomers   **D. none of the above**

D is correct.

Citronellol and citronellal have no isomer relationship; they have different molecular formulas, whereby citronellol is an alcohol and citronellal is an aldehyde.

A: enantiomers are chiral molecules with a non-superimposable mirror image. If the mirror images are superimposable, the molecules are nonchiral – a carbon that is not attached to 4 different substituents. A chiral molecule and its mirror image are enantiomers (stereoisomers).

B: diastereomers result from chiral molecules with 2 or more chiral carbons (stereogenic centers). The diastereomers are not the mirror image – the mirror image is the enantiomer.

C: geometric isomers are a special class of diastereomers where a double bond is present in the molecule. Geometric isomers are designated *cis* or *trans* if the same substituents are attached to each side of the double bond. If the atoms are different on each side of the double bond, E and Z are used to designate the geometric isomer. E is analogous to *trans* and Z (zame side) to *cis*. Determination of E or Z requires prioritizing the substituents according to atomic number (Cahn-Ingold-Prelog priorities).

Passage 6
(Questions 39–43)

Beta-oxidation is the process when fatty acids are broken down in the mitochondria. Before fatty acids are oxidized, they are covalently binded to coenzyme A (CoA) on the mitochondrion's outer membrane. The sulfur atom of CoA attacks the carbonyl carbon of the fatty acid and H_2O dissociates. The hydrolysis of two high-energy phosphate bonds drives this reaction, producing acyl-CoA.

Special transport molecules shuttle the acyl-CoA across the inner membrane and into the mitochondria matrix. Further fatty acids beta-oxidation involves four recurring steps, whereby acyl-CoA is broken down by the sequential removal of two-carbon units in each cycle to form acetyl-CoA. Acetyl-CoA is the initial molecule that enters the Krebs cycle.

The beta-carbon of the fatty acyl-CoA is oxidized to a carbonyl that is attacked by the lone pair of electrons on the sulfur atom of another CoA. The CoA substrate molecule and the bound acetyl group dissociate. The acetyl-CoA, produced from fatty acid oxidation, enters the Krebs cycle and is further oxidized into CO_2. The Krebs cycle yields 3 NADH + 1 $FADH_2$ + 1 GTP, which is converted into ATP.

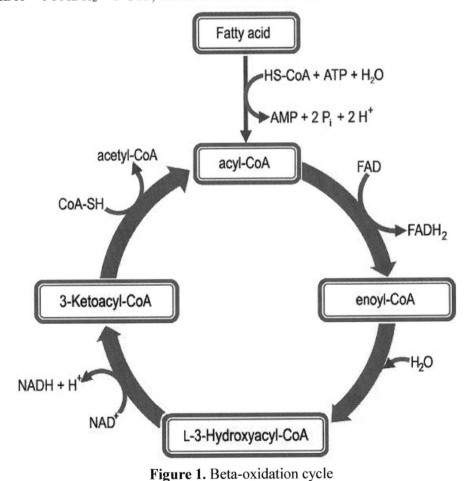

Figure 1. Beta-oxidation cycle

39. For an 18-carbon fatty acid to be completely oxidized, how many turns of the beta-oxidation cycle must be completed?

   A. 1   **B. 8**   **C.** 9   **D.** 18

B is correct.

To complete the oxidation of 18-carbon fatty acid, 8 rounds of beta-oxidation need to be completed, because each round removes 2 carbon units.

40. How many ATP would be produced if a 12-carbon fatty acid was completely oxidized to CO_2 and H_2O?

   A. 5ATP   **B.** 51 ATP   **C. 78 ATP**   **D.** 80 ATP

C is correct.

To complete the oxidation of 12-carbon fatty acid, 5 rounds of beta-oxidation need to be completed. Each cycle produces 5 NADH, 5 $FADH_2$, and 6 acetyl-CoA. Every acetyl-CoA enters the Krebs cycle and yields 3 NADH, 1 $FADH_2$, and 1 GTP per turn. The 6 acetyl-CoA produce a total of 18 NADH, 6 $FADH_2$ and 6 GTP. Adding the products of β-oxidation and Krebs cycles yields: NADH = 18 + 5 = 23, $FADH_2$ = 5 + 6 = 11 and GTP = 6.

During oxidative phosphorylation (e.g. electron transport chain), one NADH produces 2.5 ATP and one $FADH_2$ produces 1.5 ATP. Total ATP production is (23 NADH x 2.5 ATP) + (11 $FADH_2$ x 1.5 ATP) + (6 GTP x 1 ATP) = 80 ATP. Deduct 2 ATP that are required to activate the fatty acid, which results in a total of 78 ATP.

41. Which of the following enzymes is involved in the conversion of acyl-CoA to enoyl-CoA?

Acyl-CoA   trans-Δ^2-Enoyl-CoA

   A. reductase   **B.** ketothiolase   **C.** isomerase   **D. dehydrogenase**

D is correct.

Dehydrogenase catalyzes the formation of a trans alkene (double bond) from the alkane of the acyl-CoA thioester substrate.

A: reductase catalyzes the reduction (addition of Hs) across a double bond.

C: isomerase converts the molecule into a related structural isomer (same molecular formula but different connectivity among the atoms) by catalyzing breakage/formation of bonds during this conversion, and acyl-CoA is not an isomer of acetyl-CoA.

42. The equation for one turn of the fatty acid degradation cycle is:

A. C_n-acyl-CoA + H_2O → acetyl-CoA

B. C_n-acyl-CoA → C_{n-2}-acyl-CoA + acetyl-CoA

C. C_n-acyl-CoA + NAD^+ + FAD + H_2O → C_{n-2}-acyl-CoA + NADH + $FADH_2$ + acetyl-CoA

D. **C_n-acyl-CoA + NAD^+ + FAD + H_2O + CoA → C_{n-2}-acyl-CoA + NADH + $FADH_2$ + acetyl-CoA + H^+**

D is correct.

The balanced equation includes H_2O as a reactant and changes in NAD^+ (reduced to NADH) and FAD (reduced to $FADH_2$) redox states. The resulting acyl-CoA (formed after one turn of the cycle) is two carbons shorter than the original acyl-CoA.

A: the equation does not include NAD^+ and FAD as redox reactants.

B: the equation is not a balanced equation and does not include changes in the redox state of NAD^+ and FAD.

C: the equation is not balanced, because reactants on the left side lack CoA and the products on the right side lack H^+.

43. Which of the following traits are shared by the reactions of beta-oxidation and fatty acid biosynthesis?

A. both biochemical pathways use or produce NADH

B. **both biochemical pathways use or produce acetyl alcohol**

C. both biochemical pathways occur in the mitochondrial matrix

D. both biochemical pathways use the same enzymes

B is correct.

Fatty acid biosynthesis builds fatty acids from two-carbon units of acetyl-CoA. Beta-oxidation produces acetyl-CoA by the cleavage of two-carbon units during degradation of fatty acids.

A: fatty acid biosynthesis requires NADPH as a reducing agent, while beta-oxidation produces NADH.

C: fatty acid biosynthesis takes place in the cytosol, while beta-oxidation takes place within the matrix of the mitochondria.

D: since fatty acid biosynthesis and beta-oxidation are opposing biochemical pathways, they require different enzymes to catalyze the reactions.

> Questions 44 through 47 are not based on any
> descriptive passage and are independent of each other

44. The deletion of nucleotides occurs during DNA replication. For mutations involving the addition or deletion of three base pairs, the protein encoded for by the mutated gene is relatively normal. A reasonable explanation for this observation is that:

    A. cellular function is not affected by most DNA mutations
    B. the size of amino acid codons often varies
    C. the original reading frame is retained after removal of three nucleotide multiples
    D. non-mutated mRNA are translated successfully by ribosome one-third of the time

C is correct.

Codons consist of three nucleotides (base pairs: A, C, G, U) located on the mRNA. The deletion of one or two nucleotides (bases) changes the reading frame along the entire mRNA and (often) results in a completely nonfunctional protein past the point of the base pair deletion. This mutation (i.e. change in nucleotides) is referred to as a frame-shift mutation, because the reading frame (and corresponding amino acids incorporated into the growing polypeptide) has changed.

An addition or deletion of three base pairs, however, deletes one entire codon which codes for one amino acid of the protein. Such mutation retains the original reading frame, but results in one less amino acid in the protein. The loss of one amino acid is a subtle change compared to changing the entire reading frame of a protein. Therefore, with an alteration of 3 nucleotides (1 amino acid) the protein may fold and function normally.

45. Which sequence is the correct cycle of spermatogenesis?

    A. spermatids → spermatogonia → spermatocytes → spermatozoa
    B. spermatids → spermatogonia → spermatozoa → spermatocytes
    C. spermatogonia → spermatids → spermatozoa → spermatocytes
    D. spermatogonia → spermatocytes → spermatids → spermatozoa

D is correct.

Spermatogenesis is the process that produces gametes in males and proceeds from spermatogonia → spermatocytes → spermatids → spermatozoa.
In the testis of males, primary spermatocytes (i.e. diploid as 2n) with 46 chromosomes divide to form two secondary spermatocytes (i.e. haploid as 1n), each with 23 duplicated chromosomes.

Secondary spermatocytes divide to produce four spermatids (i.e. 1n), also with 23 daughter chromosomes.

The spermatid is a round, unflagellated cell that looks nothing like a mature vertebrae sperm. Spermatids then differentiate into spermatozoa (i.e. sperm). The process of meiosis in males produces 4 haploid cells that become sperm.

Each day, some 100 million sperm are made in each testicle, and each ejaculation releases 200 million sperm. Unused sperm are either reabsorbed or passed out of the body in urine.

46. What is the IUPAC name for the molecule shown below?

A. (S)-4,5 dimethyl-(Z)-2-hexene
B. (S)-4,5 dimethyl-(E)-2-hexene
C. (R)-4,5 dimethyl-(Z)-2-hexene
D. (R)-4,5 dimethyl-(E)-2-hexene

A is correct.

The longest possible carbon backbone contains 6 carbons and corresponds to hexene. In naming organic molecules containing double bonds, the E (i.e. *trans*) and Z (i.e. *cis*) notation is required for alkenes. R and S refer to stereospecificity, according to Cahn-Inglold-Prelog priorities.

For R and S: refer to the chiral (stereogenic) center with 4 different substituents, assign priorities according to atomic number (from first point of difference). The alkene branch is labeled as (1), the isopropyl is labeled as (2), the methyl as (3) and the hydrogen (not shown and pointing into the page) as (4). Orientation is counterclockwise and thus, (S).

The molecule is (Z) because the highest priorities across the double bond (isopropyl and alkene) are on the same (*cis*) side of the double bond in the alkene.

47. Which of the following is the site for collagen polypeptide synthesis?

    A. lysosome   **C.** smooth endoplasmic reticulum
    B. mitochondrion   **D. rough endoplasmic reticulum**

D is correct.

Rough endoplasmic reticulum (rough ER) contains ribosomes, which serve as the site for protein synthesis.

A: lysosomes are cytoplasmic organelles involved in cellular digestion (recycle macromolecule building blocks).

B: the mitochondrion is the "powerhouse" of the cell and produces ATP during cellular respiration. The three stages of cellular respiration are: 1) glycolysis (occurs in cytoplasm), 2) Krebs (TCA) cycle (occurs in mitochondrion), and 3) electron transport chain (ETC) (occurs in intermembrane space between the inner and outer membrane of mitochondrion).

C: smooth endoplasmic reticulum (smooth ER) is responsible for cell detoxification (i.e. liver cells) and lipid synthesis.

Passage 7
(Questions 48–52)

With the advent of recombinant biology, *gene therapy* is a technique used to insert foreign genes into cells. Researchers are now able to introduce DNA into cells to treat genetic defects. One technique for gene therapy uses a small bore pipette to microinject a gene into a target cell. This technique worked in many cases but is very time consuming and requires high technical skills. Another method is electroporation, whereby cells undergo electric shock to increase the permeability of the plasma membrane and DNA can enter cells. However, this procedure can destroy the cell. Alternative and highly effective gene therapy technique is when foreign genes are introduced into cells via a viral vector, where foreign genes enter the cell through the mechanism of normal viral infection.

Viral genomes consist of DNA or RNA, and the nucleic acid can be either single- or double-stranded. Simple RNA viruses use a mechanism where their genome is directly translated into mRNA (by the RNA *replicase* enzyme) without integration into host's DNA. On the other hand, when a DNA virus enters a cell, its DNA may be inserted into the host's genome via the lysogenic cycle. After integration into the host's genome, viral genes can be transcribed into mRNA and, subsequently, into proteins.

Retroviruses contain an RNA (either single- or double-stranded) genome and viral genome is transcribed into DNA by the enzyme *reverse transcriptase*. The newly synthesized DNA is then inserted into the host's genome, and viral genes can then be expressed to synthesize viral RNA and proteins. Retroviruses consist of a protein core that contains viral RNA and reverse transcriptase, and are surrounded by an outer protein envelope. The RNA of a retrovirus is made up of three coding regions – *gag, pol* and *env* – which encode for core proteins, reverse transcriptase and coat protein, respectively.

Retroviruses present a more promising gene therapy technology than simple RNA viruses or DNA viruses. A retrovirus, carrying a specific gene, enters a target cell by receptor-mediated endocytosis. Its RNA gets transcribed into DNA, which then randomly integrates into the host's DNA, forming a provirus. The provirus would be copied along with the chromosomal DNA during the S phase of cell division. Retroviral vectors are constructed in a way that the therapeutic gene replaces *gag* or *env* coding region.

However, there are some practical problems associated with retroviral vector gene therapy because of the risk of random integration leading to the activation of *oncogenes*. Oncogenes arise when newly integrated fragments of nucleic acids stimulate the cell to divide and increase protein production beyond desirable levels. A major limitation is that due to the randomness of the virus vector integration into the host's genome, gene expression of desired genes can't be controlled. Future research is underway to target integration of the virus vector into specific regions of the host's genome; similar to transposons in maze described by Nobel laureate Barbara McClintock. Additionally, integration can take place only in the cells that can divide.

48. To successfully integrate a retrovirus into the cell's genome, which of the following events must take place?

A. New virions must be produced
B. The retroviral proteins encoded by *gag*, *pol* and *env* must be translated after integration
C. Reverse transcriptase must translate the retroviral genome
D. The retroviral protein envelope must bind to the cell's surface receptors

D is correct.

Several events must take place for a retrovirus to successfully infect a cell and integrate into the host's genome. Firstly, the retrovirus must enter the cell, which occurs when viral protein tail fibers bind to the cell's surface receptors. Then, the retroviral RNA is reverse transcribed into DNA by reverse transcriptase.

A: to produce virions, the virus needs to enter a lytic cycle in which case the host cell would be destroyed. This is not the desired outcome and does not occur in successful gene therapy.

B: would not take place during gene therapy because the proteins encoded by *gag*, *pol* and *env* genes are not synthesized after integration. Since *gag* encodes for the retroviral core proteins and *env* encodes for the protein envelope, these proteins are synthesized only if the retrovirus enters a lytic cycle. *Pol* encodes for reverse transcriptase and because it is necessary for integration, it must be synthesized before integration into host's DNA.

C: translation (mRNA → protein) is different from transcription (DNA → mRNA). Transcription is the process of synthesizing genetic information from nucleic acids – DNA or RNA are converted to another form of nucleic acids (e.g. DNA to RNA per the central dogma of molecular biology, or retrovirus RNA to DNA via reverse transcriptase as reverse transcription)

49. All of these cells would be good targets for retroviral gene therapy, EXCEPT:

A. hepatocytes
B. neuronal cells
C. bone marrow cells
D. epidermal cells

B is correct.

Neuronal cells are not good targets for retroviral gene therapy, because they do not divide and the therapeutic gene cannot integrate. A retrovirus integrates its DNA reverse-transcribed from RNA into host's DNA during host cell replication. Therefore, cells that do not undergo division are not able to integrate reverse-transcribed viral DNA into their chromosomes. Of the four cell types in the answer choices, only nerve cells remain in G_0 and cannot divide.

A: hepatocyte is a liver cell. Liver cells are productive targets for retroviral gene therapy, because they continuously divide and the therapeutic gene would be replicated along with the host's DNA during division. After cell replication, each daughter cell inherits the integrated therapeutic gene in its DNA for expression of the therapeutic protein.

C: bone marrow cells are good targets for retroviral vector gene therapy. While the procedure would require the removal of bone marrow cells from the body to infect them, they can be placed back into the body. Furthermore, these cells divide and give rise to important blood cells (red blood cells, white blood cells and platelets) and therefore are a good cell type for gene replacement therapy. Clinically, bone marrow replacement procedures are used to treat lymphomas.

D: while the top layer of the skin consists of the epithelial skin cells, which are dead and continually sloughed from the surface of the epidermis, they are replaced through cell division by living precursor skin cells. Only these precursor cells could be successfully infected by a retrovirus, because they undergo cell division. Once the retrovirus infects this cell, the therapeutic gene would be inherited by daughter cells.

50. From in vitro gene therapy experiments, the retroviral delivery system is preferred over physical techniques (i.e. microinjection or electroporation) of introducing therapeutic genes into cells. Which of the following statements is the most likely explanation for this?

   A. Retroviral gene delivery allows more control over the site of integration
   B. Retroviral gene delivery results in more cells that integrate the new gene successfully
   C. Retroviral gene delivery is less damaging to the cells and less labor-intensive
   D. Retroviral gene delivery permits the insertion of therapeutic genes into all cell types

C is correct.

Microinjection is very time consuming and requires a high level of technical skills, while electroporation is traumatic to the cells. These drawbacks do not apply to retroviral gene delivery because it occurs through a regular viral infection mechanism (receptor-mediated endocytosis). Inducing a retroviral infection simply involves mixing the virus with the cells to be infected. This technique does not harm the cells' integrity during the infection and the virus integrates in the host's genome and enters a lysogenic (not lytic, where virions are produced) cycle.

A: the site of gene integration cannot be predetermined in retroviral vector delivery because, from the passage, the retroviral DNA integrates into the host's DNA randomly. B: the passage contains no evidence that a retroviral gene delivery results in a greater number of cells to integrate the therapeutic gene as compared to electroporation or microinjection. In fact, as far as integration ratio numbers, microinjection is the most efficient method of gene therapy.

D: not all cell types are suitable for retroviral gene therapy, because provirus integration takes place during DNA replication. Therefore, cells that do not divide cannot be treated by retroviral gene therapy.

51. Simple RNA viruses are not suitable for gene therapy vectors, because:

A. a therapeutic gene introduced within a viral RNA cannot be replicated
B. the RNA genome becomes unstable due to an insertion of a therapeutic gene
C. their genome size is not sufficient to carry a therapeutic gene
D. only specific cell types can be infected by simple RNA viruses

A is correct.

Simple RNA viruses are not optimal for gene therapy vectors, while retroviruses make good vectors. The reason for this is related to the cellular mechanism of retroviruses.

If simple RNA viruses were used as the viral vector for a therapeutic gene, the cell's DNA genome would not express the genes contained in the virus. DNA integration is a necessary step of successful gene therapy and can take place only if the foreign gene is reverse transcribed into DNA. Since DNA integration cannot occur for simple RNA viruses, the viral RNA (containing the therapeutic gene) gets degraded by the cell. By contrast, the retrovirus has an RNA genome that is not directly transcribed into messenger RNA, but instead is reverse transcribed into a DNA.

B: the passage contains no evidence that incorporation of a therapeutic gene into an RNA genome makes it unstable for being used as a vector. Opposite to that, the passage states that all viruses can contain therapeutic genes but retroviruses, due to other reasons, are the best vectors.

C: the passage contains no evidence that simple RNA viruses have smaller genomes than DNA viruses or retroviruses and cannot carry a therapeutic gene.

D: certain viruses are able to infect only specific cell types – this is known as host specificity. Host specificity applies to all viruses, not only simple RNA viruses; therefore, this cannot be the reason why simple RNA viruses are a poor choice for gene therapy.

52. Following an integration of a therapeutic gene into a cell's DNA, the retroviral DNA:

A. causes nondisjunction to correct the genetic defect
B. is deemed "foreign" by the host's immune system and degraded
C. replicates and produces infectious virions
D. remains in the cell in a noninfectious form

D is correct.

The purpose of successful viral gene therapy is to introduce a therapeutic gene into a genetically defective cell and have the cell produce desired protein without causing an infection. Therefore, the retroviral DNA must remain in the host's DNA in a noninfectious form.

A: nondisjunction is a failure of either sister chromatids (during mitosis) or homologous chromosomes (during meiosis) to properly separate during anaphase. Nondisjunction during mitosis or meiosis results in some daughter cells inheriting multiple copies of one chromosome while others lack the chromosome completely. In either case, it is not desirable and often is lethal. Therefore, it is unlikely for a therapeutic gene to cause nondisjunction. Additionally, nondisjunction would not correct a genetic defect.

B: the host's immune system is not able to recognize the retroviral DNA as foreign, because it integrates into the host cell's genome along with the therapeutic gene.

C: to produce infectious virions, the virus must enter a lytic cycle and destroy the host cell. This is not the desired outcome and does not occur in successful gene therapy.

> Questions 53 through 59 are not based on any descriptive passage and are independent of each other

53. Incomplete proteins lack one or more:

A. essential amino acids

B. nonpolar amino acids

C. sulfur-containing amino acids

D. polar amino acids

A is correct.

A complete protein is a protein that contains all nine essential amino acids. Complete proteins come from animal products (meat, poultry, dairy, eggs, fish etc.), soy and quinoa (a grain). Incomplete proteins contain fewer than all nine essential amino acids and come from plant-based foods (beans, rice, grains, vegetables and legumes other than soy). In a diet, incomplete proteins can be combined in meals to make a complete protein. Incomplete proteins do not need to be consumed at the same time in order to be used by the body to build protein, but may be consumed within about a 24 hour period.

54. Which statement regarding the number of initiation and STOP codons is correct?

A. There are multiple initiation codons, but a single STOP codon

B. There are two STOP codons and four initiation codons

C. There is a single STOP codon and single initiation codon

D. There are multiple STOP codons, but a single initiation codon

D is correct.

55. How many carbon atoms are in a molecule of stearic acid?

A. 12　　　　　**B.** 14　　　　　**C.** 16　　　　　**D. 18**

D is correct.

Stearic acid is a waxy solid 18-carbon chain saturated fatty acid (IUPAC: octadecanoic acid) with the molecular formula $CH_3(CH_2)_{16}CO_2H$. The salts and esters of stearic acid are called stearates. Stearic acid is one of the most common saturated fatty acids found in nature following palmitic acid.

56. Fatty acids that mammals must obtain from nutrition are:

A. essential　　　　**B.** saturated　　　　**C.** dietary　　　　**D.** esters

A is correct.

Essential fatty acids (EFAs) are fatty acids required for biological processes but do not include the fats that only act as fuel. Humans and other animals cannot synthesize them and therefore these fatty acids must be ingested with food because they are required by the body. Only two fatty acids are known to be essential for humans: alpha-linolenic acid (omega-3) and linoleic acid (omega-6). Some other fatty acids are sometimes considered *conditionally essential*, meaning that they may become essential under some physiological conditions.

57. What type of amino acid is phenylalanine?

A. basic　　　**B.** acidic　　　**C.** polar　　　**D. hydrophobic aromatic**

D is correct.

Phenylalanine has a benzyl side chain and is a precursor for tyrosine. It also is a precursor for the monoamine signaling molecules epinephrine (adrenaline), norepinephrine (noradrenaline) and dopamine along with melanin (skin pigment).

58. The simplest lipids that can also be a part of or a source of many complex lipids are:

A. terpenes　　　**B.** sterols　　　**C.** waxes　　　**D.** triglycerols

A is correct.

59. What type of macromolecule is a saccharide?

A. protein　　　**B.** nucleic acid　　　**C. carbohydrate**　　　**D.** lipid

C is correct.

The carbohydrates (i.e. saccharides) are divided into four groups: monosaccharides, disaccharides, oligosaccharides and polysaccharides. Monosaccharides and disaccharides are smaller (i.e. lower molecular weight) and are generally referred to as sugars.

Biological & Biochemical Foundations of Living Systems
MCAT® Practice Test #3 – Answer Key

Passage 1
1 : A
2 : D
3 : C
4 : D
5 : C
6 : B

Passage 2
7 : D
8 : A
9 : A
10 : C
11 : B

Independent questions
12 : C
13 : A
14 : A
15 : C

Passage 3
16 : D
17 : A
18 : C
19 : B
20 : D
21 : A
22 : C

Passage 4
23 : D
24 : C
25 : B
26 : D
27 : A
28 : D

Independent questions
29 : B
30 : C
31 : B
32 : B
33 : A

Passage 5
34 : A
35 : B
36 : C
37 : C
38 : B
39 : B

Passage 6
40 : D
41 : C
42 : B
43 : D

Independent questions
44 : A
45 : A
46 : A
47 : D

Passage 7
48 : A
49 : C
50 : A
51 : B
52 : D

Independent questions
53 : C
54 : A
55 : B
56 : C
57 : C
58 : A
59 : C

Passage 1
(Questions 1–6)

Aerobic respiration is the major process that provides cellular energy for oxygen requiring organisms. During cellular respiration, glucose is metabolized to generate chemical energy in the form of ATP:

$$C_6H_{12}O_6 + 6O_2 \rightarrow 6CO_2 + 6H_2O + 36 \text{ ATP}$$

Mitochondrion is the biochemical machinery within the cell utilized for cellular respiration. Mitochondria are present in the cytoplasm of most eukaryotic cells. The number of mitochondria per cell varies depending on tissue type and individual cell function.

Mitochondria have their own genome independent from the cell's genetic material. However, mitochondrial replication depends upon nuclear DNA to encode essential proteins required for replication of mitochondria. Mitochondria replicate randomly and independently of cell cycle.

The mitochondrial separate genome and the ribosomes of the protein synthesizing machinery became the foundation for the endosymbiotic theory. Endosymbiotic theory proposes that mitochondria originated as a separate prokaryotic organism that was engulfed by a larger anaerobic eukaryotic cell millions of years ago. The two cells formed a symbiotic relationship and eventually became dependent on each other. The eukaryotic cell sustained the bacterium, while the bacterium provided additional energy for the cell. Gradually, the two cells evolved into the present-day eukaryotic cell, with the mitochondrion retaining some of its own DNA. Mitochondrial DNA is inherited in a non-Mendelian fashion, because mitochondria, like other organelles, are inherited from the maternal gamete that supplies the cytoplasm to the fertilized egg. The study of individual mitochondria is used to investigate evolutionary relationships among different organisms.

1. Which of the following statements distinguishes the mitochondrial genome from the nuclear genome?

A. Most mitochondrial DNA nucleotides encode for protein
B. Specific mitochondrial DNA mutations are lethal
C. Mitochondrial DNA is a double helix structure
D. Some mitochondrial genes encode for tRNA

A is correct.

The nuclear genome is comprised of double helix DNA that encodes for mRNA, tRNA and rRNA. The mitochondrial genome is small compared to the size of the nuclear genome. Almost every nitrogen base of mitochondrial genome encodes for a protein and, like bacterial genomes, does not contain noncoding regions. Bacteria, mitochondria and chloroplasts do not have noncoding sequences because they lack introns within the transcribed mRNA molecule. Coding/noncoding refer to bases on the DNA nucleotide strand, while exon/intron refer to bases on the RNA nucleotide strand. Three nucleotides on the mRNA strand are referred to as a codon. Anticodons correspond to the codons and are located on the tRNA.

B: nuclear genome mutations can render a necessary characteristic of the nuclear genome ineffective. Although the nuclear genome encodes for many products, most of the bases of DNA are noncoding, because these nucleotides regulate gene expression and do not directly encode for protein. Mitochondria are vital to cell function and their replication is highly accurate. Mutations that change the mitochondrial DNA dramatically affect a cell's ability to produce proteins needed for ATP production and are lethal to the cell. Therefore, statement B is true, but it does not distinguish mitochondrial genome from the nuclear genome.

C: mitochondrial DNA is a double helix, but this does not answer the question.

D: is false and describes the nuclear, not mitochondrial, genome.

2. In which phase(s) of the eukaryotic cell cycle does mitochondrial DNA replicate?

    I. G_1 II. S   III. G_2 IV. M

  A. I only   **B.** II only   **C.** II and IV only   **D. I, II, III and IV**

D is correct.

From the passage, mitochondria replicate randomly and independently of the phase of the cell cycle and from other mitochondria. Mitochondrial DNA must replicate prior to the mitochondria dividing into daughter mitochondria. It is inferred that mitochondrial DNA replicates throughout the cell cycles: G_1, S, G_2, and M.

During G_1, the cell undergoes intense biochemical activity associated with cell growth. During S (synthesis), the nuclear DNA replicates. During G_2, other organelles replicate, nuclear DNA condenses, and structures used during mitosis (e.g. spindle fibers) begin to assemble.

During M (mitotic), mitosis occurs: the nuclear envelope disintegrates, spindle fibers assemble, condensed DNA segregates to opposite poles of the cell, replicated organelles (e.g. mitochondria and others) are partitioned within the cell, and the cell divides (cytokinesis), forming two identical daughter cells.

3. A wild-type strain of cyanobacteria (algae) is crossed with the opposite mating type of a mutant strain of cyanobacteria. All mitochondrial functions of the mutant strain are lost because of deletions within the mitochondrial genome. All progeny also lack mitochondrial functions. From the passage, which of the following best explains this observation?

    A. The presence in mitochondria of genetic material distinct from nuclear DNA
    B. Recombination of mitochondrial DNA during organelle replication
    C. Non-Mendelian inheritance of mitochondrial DNA
    D. The endosymbiotic hypothesis

C is correct.

Mating type is analogous to males and females for species that do not have opposite genders (e.g. algae and yeast). The progeny lack functional mitochondria, because the offspring have the deleted mitochondrial genome like the parental mutant strain. Precisely, the mutant strain must have been the organelle-donating parent (e.g. female). Therefore, the non-Mendelian inheritance pattern of mitochondrial DNA best explains the result of the experiment. If the wild-type strain had been the organelle-donating parent, all progeny would have wild-type mitochondrial function.

The endosymbiotic theory explains the origin of mitochondria in eukaryotic cells but not the pattern of mitochondrial inheritance.

A: is a correct statement, but does not explain the inheritance patterns observed in this cross.

B: the term "recombination" indicates the formation of new gene combinations from crossing over during reproduction (e.g. prophase I of meiosis in eukaryotes). If recombination occurred, some of the offspring would regain mitochondrial functions, because wild-type mitochondrial DNA would replace the deleted segments of DNA.

4. Four human cell cultures (colon cells, epidermal cells, erythrocytes and skeletal muscle cells) were grown in a radioactive adenine medium. After several days of growth, centrifugation was used to isolate the mitochondria. The radioactivity level of the mitochondria was measured by a liquid scintillation counter. Which of the following cell types would have the highest level of radioactivity?

    A. colon cells   **C.** erythrocytes
    B. epidermal cells   **D. skeletal muscle cells**

D is correct.

During DNA replication, cells incorporate radioactive adenine. Since all autosomal human cells have the same amount of nuclear DNA, the difference in radioactivity is related to mitochondrial DNA. Cells with the largest number of mitochondria have the highest radioactive count. The cell type with the greatest number of mitochondria depends on the energy needs of the tissue. Skeletal muscle cell is the correct choice because muscle cells have high energy demands needed for contraction.

A and B: the epidermal (deep skin) and colon (large intestine) cells do not have any special energy requirements.

C: the erythrocytes (red blood cells) are enucleated (without a nucleus) and do not contain any mitochondria. If red blood cells were metabolically active, they would consume a portion of the O_2 they carry to tissues.

5. Which of the following statements does NOT support the endosymbiotic theory?

    A. Mitochondrial DNA is circular and not enclosed by a nuclear membrane
    B. Mitochondrial DNA encodes for its own ribosomal RNA
    C. Mitochondrial ribosomes resemble eukaryotic ribosomes more than prokaryotic ribosomes
    D. Many present day bacteria live within eukaryotic cells and digest nutrients within the hosts

C is correct.

The endosymbiotic theory originated from the hypothesis that mitochondrion was once an independent unicellular organism, prokaryotic in origin, which formed a symbiotic, mutually beneficial relationship within a eukaryotic cell. If mitochondria were prokaryotic in origin, then similarities between mitochondria and bacteria support the hypothesis.

The statement that mitochondrial ribosomes resemble eukaryotic ribosomes more than prokaryotic ribosomes is false. If true, this fact would not support the endosymbiotic theory. Mitochondrial ribosomes do resemble prokaryotic ribosomes, thereby providing further support for the endosymbiotic hypothesis.

A: mitochondrial DNA is circular and not enclosed by a nuclear membrane. Bacteria have a single circular chromosome (like mitochondria), located in a cytoplasmic region of the prokaryotic cell known as the nucleoid. The nucleoid region is not enclosed by a membrane. These observations are correct and support the endosymbiotic hypothesis.

B: the fact that mitochondrial DNA encodes for its own ribosomal RNA provides evidence that mitochondria may have existed as independent cells capable of directing their own protein synthesis and cell division. These processes of protein synthesis and replication are cellular activities associated with independently living organisms.

D: the fact that many present day bacteria live within eukaryotic cells, digesting nutrients within their hosts, supports the endosymbiotic theory. If many present day bacteria have symbiotic relationships within eukaryotic cells, this supports the hypothesis that the mitochondrial ancestor may have lived within an ancestral eukaryotic cell in a mutualistic relationship.

6. Experimental data shows that mitochondrial DNA of humans mutates at a relatively low frequency. Due to mitochondria having an important role in the cell, these mutations most likely are:

    A. nondisjunctions
    B. point mutations
    C. frameshift mutations
    D. lethal mutations

B is correct.

Mitochondria supply the cell with energy in the form of ATP. Mitochondrial DNA produces mitochondrial proteins that are essential for cell survival. Mitochondria are vital to the eukaryotic cell, and replication of mitochondrial DNA is very accurate. Mutations that cause a dramatic change in the mitochondrial DNA and its ability to produce proteins needed for ATP production would be lethal to the cell.

Since some mutations do occur, the most likely type of mutation would be the type that causes the least damage. A point mutation is a single change of a nitrogenous base. For example, a cytosine is substituted for an adenine during replication. Point mutations are not usually lethal because of the redundancy of the genetic code. Redundancy means that most amino acids are coded for by more than one codon. For example, glycine is coded for by codons: GGU, GGC, GGA, and GGG. If the codon GGU undergoes a point mutation at the third base, then any of the three remaining bases (C, A, G) is substituted for U (uracil); the amino acid product is still glycine. Therefore, point mutations are least likely to affect the cell function.

A: nondisjunction is the failure of homologous chromosomes to separate during meiosis. Only specialized eukaryotic cells (e.g. gametes) in sexually reproducing organisms undergo meiosis to produce egg or sperm. Mitochondria are not gametes and, therefore, do not undergo meiosis.

C: a frameshift mutation causes bases to be either inserted or deleted during DNA replication (or during transcription). Frameshift mutations shift the reading frame of the mRNA strand being translated, usually forming nonfunctional polypeptides. Changes in protein synthesis would most likely be dangerous for the mitochondria and the cell itself.

D: lethal mutations cause the mitochondria to become nonfunctional.

Passage 2
(Questions 7–11)

Protons adjacent to a carbonyl functional group are referred to as α and are significantly more acidic than protons adjacent to carbon atoms within the hydrocarbon chain. The increased acidity characteristic for α hydrogens results from the electron withdrawing effect of the neighboring carbon-oxygen double bond. In addition, the resulting anion is stabilized by the resonance shown below:

A reaction of the enolate anion with an alkyl halide or carbonyl compound forms a carbon-carbon bond at the α position. Condensation of an enolate with an aldehyde or ketone forms an unstable alcohol, which is a reaction intermediate and not an isolated product. The intermediate spontaneously reacts, via dehydration, to form an α,β-unsaturated compound.

7. Which of the following ketones would NOT react with the strong base LDA?

A.

B.

C.

D.

D is correct. Ketone D has no α protons to react with LDA.

8. Which of the following compounds would be the intermediate alcohol from the condensation reactions shown below?

A.

B.

C.

D.

A is correct.

Attack of the enolate of 2-propanone occurs at the carbonyl carbon of 2-methylcyclohexanone and yields a tertiary alcohol adjacent to the methyl group on the ring.

9. What is the order of decreasing basicity for the following reagents?

I. $H_3C—C\equiv C^-Na^+$ **IV.**

II. $CH_3O^-Na^+$

III. $NaHCO_3$

A. IV > I > II > III
B. II > I > IV > III

C. IV > II > III > I
D. III > IV > I > II

A is correct.

The more stable the negatively-charged anion, the less basic the molecule.

Resonance stabilization or powerful electron withdrawing groups decrease basicity. The only anion fitting such criteria is HCO_3^-, which has resonance structures.

10. Which carbonyl compound has the most acidic proton?

A.

B.

C.

D.

C is correct.

The α protons between two carbonyl groups would be most acidic.

A and B: have about the same acidity, but far less acidity than the correct choice.

D: does not have any α protons.

11. Which set of the following reactants would result in the formation of ethyl-2-hexanoate?

  A. step 1: propanol, ethyl acetate and LDA; step 2: H$^+$
  B. step 1: butanal, ethyl acetate and LDA; step 2: H$^+$
  C. step 1: pentanal, ethyl acetate and LDA; step 2: H$^+$
  D. step 1: hexanal, ethyl acetate and LDA; step 2: H$^+$

B is correct.

Ethyl-2-hexanoate contains eight carbons. All answer choices have the same functional groups but differ in chain length of the parent molecule. Ethyl acetate contains four carbons, so butanal (aldehyde with a four carbon chain) must be the correct answer. LDA is a strong base that abstracts α protons in this reaction.

Ethyl acetate   Butanal

Ethyl-2-hexanoate

Questions 12 through 15 are not based on any descriptive passage and are independent of each other

12. In the graph shown, the solid line represents the reaction profile $A + B \rightarrow C + D$ in the absence of a catalyst. Which dotted line best represents the reaction profile in the presence of a catalyst?

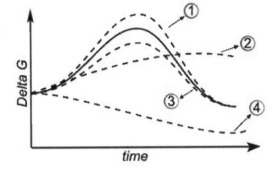

A. 1   C. 3
B. 2   D. 4

C is correct.

Catalysts are typically enzymes (i.e. proteins) that increase the rate of reaction by lowering the energy of activation. The activation energy is the energy required by the reactants to form a product. Catalysts are neither altered nor consumed during the reaction. Furthermore, catalysts have no effect on the reactant's initial potential energy or the product's potential energy. Catalysts do not change the delta G of a reaction.

In the graph, the solid curve represents the reaction rate without a catalyst. In the presence of a catalyst, the dotted line must begin (reactant) and end (products) at the same points as the solid line. Since the activation energy of the uncatalyzed reaction (solid line) corresponds to the potential energy of the reactant, and the potential energy is highest at the peak, the activation energy of the catalyzed reaction would be lower. In the catalyzed reaction, the difference between the highest potential energy and the initial potential energy is smaller.

13. How would the beta-oxidation cycle be affected by depleting oxygen within the cell?

A. **NADH and FADH₂ accumulate, and the cycle slows**
B. Krebs cycle replaces beta-oxidation
C. CoA availability decreases
D. Beta-oxidation accelerates to satisfy energy needs

A is correct.

Acetyl-CoA is the initial molecule entering the Krebs cycle. With O_2 depletion, the electron transport chain is inhibited and acetyl-CoA accumulates as each turn of the cycle produces additional NADH and $FADH_2$. NADH and $FADH_2$ are high-energy intermediates used by the electron transport chain for oxidative phosphorylation of ATP. Without entry into the electron transport chain, NADH and $FADH_2$ products accumulate and slow the beta-oxidation cycle.

14. Which of the following is the correct ranking of C-O bond length from shortest to longest?

A. $CO < CO_2 < CO_3^{2-}$ **C.** $CO_3^{2-} < CO < CO_2$

B. $CO < CO_3^{2-} < CO_2$ **D.** $CO_3^{2-} < CO_2 < CO$

A is correct.

Bond length depends on the hybrid orbitals forming the bond. The *sp* hybridized orbitals form shorter bonds than sp^2 orbitals, because *sp* hybridization contains more s character. The sp^2 hybridized orbitals form shorter bonds than sp^3 orbitals, because sp^2 hybridization contains more s character.

Therefore, CO and CO_2 have shorter bond lengths than CO_3^{2-}, since their carbon atom is *sp* hybridized, while the carbon in CO_3^{2-} is sp^2 hybridized. CO has a shorter bond length than CO_2, since oxygen orbitals are *sp* hybridized with one σ and two π bonds towards the single O. The hybridized orbital in CO_2 is *sp* with one σ and one π bond towards each O.

15. Which of the following properties distinguish fungal and animal cells from bacterial cells?

I.   Presence of cell walls   III. Asexual reproduction

II.   Presence of ribosomes   **IV. Presence of membrane bound organelles**

A. I and II only   **B.** III and IV only   **C. IV only**   **D.** I, II and IV only

C is correct.

All animal and plant cells are eukaryotic. Bacterial cells are prokaryotic. Although fungi have their own kingdom, they were originally classified in the plant kingdom. Fungal cells are eukaryotic and heterotrophic (i.e. use organic substances to derive chemical energy) organisms of a variety of shapes and sizes. Fungi can be either multicellular (e.g. mushrooms) or unicellular (e.g. yeast). Like plant cells, fungi have cell walls and other membrane bound organelles present within eukaryotic cells.

I: bacteria have cell walls (i.e. peptidoglycan) different in structure from plant (cellulose) and fungal (glucosamine polymer such as chitin) cell walls. However, the plasma membrane of animal cells is not enclosed by a cell wall.

II: both animal cells and fungal cells are eukaryotic and have ribosomes. Ribosomes are organelles responsible for translation-conversion of mRNA (nucleotides) into protein (amino acids). Bacteria also use ribosomes to synthesize proteins. Note: prokaryotic ribosomes (30S small subunit + 50S large subunit = 70S complete unit) are structurally different from eukaryotic ribosomes (40S small subunit + 60S large subunit = 80S complete unit). However, ribosomes are common to both cell types.

III: animals reproduce sexually, while the primary method of reproduction in fungi is asexual (via spores). Bacteria reproduce asexually (via binary fission). Therefore, asexual reproduction is not a common characteristic of animal and fungal cells and can be eliminated as an answer choice. The only property characteristic to animal and fungal cells that is not found in bacterial cells is the presence of membrane bound organelles.

Passage 3
(Questions 16–22)

Viruses are classified into two major groups: DNA viruses and RNA viruses. Herpes simplex virus type 1 (HSV-1) infection, also known as Human Herpes Virus 1 (HHV-1) is almost universal among humans.

HSV-1 infects humans and hides in the nervous system via retrograde movement through afferent sensory nerve fibers. During latency period, the nervous system functions as a viral reservoir from which infection can recur, and this accounts for a virus's durability in a human body. Reactivation of the virus is usually expressed by watery blisters commonly known as cold sores or fever blisters. During this phase, viral replication and shedding occur as the most common way of herpes simplex transmission.

Following initial contact, production of the herpes virus growth mediators takes place. Viral growth factors bind axon terminal receptors and are related to tumor necrosis factors.

The structure of herpes viruses consists of a relatively large double-stranded, linear DNA genome encased within an icosahedral protein cage called the capsid, which is wrapped in a lipid bilayer called the envelope. The envelope is joined to the capsid by means of a tegument. This complete particle is known as the virion. Replication and assembly of the virus takes place via nuclear machinery.

HSV-1 infection is productive if the cell is permissive to the virus and allows viral replication and virion release. HSV-1 cell infection is often not productive due to a viral genome integration block that occurs upstream. However, stimulation of an infected cell will eliminate this block and allow for virion production. Abortive infection results when cells are non-permissive. In this case, restrictive attacks occur when a few virion particles are produced. Viral production then ceases, but the genome integration persists.

Figure 1. Steps of HSV-1 infection

---

16. Where in the nervous system will the latent virus of herpes simplex be localized?

    A. The neurotransmitter   **C.** Lower motor neuron dendrites

    B. The axon hillock   **D. The afferent nervous system ganglion**

D is correct.

Figure 1 of the passage describes the steps of HSV infection. It indicates that, immediately before re-infecting the skin, the virus leaves a ganglion (collection of neuron cells bodies) to return to the surface of the skin. Therefore, latent HSV virus must be localized there.

17. The spreading of HSV-1 virus occurs during shedding by direct contact with the lesion. Which of the following locations is the source for the virus to acquire its glycoprotein-covered envelope?

    A. Nuclear membrane after transcription   **C.** Outer cell wall during lysis

    B. Storage vacuoles during lysis   **D.** Rough ER during protein synthesis

A is correct.

Most viruses acquire their envelopes from the plasma membrane, which is not an answer choice.

The second logical answer would be a nuclear membrane, since the passage states that the viral assembly takes place in the nucleus.

C: can be eliminated because human cells lack a cell wall.

18. Which infection type(s) result(s) in the integration of the viral genome into the host cell chromosome?

    I. restrictive   **II. productive**   III. abortive

    A. I only   **B.** II only   **C. I and II only**   **D.** I, II and III

C is correct.

From the passage, productive infection is a type of infection when the cell is permissive to the virus and allows for viral integration, replication and virion release. During restrictive attacks, viral production ceases, but the genome integration still persists.

Abortive infection occurs when cells are non-permissive and do not allow the viral genome to integrate into the host cell's chromosome.

19. If the infectivity/particle ratio of picornaviruses is about 0.1%, what is the number of infectious particles present in a culture of 25,000 virions?

    A. 5   **B. 25**   **C.** 250   **D.** 2500

B is correct.

0.1% of 25,000 is 25.

Picornavirus is a non-enveloped, positive-stranded RNA virus with an icosahedral capsid. The genome RNA is unusual, because it has a protein on the 5' end that is used as a primer for transcription by RNA polymerase. The name is derived from "pico" meaning "small," so "picornavirus" literally means "small RNA virus."

20. Which of the following statements is NOT the cause of the abortive viral cycle?

    A. Infected esophagus cells lack DNA replication machinery
    B. Hepatitis C patients lack the majority of viral liver cell receptors
    C. Host autoimmune antibodies bind to the viral antigen and prevent infection
    D. Random mutations of influenza virus plasma membrane antigens cause genetic drift

D is correct.

From the passage, abortive viral infection results from non-permissive cells where no virion particles are produced. The host does not present symptoms of infection. Viruses, bacteria and fungi are infecting organisms that possess antigens (e.g. surface markers) that are detected by the host's immune system. When the influenza virus undergoes rapid random mutation, its ability to cause an infection (i.e. virulence) increases, because the immune system has difficulty detecting rapidly changing surface markers. Therefore, the infection is productive and not abortive.

All other statements are characteristic of abortive infection.

A: esophagus cells that lack DNA replication machinery cannot replicate, and therefore they are unable to produce new virions.

B: viral particles of hepatitis C are not able to bind to liver tissue cells, which lack cell surface receptors.

C: viral surface markers (antigens) that match the host's antibodies will be detected and suppressed by the immune system.

21. Where will radioactive tegument dye be localized?

    A. The protein-filled area between capsid and envelope
    B. The protein-filled area between envelope and extracellular glycoprotein
    C. The protein-filled area between DNA core and nucleosome
    D. The protein-filled area between capsid and DNA core

A is correct.

From the passage, the envelope is joined to the capsid by means of a tegument (viral matrix), which is a protein-filled area. Therefore, radioactive tegument dye would adhere to that area between the capsid and the envelope.

22. From the information provided in the passage, which statement must be true for tumor necrosis factors (TNFs)?

    A. TNFs are taken up by dendrites and transported toward the neuron cell body

    B. TNFs are produced following a malignant cancerous spread through the basement membrane

    C. TNF uptake and transport are inhibited following an injury to the axon terminal

    D. TNFs function with nerve growth factors to stimulate voltage gated Na^+ channels

C is correct.

According to the passage, tumor necrosis factors (TNF) are similar to viral growth factors, which bind the axon terminal receptors. Therefore, it can be assumed that tumor necrosis factors also bind axon terminal receptors, and axon terminal injury will prevent TNF transport.

Tumor necrosis factors refer to a group of cytokines family that can cause cell death. In 1975, a protein responsible for this process was identified and named tumor necrosis factor alpha – TNF-alpha. TNF-α is the most well-known member of this class and is sometimes referred to when the term "tumor necrosis factor" is used. TNF-β is a cytokine that is induced by interleukin 10.

TNF acts via the TNF Receptor (TNF-R) and is part of the extrinsic pathway for triggering apoptosis. TNF-R is associated with procaspases through adapter proteins that can cleave other inactive procaspases and trigger the caspase cascade, irreversibly leading the cell to apoptosis (programmed cell death).

TNF interacts with tumor cells to trigger cytolysis or cell death. TNF also interacts with receptors on endothelial cells, which leads to increased vascular permeability, allowing for leukocytes to access the site of infection – localized inflammatory response.

Passage 4
(Questions 23–28)

Translation is a mechanism of protein synthesis. Proteins are synthesized on ribosomes that are either free in the cytoplasm or bound to the rough endoplasmic reticulum (rough ER). The *signal hypothesis* states that about 8 initial amino acids (known as a leader sequence) are joined initially to the growing polypeptide. In the absence of a leader sequence, the ribosomes remain free in the cytosol. If the leader sequence is present, translation of the nascent polypeptide pauses, and the ribosomes, along with the attached mRNA, migrate and attach to the ER.

Proteins that are used for transport to organelles, the plasma membrane, or to be secreted from the cell have *N-terminus signal peptide* of about 8 amino acids, which are responsible for the insertion of the nascent polypeptide through the membrane of the ER. After the leading end of the polypeptide is inserted into the lumen of the ER, the leader sequence (i.e. signal peptide) is cleaved by an enzyme within the ER lumen.

With the aid of chaperone proteins in the endoplasmic reticulum, proteins produced for the secretory pathway are folded into tertiary and quaternary structures. Those that are folded properly are packaged into transport vesicles that bud from the membrane of the ER via endocytosis. This packaging into a vesicle requires a region on the polypeptide that is recognized by a receptor of the Golgi membrane. The receptor-protein complex binds to the vesicle and then brings it to its destination, where it fuses to the cis face (closest to the ER) of the Golgi apparatus.

A pathway of vesicular transport from the Golgi involves lysosomal enzymes that carry a unique mannose-6-phosphate (M6P) marker that was added in the Golgi. The marker is recognized by specific M6P-receptor proteins that concentrate the polypeptide within a region of the Golgi membrane. These isolations of the M6P-receptor proteins facilitate their packaging into secretory vesicle, and after vesicle buds from the Golgi membrane, it moves to the lysosome and fuses with the lysosomal membrane. Because of the low pH of the lysosome, the M6P-receptor releases its bound protein. The lysosomal high H^+ concentration also produces the conformation change of the lysosomal enzymes.

23. The lumen of the endoplasmic reticulum most closely corresponds to the:

    A. cytoplasm   **C.** intermembrane space of the mitochondria

    B. ribosome   **D. extracellular environment**

D is correct.

The interior of endoplasmic reticulum (the ER lumen) is similar to the interior of the Golgi. The interior of secretory vesicles is similar to the interior of the transport vesicles (proteins from ER to Golgi). The Golgi and the extracellular environment are similar because the contents of the ER are transported via secretory vesicles to the Golgi, an organelle, or to the extracellular space (e.g. peptide hormones).

A: cytoplasm is the gel-like substance (70-90% water) within the cell membrane that holds all the cell's organelles outside the nucleus. All the contents of prokaryotic cells are contained within the cytoplasm, while in eukaryotes the nucleus is separated from the cytoplasm. Most cellular activities (including glycolysis and processes of cell division) occur within the cytoplasm. The inner granular mass is called the *endoplasm* and the outer clear layer is the cell cortex, or the *ectoplasm*.

B: ribosome is a large complex molecular machinery found in all living cells and serves as the primary site of protein synthesis – translation. It is made from complexes of RNAs and proteins (making it a *ribonucleoprotein*) and is divided into two subunits: the smaller subunit binds to the mRNA pattern, the larger subunit binds to the tRNA and the amino acids.

C: the intermembrane space of the mitochondria is used for the electron transport chain in cellular respiration and has a low pH due to the high concentration of H^+. This creates the proton motive force as the protons pass through the ATPase to synthesize ATP via oxidative phosphorylation during the last stage of cellular respiration.

24. If a protein destined to become a lysosomal enzyme was synthesized lacking a signal peptide, where in the cell is the enzyme targeted?

   A. Golgi apparatus   **B.** lysosome   **C. cytosol**   **D.** plasma membrane

C is correct.

The signal peptide is located at the N-terminus of the growing polypeptide (protein). The N-terminus is the initial amino acid residue portion within a polypeptide. The C-terminus is the final amino acid incorporated into the polypeptide chain. The N-terminus is written on the left ($-NH_2$) and the C-terminus is written on the right ($-COOH$).

A signal peptide is used by the ribosome, including the small and the large subunits (40S and 60S respectively), to adhere to the membrane of the ER for the translation completion. The ER is a continuous membrane structure with a nuclear envelope membrane and functions to fold proteins into their proper three-dimensional shape. The correct three-dimensional shape is the necessary condition for the protein to be functional and for it to be transported in vesicles out of the ER. Proteins not folded properly are destined for the proteosome to be degraded.

Without a signal peptide, the protein is translated on the free ribosomes and remains in the cytoplasm. It will not enter the secretory pathway (the ER to *cis* Golgi, *medial* Golgi and *trans* Golgi).

25. In a cell that failed to label proteins with the M6P marker, which of the following processes would be disrupted?

    A. Oxidative phosphorylation   **C.** Lysosomal formation

    B. Intracellular digestion of macromolecules   **D.** Protein synthesis

B is correct.

In the Golgi apparatus, lysosomal proteins are targeted with the M6P marker. Without this marker, the proteins are not targeted to the lysosome. If specific proteins do not get transported to the lysosome, the lysosome cannot properly hydrolyze macromolecules.

A: oxidative phosphorylation (i.e. requires oxygen) produces ATP by the electron transport chain (ETC) of cellular respiration. Both glycolysis and the Krebs cycle are substrate-level phosphorylation because oxygen is not required for the production of ATP. Note: the nucleotide analog of ATP (GTP) is produced in the Krebs cycle and then converted into ATP for use as energy.

Aerobic respiration during ETC (via oxidative phosphorylation) is different than ATP production during glycolysis and the Krebs cycle (i.e. the citric acid cycle – TCA), because glycolysis and the Krebs cycle do not use oxygen (substrate level phosphorylation). A common misconception is that the Krebs cycle is aerobic, because it does cease to function in the absence of oxygen. The reason that the Krebs cycle cannot continue in the absence of oxygen is that its products (i.e. NADH and $FADH_2$) are utilized by the ETC. The ETC does require oxygen and its inhibition (due to the lack of oxygen) causes the Krebs cycle products to accumulate, and the overall reaction is halted (i.e. Le Chatelier's principle).

D: the M6P marker does not target polypeptides meant for other organelles, the plasma membrane or the secretory pathway (e.g. peptide hormones) out of the cell.

26. Within the cell, where is the M6P receptor transcribed?

    A. nucleolus   **B.** smooth ER   **C.** ribosome   **D. nucleus**

D is correct.

Transcription is the conversion of DNA nucleotide sequences into messenger RNA. The enzyme that completes RNA synthesis from the sense strand of DNA is RNA polymerase. In eukaryotes, transcription (like replication, copying of the DNA during S phase of interphase in the cell cycle) occurs in the nucleus.

A: the nucleolus is inside the nucleus and is involved in rRNA synthesis. The nucleolus is often visualized via staining that is denser than the positive stain that highlights the nucleus, because the rRNA nucleotides in the nucleolus are more concentrated than the DNA in the larger nucleus. rRNA is transported into the cytoplasm and anneals with proteins to form the ribosomes.

C: translation is the conversion of mRNA into proteins (using ribosomes), which occurs in the cytoplasm of the cell.

27. Which of these enzymes functions in an acidic environment?

   A. pepsin   **B.** endonuclease   **C.** signal peptidase   **D.** salivary amylase

A is correct.

Pepsin is a digestive enzyme that breaks down proteins in the stomach. Therefore, its catalytic activity is optimal at a very low pH (e.g. 2 to 3), as the stomach has a very acidic environment due to the presence of hydrochloric acid.

B: endonucleases are enzymes that cleave the phosphodiester bond in a polynucleotide chain. While some cut DNA relatively nonspecifically (regardless of the sequence), many of them (e.g. restriction endonucleases or restriction enzymes) cleave only at very specific nucleotide sequences.

C: signal peptidase targets growing polypeptides into the endoplasmic reticulum (ER). The interior lumen of ER is not acidic; therefore, this enzyme would not function in an acidic environment.

D: salivary amylase is an enzyme released in the mouth in the saliva for the pre-digestion of starch – conversion of long polymers of glucose into maltose.

Saliva is a clear, tasteless, odorless, slightly acidic (pH 6.8) fluid consisting of the secretions from the parotid, sublingual and submandibular salivary glands and mucous glands of the oral cavity. Food ingested into the mouth undergoes mastication by chewing to increase surface area of the bolus (food).

28. Which of the following is required for the transport of proteins to the lysosome?

   A. Endocytosis   **C.** Acidic pH of the Golgi
   B. Absence of a leader sequence   **D. Vesicular transport from the rough ER to the Golgi**

D is correct.

Before being transported to the lysosome, proteins are synthesized and inserted into the lumen of the ER via the signal peptide. After being properly folded (via the assistance of chaperone molecules), they are transported by vesicles from the rough ER (protein synthesis site) to the Golgi for protein modification and sorting. Then, to the target organelle-lysosome.

A: endocytosis is invagination of the plasma membrane that forms transport vesicles, which take extracellular material into the cell's interior. Transporting proteins via endocytosis from the extracellular space into the cell for their degradation is a different process from targeting proteins via a signal peptide sequence for integration into the plasma membrane of the lysosome.

B: a leader sequence (also known as a signal peptide sequence) is a 6-10 amino acid sequence that targets the nascent polypeptide from the synthesis on a free (cytosolic) ribosome to the endoplasmic reticulum. Signal peptidase (targeting the leader sequence) is an enzyme that converts secretory and some membrane proteins to their mature forms by cleaving their signal peptides from their N-terminals (the start of a protein or polypeptide terminated by an amino acid with a free amine group). Absence of the leader sequence is not a condition for protein targeting to the lysosome. Proteins destined for organelles (e.g. lysosomes), the plasma membrane or for excretion from the cell contain a leader sequence.

C: the pH of the Golgi is not acidic; the lysosome is the organelle with an acidic pH (about 5).

> Questions 29 through 33 are not based on any
> descriptive passage and are independent of each other

29. Which of the following properties within a polypeptide chain determines the globular conformation of a protein?

    A. Number of individual amino acids   **C.** Relative concentration of amino acids

    B. Linear sequence of amino acids   **D.** Peptide optical activity measured in the polarimeter

B is correct.

The primary ($1°$) structure is the linear sequence of amino acids in the polypeptide.

$1°$ determines subsequent local folding for the secondary ($2°$) structure - alpha helix and beta-pleated sheets. The alpha helix and beta-pleated sheets of $2°$ structure give rise to the tertiary ($3°$) structure for the overall 3-D shape of a functional protein. The overall 3-D shape determines the function of the protein. A functional enzyme (protein) has proper folding for the formation of the active site for substrate binding.

The joining of two separate polypeptide chains defines the quaternary ($4°$) structure. A classic example of $4°$ structure is hemoglobin with 2 alpha and 2 beta chains forming a functional hemoglobin protein.

30. In the Newman projection shown below, what does the circle represent?

    A. First carbon along the C_1–C_2 axis of the bond
    B. First carbon along the C_2–C_3 axis of the bond
    C. Second carbon along the C_2–C_3 axis of the bond
    D. Second carbon along the C_3–C_4 axis of the bond

C is correct.

Newman projections represent carbon-carbon bonds for the C_2–C_3 atoms. The molecule is rotated (conformational change) to look down the C_2–C_3 bond axis. The carbon in front is C_2 and represents the intersection of the three front lines. The back carbon (obscured) is C_3 and drawn as a larger circle in the Newman projection.

31. What is the degree of unsaturation for a molecule with the molecular formula $C_{18}H_{20}$?

    A. 2   **B. 9**   **C.** 18   **D.** 36

B is correct.

The degree of unsaturation is given by the formula C_2H_{2n+2} or $(2C + 2 – H)/2$, where C is the number of carbon atoms and H is the number of hydrogen atoms. Therefore, $C_{18}H_{20}$ contains $(36 + 2 – 20)/2 = 9$ degrees of unsaturation.

A single degree of unsaturation corresponds to 2 Hs, and the molecule has a structure of either a double bond or a ring.

Two degrees of unsaturation correspond to 4 Hs, and the molecule has a structure of a triple bond, two double bonds, a double bond and a ring, or two rings.

Three degrees of unsaturation correspond to 6 Hs, and the structure is either a triple bond and a double bond, three double bonds, two double bonds and a ring, a double bond and two rings, or a three ring structure.

32. If distillation was used to separate hexanol from butanol, which product would distill first?

    A. hexanol   **B. butanol**   **C.** they distill simultaneously **D.** cannot be determined

B is correct.

Hexanol and butanol contain hydroxyl groups. Hydroxyl groups form hydrogen bonds because hydrogen is attached directly to an electronegative atom (e.g. F, O, N or Cl). The partial delta charge (i.e. due to electronegativity differences in the atoms compared to hydrogen) permits the formation of the strongest of the dipole-dipole bonds (i.e. hydrogen bonding).

With the H attached directly to O, hydrogen bonding is possible in both molecules. However, butanol (i.e. 4-carbon chain) is a smaller alcohol (i.e. less molecular weight) than hexanol (i.e. 6-carbon chain) and has a lower boiling point, making it the first compound to be distilled.

Always consider molecular weight as the greater factor in boiling point and then dipole interactions (e.g. hydrogen bonding) between molecules.

33. All of the following are involved in energy production within the mitochondria, EXCEPT:

    A. glycolysis   **C.** electron transport chain
    B. Krebs cycle   **D.** oxidative phosphorylation

A is correct.

Glycolysis is involved in the net production of 2 ATP during cellular respiration. Glycolysis is important in energy production, but it occurs in the cytoplasm, not the mitochondria. All other choices name processes that occur in the mitochondria.

Passage 5
(Questions 34–39)

Acetylsalicylic acid (known by the brand name Aspirin) is one of the most commonly used drugs. It has analgesic (pain relieving), antipyretic (fever-reducing) and anti-inflammatory properties. The drug works by blocking the synthesis of *prostaglandins*. A prostaglandin is any member of a lipid compound group enzymatically derived from fatty acids. Every prostaglandin is a 20-carbon (including a 5-carbon ring) unsaturated carboxylic acid.

Prostaglandins are involved in a variety of physiological processes and have important functions in the body. They are mediators and have strong physiological effects (e.g. regulating the contraction and relaxation of smooth muscle). These *autocrine* or *paracrine* hormones (i.e. messenger molecules acting locally) are produced throughout the human body with target cells present in the immediate vicinity of the site of their secretion.

Acetylsalicylic acid is a white crystalline substance that is an acetyl derivative and is a weak acid with a melting point of 136 °C (277 °F) and a boiling point of 140 °C (284 °F). Acetylsalicylic acid can be produced through acetylation of salicylic acid by acetic anhydride in the presence of an acid catalyst, and is shown in the following reaction:

salicylic acid   acetic anhydride   acetylsalicylic acid   acetic acid

Reaction 1. Synthesis of acetylsalicylic acid

The acetylsalicylic acid synthesis is classified as an *esterification* reaction. Salicylic acid is treated with acetic anhydride, an acid derivative, which causes a chemical reaction that turns salicylic acid's hydroxyl group into an ester group (R-OH → R-OCOCH$_3$). This process yields acetylsalicylic acid and acetic acid, which for this reaction is considered a byproduct. Small amounts of sulfuric acid (and sometimes phosphoric acid) are almost always used as a catalyst.

Reaction 2. Mechanism of acetylsalicylic acid synthesis

In a college lab, this synthesis was carried out via the following procedure:

10 mL of acetic anhydride, 4 g of salicylic acid and 2 mL of concentrated sulfuric acid were mixed, and the resulting solution was heated for 10 minutes. Upon cooling the mix in an ice bath, a crude white product X precipitated. 100 mL of cold distilled water was added to complete the crystallization. By suction filtration, the product X was isolated and then washed with several aliquots of cold water.

Product X was dissolved in 50 mL of saturated sodium bicarbonate and the solution was filtered to remove an insoluble material. Then, 3 *M* of hydrochloric acid was added to the filtrate and product Y precipitated. It was collected by suction filtration and recrystallized in a mixture of petroleum ether (benzine) and common ether.

After analyzing product X, it showed the presence of acetylsalicylic acid, trace levels of salicylic acid and a contaminate of high molecular weight.

34. In the experiment described in the passage, salicylic acid primarily acts as an alcohol. What is the likely product when salicylic acid is reacted with an excess of methanol in the presence of sulfuric acid?

A. methyl salicylate   **B.** benzoic acid   **C.** phenol   **D.** benzaldehyde

A is correct.

Salicylic acid has two different functional groups – an alcohol and a carboxylic acid – both of which can undergo esterification reactions. From the passage, in the synthesis of acetylsalicylic acid, the alcohol functional group of salicylic acid reacts with acetic anhydride to form an ester.

Under acidic conditions, the carboxylic acid group forms an ester linkage when it is reacted with an excess of alcohol. The oxygen in methanol (i.e. nucleophile) attacks the carboxyl carbon in salicylic acid and salicylic acid acts as a carboxylic acid.

The reaction mechanism in the problem stem is similar to salicylic acid and acetic anhydride, whereby a series of protonation/deprotonation steps lead to the formation of the ester (e.g. methyl salicylate). This is nucleophilic acyl substitution with the OH group on the carboxylic acid being substituted (i.e. not the hydroxyl group).

B: the hydroxyl group would be removed from the aromatic ring, but this is unlikely, because the aromatic ring is stable and the hydroxyl group remains attached.

C: if phenol was formed, salicylic acid would have to undergo decarboxylation. However, under these conditions, decarboxylation is highly unlikely. For decarboxylation, high temperatures and either 1,3-dicarboxylic acids or β-keto acids spontaneously release carbon dioxide.

D: the hydroxyl group would need to be removed from benzene, and the carboxyl group would have to be reduced to an aldehyde. Reduction of the carboxylic acid would occur with a strong reducing agent, such as lithium aluminum hydride ($LiAlH_4$).

35. When acetylsalicylic acid is exposed to humid air, it acquires a vinegar-like smell, because:

   A. moist air reacts with residual salicylic acid to form citric acid
   B. it undergoes hydrolysis into salicylic and acetic acids
   C. it undergoes hydrolysis into salicylic acid and acetic anhydride
   D. it undergoes hydrolysis into acetic acid and citric acid

B is correct.

Since acetylsalicylic acid is an ester, it reacts with water, whereby the ester linkage is cleaved and forms an alcohol and a carboxylic acid. From moisture (i.e. humidity), acetylsalicylic acid is cleaved to produce salicylic acid and acetic acid. Acid is present as H_3O^+, and through a series of intermediates, the ester linkage is cleaved in acetylsalicylic acid, yielding salicylic acid (alcohol) and acetic acid (carboxylic acid). Acetic acid generates the aroma of vinegar.

A: there should not be any residual salicylic acid in acetylsalicylic acid. Even if small levels of salicylic acid were present, salicylic acid does not react with water-saturated air to form citric acid.

C: acetic anhydride will not be formed. Acetic anhydride is often a reactant in the synthesis of molecules of acetic acid with the side product of water. However, the question states that acetylsalicylic acid undergoes hydrolysis, and the hydrated product (not the dehydrated product) is formed. Acetic acid (not acetic anhydride) is formed with salicylic acid.

D: acetylsalicylic acid does cleave to produce citric acid (smell of lemon juice) and acetic acid. For citric acid to form, the ester would have to be aliphatic (e.g. hydrocarbon chain) and not aromatic (e.g. benzene). Acetylsalicylic acid contains an aromatic ring, so upon hydrolysis (i.e. cleavage by the addition of water), a phenyl (i.e. aromatic) group would be one of the products. Neither citric nor acetic acid contain a phenyl group.

36. What is the purpose of dissolving product X in saturated $NaHCO_3$ in the experiment conducted in a college lab?

    A. To precipitate any side product contaminants as sodium salts
    B. To remove water from the reaction
    C. To form the water-soluble sodium salt of aspirin
    D. To neutralize any remaining salicylic acid

C is correct.

Bicarbonate ($NaHCO_3$) is commonly used for syntheses and extractions. In the experiment, acetylsalicylic acid was formed when the solution of acetic anhydride, salicylic acid and sulfuric acid was heated. The formation of the crude white precipitate containing acetylsalicylic acid following the cooling indicates that acetylsalicylic acid is relatively insoluble in water.

Acetylsalicylic acid has two functional groups: a carboxylic acid and an ester. Therefore, when dissolving product X in sodium bicarbonate, acetylsalicylic acid dissolves in this solution, because the proton of the carboxylic acid dissociates (i.e. –COOH into –COO⁻ Na⁺). The hydrogen on the carboxyl group is slightly acidic with a pK_a of about 3.5, and acetylsalicylic acid is converted into its corresponding sodium salt.

Salicylic acid is present in product X as an impurity and is converted to its corresponding sodium salt, which is removed in the recrystallization step. By filtration, the acetylsalicylic acid salt is then isolated in the filtrate and can be converted back to its solid form by acidification with hydrochloric acid (HCl).

A: the contaminant cannot form a water soluble sodium salt because acetylsalicylic acid forms a water soluble sodium salt. If the contaminant could be dissolved in water as its corresponding salt, it would mix with acetylsalicylic acid, preventing its isolation.

B: sodium bicarbonate is not a desiccant that would dry the solution.

D: sodium bicarbonate converts acetylsalicylic acid into its corresponding sodium salt. Bicarbonate (NaHCO$_3$) is often used to deprotonate a weak acid, which (as an ion) becomes soluble. The choice of sodium hydroxide would not be proper because –OH is a strong base.

37.

Phenyl salicylate is a molecule different from acetylsalicylic acid, but also possesses analgesic properties. Which of the following could be reacted with salicylic acid in the presence of sulfuric acid to produce phenyl salicylate?

A. PhCH$_2$OH   **B.** PhCO$_2$H   **C. PhOH**   **D.** Benzene

C is correct.

This question tests the basic concepts of carboxylic acid and alcohol reactions similar to the mechanism in the synthesis of acetylsalicylic acid (Reaction 1). Under acidic conditions, the oxygen of phenol is a nucleophile that attacks and adds to the carboxyl carbon of salicylic acid. Through a series of intermediates, water dissociates (i.e. dehydration), and the product is the substitution of the carboxyl hydroxyl by the aromatic ring. This dehydration forms an ester linkage between the carboxyl group (salicylic acid) and the alcohol (phenol) to form phenyl salicylate.

A: note the extra CH$_2$ group. Even though this molecule contains a nucleophilic alcohol, the product would not be phenyl salicylate.

B: salicylic acid would function as an alcohol undergoing nucleophilic attack of its hydroxyl oxygen on the carboxyl carbon of benzoic acid, resulting in *o*-benzoylbenzoic acid.

D: benzene is very stable and would not react directly with salicylic acid. Even under extreme conditions (e.g. high temperature), a reaction between the two molecules is not likely.

38. For the synthesis of acetylsalicylic acid, what is the reaction mechanism?

A. Nucleophilic addition   **C.** Nucleophilic aromatic substitution
B. Nucleophilic acyl substitution   **D.** Electrophilic aromatic substitution

B is correct.

Acetylsalicylic acid is synthesized when a molecule of salicylic acid reacts with a molecule of acetic anhydride. Anhydrides are formed during dehydration of either two carboxylic acids or a carboxylic acid and an alcohol. The oxygen on the alcohol is the nucleophile, which attacks and adds to one of the carbonyl carbons in acetic anhydride. The carbonyl oxygen of acetic anhydride is protonated by sulfuric acid (i.e. acid catalyzed reaction) which makes it more susceptible to a nucleophilic attack, because the O is deficient in electron density (i.e. yielding a greater partial plus on the O). A series of intermediates is formed, which leads to the formation of acetylsalicylic acid and the dissociation of acetic acid.

A: no addition reaction occurs for benzene, because this would interrupt aromaticity, and the overall molecule would be less stable. From the product, the hydrogen on the phenol group has been replaced (i.e. substituted) by an acyl group.

C and D: in the synthesis of acetylsalicylic acid, the stable benzene ring does not undergo a reaction, but the reaction occurs with the functional groups attached to stable (i.e. aromatic) benzene. Under relatively mild reaction conditions, the benzene ring is unlikely to be attacked by either electrophilic (EAS) or nucleophilic aromatic substitution (NAS). Electrophilic aromatic substitution is restricted to a few reactions (e.g. halogenations, nitration, sulfonation, Friedel-Crafts alkylation and Friedel-Crafts acylation) and each requires a Lewis acid as a catalyst to generate a "carbocation" that the electrons of benzene attack.

39. Which of the following is the likely structure of the high-molecular weight contaminant in product X?

B is correct.

Because the contaminant must be a derivative of salicylic acid, analyze the structure of salicylic acid and consider other possible reactions that it can undergo in an acidic environment. Salicylic acid has an alcohol and two carboxylic acid functional groups.

These two functional groups both react with other molecules (i.e. intermolecular attack) and also react with each other (i.e. intramolecular attack). The contaminant is the product of the hydroxyl group of one of the salicylic acid molecules, forming an ester linkage with the carboxyl group of another salicylic acid. The oxygen (i.e. hydroxyl group) in salicylic acid acts as a nucleophile and attacks the carboxyl carbon of another salicylic acid molecule to form a protonated intermediate.

Water can then dissociate from this intermediate with an ester linkage between the two molecules. The hydroxyl and carboxyl groups remaining at each end can react further. A large number of molecules can react via polymerization of these repeating units (i.e. benzene ring attached to an ester moiety). However, the length of the polymer is limited by entropy and by depletion of the substrate. The polymer has repeating units and is formed via dehydration, whereby the oxygen of the hydroxyl group attacks the carbon of the carbonyl, and water is released when the ester linkage is formed.

Passage 6
(Questions 40–43)

The ovaries of a female at birth contain on average 300,000 follicles (with a range from 35,000 to 2.5 million). These follicles are immature (*primordial*), and each contains an immature primary oocyte. By the time of puberty, the number decreases to an average of 180,000 (the range is 25,000-1.5 million). Only about 400 follicles ever mature and produce an oocyte. During the process of *folliculogenesis* (i.e. maturation), a follicle develops from a *primary follicle* to a *secondary follicle*, then to a *vesicular* (Graafian) follicle. The whole process of folliculogenesis, from primordial to a preovulatory follicle, belongs to the stage of *ootidogenesis* of *oogenesis*. A secondary follicle contains a secondary oocyte with a reduced number of chromosomes. The release of a secondary oocyte from the ovary is called *ovulation*.

Unlike male *spermatogenesis*, which can last indefinitely, folliculogenesis ends when the remaining follicles in the ovaries are incapable of responding to the hormonal signals that previously prompted some follicles to mature. The depletion in follicle supply sets the beginning of menopause in women.

The ovarian cycle is controlled by the *gonadotropic hormones* released by the pituitary: follicle-stimulating hormone (FSH) and luteinizing-hormone (LH). Imbalances of these hormones may often cause infertility in females. For treatment of many female reproductive disorders, therapies that act similar to FSH and LH are often used successfully.

In a pharmaceutical laboratory, scientists test two of such drugs. Drug X binds to LH receptors, while drug Y binds to FSH receptors. The scientists separated 15 mice with fertility disorders into three experimental groups. The mice in Group I were administered drug Y, while the mice in Group II were administered drug X, and the mice in Group III received a placebo. After 1 month, the scientists performed an *ovariectomy* (i.e. surgical removal of ovaries in laboratory animals) and counted the number of developing follicles in the mice ovaries.

Note: a normal female mouse has on average 10-12 developing follicles at any point in the menstrual cycle.

Mice	Group I	Group II	Group III
#1	5	6	6
#2	11	4	5
#3	8	16	6
#4	11	11	4
#5	8	5	9

Table 1. Number of developing follicles per mouse

40. From the data, which of the following conditions most likely is the cause of infertility observed in mice #3 in all three groups, given that they all are affected by the same reproductive disorder?

    A. Inability of FSH to bind FSH receptors   **C.** Elevated levels of LH

    B. Benign tumor of the pituitary   **D.** **Gene mutation LH hormone**

D is correct.

The LH receptors are likely functional in all mice # 3, because the LH agonist induced follicular development. An agonist is a molecule that combines with receptors to initiate (e.g. drug) actions, because the agonist possesses affinity and intrinsic activity.

The cause for infertility is either insufficient LH synthesis or the synthesis of nonfunctional LH. A mutation of the LH gene can result in nonfunctional LH.

41. Which of the following conditions is LEAST likely to result in female infertility?

    A. downregulation of LH receptors   **C.** **release of multiple follicles**

    B. inflammation of oviducts   **D.** FSH gene mutation

C is correct.

The release of multiple follicles may lead to the occurrence of multiple conceptions. This effect is the opposite of infertility and is often used in *in vitro* fertilization, where hyperovulation is induced in a woman, and multiple fertilized eggs are transferred into the uterus for implantation.

A and D: from the passage, the imbalances of FSH and LH hormones often result in fertility problems.

B: a released egg must travel down the oviduct (i.e. fallopian tube) to be fertilized; therefore an inflammation of the oviducts may interfere with successful zygote implantation.

42. Overstimulation of follicular development during reproductive therapies increases the probability of multiple ovulations often resulting in multiple pregnancies. Which of the test subjects is the best example for this case?

    A. Mouse #2 of Group I   **C.** Mouse #4 of Group II

    B. **Mouse #3 of Group II**   **D.** Mouse #5 of Group III

B is correct.

According to the passage, the average female mouse has 10-12 mature follicles. Mouse #3 in Group II had 16 mature follicles and was the only mouse with a greater (than average) number of mature follicles. Therefore, this mouse exhibits therapeutic follicular overstimulation. To demonstrate a therapeutic effect, the mouse must be in an experimental group (Groups I and II) and not in the placebo group (Group III).

43. Which treatment is most likely responsible for the number of maturing follicles observed in mouse #5 in Group III?

    A. Stimulation of the pituitary   **C.** LH receptor stimulation

    B. FSH receptor inhibition   **D. No relationship to treatment**

D is correct.

The passage states that Group III is the control group that received a placebo. A placebo is a medicinally inactive compound that is administered in drug testing for its suggestive effect. Therefore, the number of follicles observed in all the mice of group III is unrelated to the treatment.

Questions 44 through 47 are not based on any descriptive passage and are independent of each other

---

44. During DNA replication, individual dNTP nucleotides are joined by bond formation that releases phosphate. Which of the following describes the bond type between two dNTP nucleotides?

    A. covalent bond   **B.** peptide bond   **C.** van der Waals bond   **D.** ionic bond

A is correct.

Covalent bonds involve equal (or about equal) sharing of electrons between two atoms when the two atoms have the same electronegativity (attraction for electron density). Covalent bonds are the most common intramolecular bond (i.e. covalent or ionic), because carbon (which comprises the backbone of organic molecules) has an intermediate electronegativity and shares electrons almost equally with most other atoms.

B: peptide bonds refer to a bond between adjacent amino acids formed during dehydration, whereby the lone pair of electrons on the nitrogen (amino group) attacks the carbonyl carbon (carboxylic acid) of the adjacent amino acid and is not applicable to this question. A peptide bond is rigid (no rotation around a single bond) because of the double bond character (due to resonance) between the amino end (NH) of one amino acid and the carboxyl end (COO) of the adjacent amino acid. The resonance of the lone pair of electrons of the NH being shared to form a double bond with the carboxyl group provides the rigidity of the peptide bond and is important for protein shape (protein shape determines function).

C: van der Waals (also known as London dispersion forces) results from an attraction between molecules based on the momentary flux of electron density within/among molecules that results in a weak (and short ranged) attraction between the oppositely charged polarity within the molecules. Van der Waals forces are the weakest of the intermolecular forces (between molecules). The strongest intermolecular force results from hydrogen bonding, where H is attached directly to a strongly electronegative atom such as F, O, N or Cl (see explanation to question 46 in *Biological and Biochemical Foundations Practice Test 1*

---

regarding Cl). Weaker than hydrogen bonding is dipole-dipole interactions, which do not have as strong of an electronegativity difference as in H-bonding. Dipole–induced dipole is the third in the series of intermolecular forces, followed by van der Waals (London dispersion forces).

D: ionic bonds involve unequal sharing of electrons and occur between two atoms with great differences in electronegativity (e.g. salts such as KCl: K^+ cations and Cl^- anions). Ionic bonds dissociate in water, because the ions each interact with the polar water molecule. For example, the cation associates with the partial negative charge on the O in water, while the anion associates with the partial plus charge on the H of water.

45. Which of the following is true about polar amino acids?

  A. Side chains project towards the exterior of the protein chain
  B. Side chains contain only hydrogen and carbon atoms
  C. Side chains are hydrophobic
  D. Side chains have neutral moieties

A is correct.

The R groups of the polar side chains project towards the exterior of the protein chain, because the polar side chains (hydrophilic moieties) hydrogen bond with the H_2O solution in biological systems.

Hydrocarbons include only hydrogens and carbons without any heteroatom (i.e. atoms other than H and C), such as electronegative O or N that create polarity due to the unequal sharing of bonded electrons (polar covalent bonds). This unequal sharing generates hydrophilic regions that interact with H_2O either by hydrogen bonds or electrostatic interactions (e.g. dipole or ionic bonds).

46. What is the net number of ATP produced per glucose in an obligate anaerobe?

  A. 2 ATP   **B.** 4 ATP   **C.** 36 ATP   **D.** 38 ATP

A is correct.

Obligate anaerobes require the absence of oxygen. Obligate anaerobes produce ATP only via fermentation, which includes both glycolysis and the reactions necessary to regenerate NAD^+ needed for subsequent glycolysis. Obligate anaerobes produce a net of 2 ATP produced during glycolysis with no additional ATP produced during fermentation, where pyruvate is converted to lactic acids (i.e. mammals) or to ethanol (i.e. yeast).

B: glycolysis produces a total (gross) of 4 ATP, but the initial process of glycolysis requires the hydrolysis (investment) of 2 ATP to add phosphates to each end of the glucose molecule at the onset of the process.

C and D: aerobic eukaryote organisms produce a net of 36 ATP per glucose, while prokaryotes (e.g. bacteria) produce a net of 38 ATP per glucose. This is because in prokaryotes, the NADH produced during glycolysis loses energy by needing to be shuttled into the double membrane-layered mitochondria. In prokaryotes, glycolysis, the Krebs cycle and the electron transport chain all occur in the cytoplasm. The reported ATP values (e.g. 36 vs. 38) are theoretical, and the actual yield is often less due to "leaky" membranes of mitochondria.

47. All of the following hormones are released by the anterior pituitary gland, EXCEPT:

A. luteinizing hormone	**C.** thyroid stimulating hormone
B. prolactin	**D. Vasopressin**

D is correct.

Vasopressin (aka ADH - antidiuretic hormone) and oxytocin are secreted by the posterior pituitary. ADH targets the kidneys for water retention and arterioles for vasoconstriction to raise blood pressure. Oxytocin targets the uterus for contractions during child birthing and the mammary glands for lactation.

The anterior pituitary synthesizes seven hormones:
- Adrenocorticotropic hormone (ACTH) targets the adrenal glands for the secretion of glucocorticoid and mineralcorticoid;
- Beta-endorphin targets the opioid receptor for inhibition of pain perception;
- Thyroid-stimulating hormone (TSH) targets the thyroid gland for the secretion of thyroid hormones;
- Follicle-stimulating hormone (FSH) targets the gonads for growth of the reproductive system;
- Luteinizing hormone (LH) targets the gonads for sex hormone production (including testosterone, estrogens and progesterone);
- Growth hormone (aka somatotropin) targets the liver and adipose tissue to promote growth, lipid and carbohydrate metabolism;
- Prolactin (PRL) targets the ovaries for secretion of estrogen and progesterone, and the mammary glands for milk production.

Passage 7
(Questions 48–52)

The genome of all cells of the human body, except germ line cells (i.e. gametes of either sperm or egg) and mature red blood cells (i.e. erythrocytes), contains identical DNA on chromosomes. Even with the same genetic material, cells of different tissue are diverse and specialized. This diversity of cellular function is due primarily to cell-specific variations in protein expression which is regulated mostly at the transcriptional level. Different genes are expressed by transcriptional controls that determine cellular function and growth.

Specifically, gene transcription is controlled by upstream regulatory sequences that include regulatory genes and promoters. Regulators and promoters are controlled by extracellular signals (e.g. hormones) and intracellular signals (e.g. calcium or glucose). Regulators stimulate or inhibit gene transcription of a gene, while activated promoters only increase transcription.

A major cause of cancer is a cell's inability to regulate the cell cycle. Genetic mutations may occur at any level of the cell growth regulation system. There are two gene categories that, if mutated, often result in cancer: *oncogenes* and *tumor suppressor genes*. Oncogenes regulate cell growth and division and a mutation of the oncogene itself or its promoters can result in uncontrolled cell growth and division. Tumor suppressor genes regulate the cell cycle and may induce cell death when a cell has abnormal function. Mutations of tumor suppressor genes impair this regulatory ability and, without this control mechanism, the malfunctioning cells are able to proliferate.

When regulators or promoter sequences for genes involved in oncogenesis (also called carcinogenesis or tumorigenesis) are identified, it is possible to use drug treatments to regulate transcription of these genes. Certain drugs are effective at controlling the growth of cancerous cells, but have significant side effects that include diarrhea, significant hair loss, decreased immunity and kidney damage.

48. Given that oncogenes and tumor suppressor genes mutations usually arise during DNA replication, which phase of the cell cycle most likely is the phase for cancerous mutations?

A. S   **B.** metaphase   **C.** cytokinesis   **D.** G_0

A is correct.

DNA is replicated in the S phase of the cell cycle, whereby the result is still a diploid cell (i.e. 2 copies of the chromosomes), but each strand is duplicated to form sister chromatids. The number of chromosomes is counted by the number of centromeres. Centromeres are a tightly coiled (i.e. heterochromatin) region that joins the chromatin arms, forming sister chromatids of the newly replicated DNA.

B and C: interphase includes the sequence of cellular growth (i.e. G_1), DNA replication (i.e. S) and organelle replication (i.e. G_2). The cell cycle is divided into interphase (i.e. G_1, S, G_2 phases) and mitosis (i.e. PMAT: prophase, metaphase, anaphase, telophase/cytokinesis). The cell spends most of its life cycle in G_1, and once it proceeds into S phase, the cell cycle checkpoints ensure that properly dividing cells undergo cytokinesis at the end of the cycle and form 2 diploid cells that are identical to the parental cell.

D: G_0 is the phase for nondividing cells (e.g. brain and spinal cord cells). Other cells can enter G_0 at the end of mitosis and then, via cell cycle signals, the cell proceeds into G_1 where the cell remains until the onset of S phase. In interphase, the DNA is accessible for transcription and is uncoiled (i.e. euchromatin).

49. What is the likely action mechanism of the cancer drugs mentioned in the passage?

    A. Changes at the nucleotide level of an oncogene
    B. Upregulation of the activator for an oncogene
    C. Increased expression of a tumor suppressor gene
    D. Blocking the promoter of a tumor suppressor gene from binding transcription factors

C is correct.

According to the passage, the drug curtails the growth of cancerous cell, whereby anticancer drugs target rapidly proliferating cells. Like cancer cells, rapidly dividing cells include hair follicles, cells of the gastrointestinal system and antibodies. Therefore, anticancer therapies result in hair loss, poor absorption of nutrients and a suppression of immune activity as side effects.

The drug must be increasing the expression of tumor suppressor genes (i.e. p53 being the most common tumor suppression gene). If the drug decreased oncogenic activity, it would suppress the expression of proteins and slow the growth of cancerous cells. Tumor suppressor genes and oncogenes work in contrast. Oncogenes increase the expression of cancer by producing protein products that yield more cell growth (i.e. uncontrolled cell growth is the hallmark of cancer cells), while tumor suppressor genes inhibit cancer by blocking the over-expression of proteins that would move the cell at an accelerated rate through the cell cycle.

50. A new cancer drug with the brand name Colcrys acts to prevent cell division by inhibiting microtubule formation. In what stage of mitosis would this drug be most effective?

    A. prophase   **B.** metaphase   **C.** anaphase   **D.** telophase

A is correct.

Microtubules assemble from the polymerization of tubulin subunits. Microtubules (i.e. spindle fibers) are essential for cell division because they connect centromeres (on the chromosomes) to the centriole (at the pole of the cell). Microtubule formation is essential for chromosomes to align along the midline of the cell (i.e. metaphase plate).

The microtubules pull the chromosomes apart by splitting the centromeres during anaphase and separating the chromatids. Without the polymerization of tubulin to form microtubules, chromosomes fail to align at the metaphase plate, separate during anaphase or become segregated into respective nuclei during telophase.

51. Along with its corresponding gene, a promoter sequence may be transcribed in one mRNA transcript. The mRNA sequence containing the transcribed promoter must be cleaved to make translation possible. Which cell region is most likely the site of this cleavage?

A. Golgi apparatus   **B. nucleus**   **C.** cytoplasm   **D.** nucleolus

B is correct.

The primary transcript (i.e. heteronuclear RNA or hnRNA) undergoes processing in the nucleus to produce mRNA. The hnRNA processing includes the addition of a 5'-G cap and a poly-A tail, excision and removal of introns, and ligation of exons. All three post-transcriptional activities (i.e. processing) must take place for the formation of mRNA. Only after hnRNA has been processed (i.e. capping, adding a tail and splicing), mRNA will migrate through the nuclear pores of the nuclear membrane and enter the cytoplasm. Once in the cytoplasm, the mRNA is the template for protein synthesis (known as translation).

A: the Golgi apparatus structure resembles a stack of flattened sacs located close to the endoplasmic reticulum. The Golgi functions in protein processing and their sorting for the secretory pathways (proteins destined for exocytosis from the cell, placement into the plasma membrane or targeted for an organelle within the cell). Secretory proteins arrive at the Golgi in vesicles that bud off from the rough endoplasmic reticulum.

C: the cytoplasm (also called cytosol) is the gel-like area outside of the nucleus. Cytosol is where organelles are located. It contains biomolecules used by the cell and is the site of translation for protein synthesis – the conversion of the nucleic acids into amino acids.

D: the nucleolus is a membrane-bound structure within the nucleus. rRNA is synthesized in the nucleolus and is then transported to the cytosol to anneal with proteins and assemble into the two subunits of the ribosomes (e.g. 30S and 50S subunits for prokaryotes and 40S and 60S subunits for eukaryotes). The complete ribosome for prokaryotes is 70S and 80S for eukaryotes.

52. A novel approach to cancer treatment employs modified tRNA molecules that carry inappropriate combinations of amino acids and anticodons. The tRNA molecule with the nucleotide triplets on one end is *charged* with mismatched amino acids on the other end. What is the likely mechanism of the anticancer action of these modified tRNA molecules?

    A. Inhibition of cancer cells to translate protein
    B. Inhibition of cancer cells to transcribe protein
    C. Inhibition of ribosomes to bind to the mRNA
    D. Change in the tertiary structure of the translated protein

D is correct.

Translation occurs in the cytoplasm and is the synthesis of proteins from mRNA. tRNAs (containing the anticodon) are used to bring the corresponding amino acid to the growing polypeptide based on the nucleotide sequence of the mRNA (containing the codon).

Translation occurs, but the synthesized proteins have incorrect amino acids (mismatch between the codon-anticodon). A change in the primary structure (linear sequence of amino acids) gives rise to a change in the overall shape of the folded protein, likely making it dysfunctional.

Without translation of the mRNA template into the correct linear sequence of amino acids, the cancerous cells cannot synthesize proteins necessary for cellular function and subsequent reproduction. Such abnormal cells would likely undergo apoptosis (i.e. programmed cell death).

Questions 53 through 59 are not based on any descriptive passage and are independent of each other

---

53. How many carbon atoms are in a molecule of oleic acid?

    A. 14   **B.** 16   **C. 18**   **D.** 20

C is correct.

Oleic acid is an odorless, colorless fatty acid that occurs naturally in many animal and vegetable fats and oils. The term "oleic" refers to oil or olive. Olive oil is predominantly composed of oleic acid, which is a monounsaturated omega-9 fatty acid, abbreviated as 18:1 cis-9.

Oleic acid has the molecular formula $CH_3(CH_2)_7CH=CH(CH_2)_7COOH$.

---

54. Amylose is different from amylopectin, because it:

A. forms a helix with no branch points
B. is highly branched, while amylopectin is linear
C. has more glucose residues than amylopectin
D. is composed of a different monomer than is amylopectin

A is correct.

55. What value is expressed by the slope in a Lineweaver-Burke plot?

A. V_{max}/K_m **B. K_m/V_{max}**   **C.** K_m **D.** $1/[S]$

B is correct.

The Lineweaver-Burke plot is a graphical representation of enzyme kinetics.

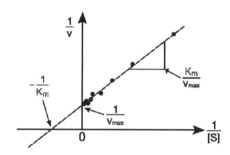

The Lineweaver-Burke plot is a graphical method for analysis of the Michaelis–

Menten equation:

$V = V_{max}[S] / K_m + [S]$

Taking the reciprocal:

$1/V = K_m + [S] / V_{max}[S] = K_m / V_{max}[S] + 1 / V_{max}$

where V is the reaction velocity (i.e. reaction rate)

K_m is the Michaelis–Menten constant

V_{max} is the maximum reaction velocity

[S] is the substrate concentration

56. Which statement about the initiation codon is correct?

A. It is part of the TATA box   **C. It specifies methionine**
B. It binds a protein complex that begins replication   **D.** It specifies uracil

C is correct.

57. Which tyrosine-derived molecule has the correct relationship?

   A. Norepinephrine – thyroid hormone   **C. Dopaquinone – precursor of melanin**
   B. Thyroxine – catecholamine   **D.** Dopamine – thyroid hormone

C is correct.

Dopaquinone is a metabolite for L-DOPA, which is a precursor for the catecholamines (e.g. dopamine, epinephrine and norepinephrine). Melanin is a natural pigment found in melanocytes for the oxidation of the amino acid tyrosine.

A: norepinephrine (noradrenaline) is the hormone and neurotransmitter most responsible for vigilant concentration, in contrast to its most chemically similar hormone, dopamine, which is primarily responsible for cognitive alertness. One of norepinephrine's most important functions is the neurotransmitter released by the sympathetic neurons to affect the heart.

B: thyroxine (T_4) is an intra-glandular precursor of a hormone triiodothyronine (T_3) produced by the thyroid gland and is primarily responsible for regulation of metabolism. Iodine is necessary for the production of T_3 and T_4.

D: dopamine is a hormone that functions as a neurotransmitter in the brain.

58. Which statement is correct about essential amino acids?

   A. They are not synthesized *de novo* by the body and must be part of the diet
   B. They are not synthesized by the body in sufficient amounts
   C. There are twelve essential amino acids
   D. They are plentiful in all animal protein

A is correct.

59. A term used for a carbohydrate polymer is:

   A. Multimer   **C. Glycan**
   B. Oligosaccharide   **D.** Polycarb

C is correct.

The IUPAC defines the terms glycan and polysaccharide as synonyms. They refer to "compounds consisting of a large number of monosaccharides linked glycosidically." In practice, *glycan* can also refer to the carbohydrate portion of a glycoconjugate (e.g. glycoprotein, glycolipid or proteoglycan), even if the carbohydrate is only an oligosaccharide (i.e. collection of approximately 12 to 18 sugars).

Biological & Biochemical Foundations of Living Systems
MCAT® Practice Test #4 – Answer Key

Passage 1
1 : B
2 : D
3 : B
4 : A
5 : A
6 : D
7 : B

Passage 2
8 : A
9 : D
10 : B
11 : C
12 : D

Independent questions
13 : D
14 : C
15 : A
16 : D

Passage 3
17 : A
18 : D
19 : C
20 : D
21 : B

Passage 4
22 : A
23 : C
24 : C
25 : D
26 : A

Independent questions
27 : C
28 : D
29 : C
30 : D

Passage 5
31 : B
32 : B
33 : C
34 : A
35 : C

Passage 6
36 : D
37 : B
38 : A
39 : D
40 : B
41 : B

Independent questions
42 : A
43 : B
44 : C
45 : C
46 : C

Passage 7
47 : D
48 : C
49 : A
50 : C
51 : A
52 : B

Independent questions
53 : C
54 : B
55 : C
56 : B
57 : B
58 : B
59 : B

Passage 1
(Questions 1–7)

There are two proteins that are involved in transporting O_2 in vertebrates; hemoglobin (Hb) is found in red blood cells and myoglobin (Mb) is found in muscle cells. The hemoglobin protein accounts for about 97% of the dry weight of red blood cells. In erythrocytes, the hemoglobin carries O_2 from the lungs to the tissue undergoing cellular respiration. Hemoglobin has an oxygen binding capacity of 1.3 ml O_2 per gram of hemoglobin, which increases the total blood oxygen capacity over seventy-fold compared to dissolved oxygen in blood.

When a tissue's metabolic rate increases, carbon dioxide production also increases. In addition to O_2, Hb also transports CO_2. Of all the CO_2 transported in blood, 7-10% is dissolved in blood plasma, 70% is bicarbonate ions (HCO_3^-) and 20% is bound to the globin to Hb as carbaminohemoglobin.

CO_2 combines with water to form carbonic acid (H_2CO_3), which quickly dissociates. This reaction occurs primarily in red blood cells, where *carbonic anhydrase* reversibly and rapidly catalyzes the reaction:

$$CO_2 + H_2O \leftrightarrow H_2CO_3 \leftrightarrow H^+ + HCO_3^-$$

Hb of vertebrates has a quaternary structure comprised of four individual polypeptide chains: two α and two β protein polypeptides, each with a heme group bound as a prosthetic group. The four polypeptide chains are held together by hydrogen bonding.

Figure 1. Hemoglobin

The binding of O_2 to Hb depends on the cooperativity of the Hb subunits. Cooperativity means that the binding of O_2 at one heme group increases the binding of O_2 at another heme within the Hb molecule through conformational changes of the entire hemoglobin molecule. This shape (conformational) change means it is energetically favorable for subsequent binding of O_2. Conversely, the unloading of O_2 at one heme increases the unloading of O_2 at other heme groups by a similar conformational change of the molecule.

Oxygen's affinity for Hb varies among different species and within species depending on multiple factors like blood pH, developmental stage (i.e. fetal versus adult), and body size. For example, small animals dissociate O_2 at a given partial pressure more readily than large animals, because they have a higher metabolic rate and require more O_2 per gram of body mass.

Figure 2 represents the O_2-dissociation of Hb (this is represented by sigmoidal curves B, C and D) and myoglobin (hyperbolic curve A), where saturation is the percent of O_2-binding sites occupied at specific partial pressures of O_2.

The *utilization coefficient* is the fraction of O_2 diffusing from Hb to the tissue as blood passes through the capillary beds. A normal value for the *utilization coefficient* is about 0.25.

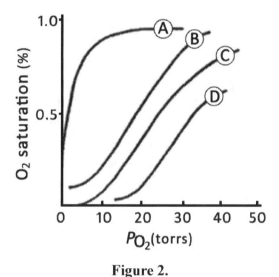

Figure 2.

In 1959, Max Perutz determined the molecular structure of myoglobin by x-ray crystallography, which led to his sharing of the 1962 Nobel prize with John Kendrew. Myoglobin is a single-chain globular protein (consisting of 154 amino acids) that transports and stores O_2 in muscle. Mb contains a heme (i.e. iron-containing porphyrin) prosthetic group with a molecular weight of 17.7 kd (kilodalton, 1 dalton is defined as 1/12 the mass of a neutral unbound carbon atom). As seen in Figure 2, Mb (curve A) has a greater affinity for O_2 than Hb. Unlike the blood-borne hemoglobin, myoglobin does not exhibit cooperative binding, because cooperativity is present only in quaternary proteins that undergo allosteric changes. A high concentration of myoglobin in muscle cells allows organisms to hold their breath for extended periods of time. Diving mammals, such as whales and seals, have muscles with abundant myoglobin levels.

1. The mountain goat has developed a type of hemoglobin adapted to unusually high altitudes. If curve C represents the O_2 dissociation curve for a cow's Hb, which curve most closely resembles the O_2 dissociation curve for a mountain goat's Hb?

A. curve A   **B. curve B**   **C.** curve C   **D.** curve D

B is correct.

At high altitudes, atmospheric pressure is low and there is less oxygen in the air than at sea level. The mountain goat has adapted to life at high altitudes by evolving a different type of hemoglobin. Since the partial pressure of O_2 is less at high altitudes, the mountain goat's hemoglobin must be able to bind oxygen with increased affinity at these lower O_2 partial pressures.

For a given value of O_2 pressure on the X-axis of Figure 2, the mountain goat's hemoglobin becomes more saturated with O_2 than the cow's hemoglobin, since cows have not adapted to living in regions of unusually high altitude. From Figure 2, the mountain goat oxygen-dissociation curve is to the left compared to the cow.

If curve C is for a cow, then the curve for a mountain goat would most closely resemble curve B.

From the passage, curves B, C and D represent O_2-dissociation for Hb (i.e. sigmoid shape curve displays cooperativity), while curve A is for the myoglobin.

2. If curve C represents the O_2-dissociation curve for a hippopotamus' Hb, which curve would most closely correspond with the Hb of a squirrel?

A. curve A   **B.** curve B   **C.** curve C   **D. curve D**

D is correct.

From the passage, small animals have higher metabolic rates (i.e. cellular respiration rate) and require more O_2 per gram of tissue than larger animals. Therefore, small animals have Hb that dissociates O_2 more rapidly than the Hb of large animals.

A high metabolic rate indicates increased aerobic respiration, where metabolically active tissues need O_2. Hb that easily dissociates O_2 is capable of delivering more oxygen to metabolically active tissue.

At a given value of O_2 partial pressure, a squirrel's Hb is less saturated with O_2 than that of a hippopotamus, because the hippopotamus is much larger than a squirrel and has a much lower metabolic rate. From Figure 2, a squirrel's Hb curve will be to the right of the hippopotamus' Hb curve.

3. If curve C represents the O_2-dissociation curve for the Hb of an adult human, which of the following best explains why curve B most closely corresponds with the curve for fetal Hb?

    A. O_2 affinity of fetal Hb is lower than adult Hb

    B. O_2 affinity of fetal Hb is higher than adult Hb

    C. Metabolic rate of fetal tissue is lower than adult tissue

    D. Metabolic rate of fetal tissue is higher than adult tissue

B is correct.

Fetal Hb has a higher affinity for O_2 than adult Hb, because oxygen is delivered to the fetus by diffusion across the placenta.

Curve B most closely resembles the oxygen-dissociation curve for fetal Hb, assuming that curve C is the curve for adult Hb. At a given oxygen pressure (P_{O_2}), fetal Hb is more saturated with O_2 than adult Hb, which implies that fetal Hb has a greater affinity for O_2 than adult Hb. Due to differences in the Hb subunits, at low P_{O_2}, fetal Hb has a 20-30% greater affinity for O_2 than adult Hb. Oxygen binds preferentially to fetal Hb in the capillaries of the placenta.

In addition, fetal blood has a 50% higher concentration of Hb than maternal blood and this, combined with greater O_2 affinity, also increases the amount of O_2 in fetal circulation.

4. Which of the following best explains the sigmoidal shape of the Hb O_2-dissociation curve?

    A. Conformational changes in the polypeptide subunits of the Hb molecule

    B. Heme groups within the Hb are being reduced and oxidized

    C. Changing $[H^+]$ in the blood

    D. Changing $[CO_2]$ transported by Hb in the blood

A is correct.

Cooperative binding of O_2 to the two α and two β polypeptide chains of Hb yields the sigmoidal shape dissociation curve. Cooperative binding of Hb is due to conformational changes in the heme group when O_2 binds to one subunit. The conformational change results in greater affinity of Hb to bind O_2 after a subunit has bound O_2. Therefore, Hb has the greatest affinity for O_2 (highest cooperativity) when three of the four heme polypeptide chains are bound to O_2.

Each heme unit is capable of binding one molecule of O_2, so Hb is capable of binding four O_2. O_2 binding to the first heme group induces a conformational (shape) change in the Hb, which causes an increase in the second heme's affinity for O_2. The binding of O_2 at the second heme group increases the affinity of the third heme for O_2. The binding of O_2 at the third heme groups increases the fourth's affinity for O_2. Because of cooperativity, the graph of percent oxygen-saturation *vs* P_{O_2} is not linear, it is sigmoidal.

Fe is a necessary component of Hb. A cofactor is a non-protein (inorganic or organic) component bound to a protein (often an enzyme) that is required for the biological activity of the protein.

Loosely bound cofactors are termed *coenzymes* (often organic molecules, such as vitamins), while tightly bound cofactors (e.g. iron in hemoglobin) are termed *prosthetic groups*.

Organic cofactors are often vitamins and many contain the nucleotide adenosine monophosphate (AMP).

An inactive enzyme (without its cofactor) is known as an *apoenzyme,* while the complete enzyme (with cofactor) is referred to as the *holoenzyme*.

While myoglobin does have a higher affinity for oxygen than hemoglobin (Figure 2), this difference in affinity does not explain the sigmoidal shape of the curve.

B: oxidation and reduction on the Hb heme groups is a true statement. O_2 is reduced when it binds to the Fe atom of the heme group. Fe is oxidized when it releases O_2. However, this does not result in the sigmoidal shape of the curve.

C: The Bohr effect is a physiological observation where Hb's O_2 binding affinity is inversely related both to the $[CO_2]$ and acidity of the blood. An increase in blood $[CO_2]$ or decrease in blood pH (increase in H^+) results in Hb releasing its O_2 at the tissue.

Conversely, a decrease in CO_2 or an increase in pH results in hemoglobin binding O_2 and loading more O_2. CO_2 reacts with water to form carbonic acid, which causes a decrease in blood pH. Carbonic anhydrase (present in erythrocytes) accelerates the formation of bicarbonate and protons, which decreases pH at the tissue and promotes the dissociation of O_2 to the tissue. In the lungs where P_{O_2} is high, binding of O_2 causes Hb to release H^+, which combines with bicarbonate to release CO_2 via exhalation. Since these two reactions are closely matched, homeostasis of the blood pH is maintained at about 7.35.

Bohr effect curves

D: $[CO_2]$ in the blood affects Hb's affinity for O_2 and therefore affects the location of the curve on the O_2-dissociation graph, but $[CO_2]$ is not the reason for the sigmoidal shape. A high $[CO_2]$ in the blood decreases Hb's affinity for O_2 and shifts the curve to the right (known as the *Bohr effect*).

5. A sample of adult human Hb was placed in a *6M* urea solution, which resulted in the disruption of nonconvalent bonds. After that, the Hb α chains were isolated. If curve C represents the O_2-dissociation curve for an adult human Hb *in vivo,* which curve most closely corresponds with the curve of the isolated α chains?

 A. curve A   **B.** curve B   **C.** curve C   **D.** curve D

A is correct.

From the passage, the four polypeptide subunits in Hb are held together by noncovalent interactions. A *6M* urea solution disrupts noncovalent interactions (hydrogen bonds, dipole–dipole, van der Waals and hydrophobic) and causes the subunits to dissociate. The alpha chains of this sample of hemoglobin were isolated; therefore, the oxygen dissociation curve for one polypeptide chain of Hb should look similar to the dissociation curve for myoglobin (single polypeptide chain).

The isolated, single chain of the dissociated Hb polypeptide does not resemble a sigmoid curve, because the unique shape of the sigmoid curve results from cooperativity of the four hemoglobin subunits. Therefore, for a single α chain dissociated by the *6M* urea solution, cooperativity is absent.

6. In response to physiological changes, the utilization coefficient of an organism is constantly being adjusted. What value most closely represents the utilization coefficient for human adult Hb during strenuous exercise?

 A. 0.0675   **B.** 0.15   **C.** 0.25   **D. 0.60**

D is correct.

Utilization coefficient is the fraction of the Hb that releases its O_2 to tissues under normal conditions and is approximately 0.25. During strenuous exercise, there is a greater demand for O_2 in cells undergoing an accelerated level of cellular respiration (e.g. skeletal muscle); therefore, a greater fraction of erythrocytes unload O_2 at the tissue, and the utilization coefficient would be greater than 0.25.

During strenuous exercise, the utilization coefficient can reach 0.70 to 0.85, where 70-85% of the Hb dissociates O_2 in the capillaries of the tissue.

7. The Mb content in the muscle of a humpback whale is about 0.005 moles/kg. Approximately how much O_2 is bound to the Mb of a humpback that has 10,000 kg of muscle (assuming the Mb is saturated with O_2)?

    A. 12.5 moles   **B. 50 moles**   **C.** 200 moles   **D.** 2×10^7 moles

B is correct.

Calculate how many moles of myoglobin are present in the humpback whale's muscles.

Calculate the moles of O_2 by determining how many molecules of O_2 bind to a single molecule of myoglobin. Myoglobin binds 1 O_2 (compared to 4 O_2 for Hb), because myoglobin has a single heme group on a single polypeptide chain.

There are 0.005 moles of myoglobin per kg of muscle, and the whale has 10,000 kg of muscle. Multiply 0.005 moles by 10,000 kg, which equals 50 moles of myoglobin. The whale has 50 moles of myoglobin in its muscles.

One molecule of myoglobin binds to one molecule of O_2. Since the whale has 50 moles of myoglobin in its muscle (each binding 1 molecule of O_2), then 50 moles of O_2 bind to myoglobin when myoglobin is completely saturated with O_2.

Passage 2
(Questions 8–12)

Corpus luteum (from the Latin "yellow body") is a temporary endocrine structure (yellow mass of cells) in female mammals. It is involved in the production of relatively high levels of progesterone and moderate levels of estradiol (predominant potent estrogen) and inhibin A. The estrogen it secretes inhibits the secretion of LH and FSH by the pituitary, which prevents multiple ovulations.

The corpus luteum is essential for establishing and maintaining pregnancy in females. It is typically very large relative to the size of the ovary (in humans, the size ranges from under 2 cm to 5 cm in diameter) and its color results from concentrating carotenoids from the diet.

The corpus luteum develops from an ovarian follicle during the luteal phase of the menstrual cycle or estrous cycle, following the release of a secondary oocyte from the follicle during ovulation. While the *oocyte* (subsequently the *zygote,* if fertilization occurs) traverses the *oviduct* (Fallopian tube) into the uterus, the corpus luteum remains in the ovary.

Progesterone secreted by the corpus luteum is a steroid hormone responsible for the development and maintenance of the endometrium – the thick lining of the uterus that provides an area rich in blood vessels in which the zygote(s) can develop. If the egg is fertilized and implantation occurs, by day 9 post-fertilization the cells of the blastocyst secrete the hormone called *human chorionic gonadotropin* (hCG), which signals the corpus luteum to continue progesterone secretion. From this point on, the corpus luteum is called the *corpus luteum graviditatis.* The presence of hCG in the urine is the indicator used by home pregnancy test kits.

If the egg is not fertilized, the corpus luteum stops secreting progesterone and decays after approximately 14 days in humans. If fertilization occurred, throughout the first trimester, the corpus luteum secretes hormones at steadily increasing levels. In the second trimester of pregnancy, the placenta (in placental animals, including humans) eventually takes over progesterone production, and the corpus luteum degrades without embryo/fetus loss.

8. Could high estrogen levels be used in home pregnancy tests to indicate possible pregnancy?

    A. No, because estrogen levels also rise prior to ovulation
    B. Yes, because estrogen is secreted at high levels during pregnancy
    C. No, because antibodies in the pregnancy test kit only recognize epitopes of proteins
    D. No, because estrogen is a steroid hormone and is not excreted into the urine by kidneys

A is correct.

High levels of estrogen would not be a good indicator of pregnancy, because estrogen levels fluctuate during the menstrual cycle and reach high levels just before ovulation (release of the egg). This occurs as a result of the ovarian follicle cells secreting estrogen in high amounts during that time. In the absence of progesterone, elevated levels of circulating estrogen actually cause active secretion of FSH and LH via a positive feedback mechanism.

Before ovulation, progesterone is at low levels, and the body uses a different mechanism for LH and FSH regulation. After ovulation (and also during pregnancy), the combination of high estrogen and moderate levels of progesterone trigger a negative feedback inhibition of FSH and LH production.

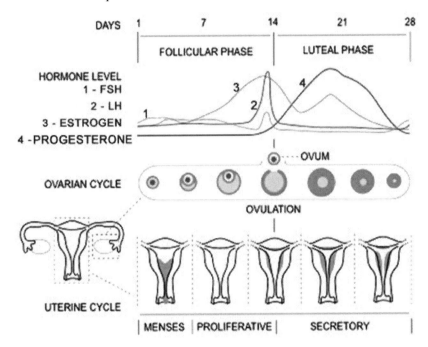

C: antibodies are composed of protein, but the epitope (i.e. what the antibodies recognize as foreign and bind to) may not be a protein.

D: steroids, including estrogen, are excreted in the urine, which is why urine is used for testing professional athletes for the use of anabolic steroids. Nevertheless, when testing estrogen levels, blood or saliva samples are more preferable since the test is done not to simply indicate the presence of estrogen (as most women would have it present to some extent), but to measure the specific level of the hormone for a diagnostic or therapeutic purpose.

9. All of these methods, if administered prior to ovulation, could theoretically be used as a method of female birth control, EXCEPT injecting:

A. monoclonal antibodies for progesterone and estrogen
B. antagonists of LH and FSH
C. agonists that mimic the actions of estrogen and progesterone
D. agonists that mimic the actions of LH and FSH

D is correct.

If agonist compounds that mimicked the activity of FSH and LH were injected, ovulation would occur and pregnancy would not be prevented. The FSH and LH hormones do not have inhibitory (i.e. negative feedback) effects on estrogen or progesterone, and these hormones are required for pregnancy. If FSH and LH agonists (i.e. analogs) were injected they would not prevent pregnancy.

A: antibodies bind to a ligand (i.e. moiety or epitope that the antibody recognizes and binds), and the ligand is either removed (from the circulatory or interstitial fluid) or inactivated. In this example, the ligand is estrogen and is bound to large antibody molecules. Estrogen and progesterone can be inactivated with monoclonal antibodies, and ovulation and (subsequent) pregnancy would be blocked, because the activity of these hormones is required for female reproductive function (see passage). This blocking of progesterone and estrogen could (theoretically) be used as a method for female birth control.

B: if FSH and LH activities are inhibited (i.e. by antagonists), ovulation is blocked and fertilization is not possible.

C: estrogen and progesterone are common in birth control pills. These hormones can be used to prevent pregnancy because these hormones have a negative feedback effect on LH and FSH, and thereby prevent ovulation (see passage). The birth control pill inhibits ovulation, because high plasma levels of progesterone and estrogen are characteristic of pregnancy.

10. How would pregnancy be affected by the removal of the ovaries in the fifth month of gestation?

  A. Not affected, because LH secreted by the ovaries is not necessary in the fifth month of gestation
  B. Not affected, because progesterone secreted by the ovaries is not necessary in the fifth month of gestation
  C. Terminated, because LH secreted by the ovaries is necessary in the fifth month of gestation
  D. Terminated, because progesterone secreted by the ovaries is necessary in the fifth month of gestation

B is correct.

The ovaries produce the female gametes (e.g. egg or ova) and are female endocrine organs that secrete estrogen and progesterone. Other endocrine organs secrete hormones that regulate the activities of the female reproductive system.

The hypothalamus secretes gonadotropin releasing hormone (GnRH) that stimulates the anterior pituitary to release follicle-releasing hormone (FSH) and luteinizing hormone

(LH). FSH and LH regulate gametogenesis and the menstrual cycle. Tropic hormones have other glands as their target, and most tropic hormones are produced and secreted by the anterior pituitary.

A mnemonic for secretions from the anterior pituitary is FLAT PEG - **F**ollicle stimulating hormone (FSH), **L**uteinizing hormone (LH), **A**drenocorticotropic hormone (ACTH), **T**hyrotropic hormone (TSH), **P**rolactin (PRL), **E**nkephalins (endorphins) and **G**rowth hormone (GH or STH for somatotropin).

The posterior pituitary stores hypothalamic hormones. The posterior pituitary secretes oxytocin and vasopressin (ADH). Oxytocin stimulates uterine contractions and stimulates release of milk from mammary glands for lactation. Vasopressin stimulates increased water reabsorption by kidneys (ADH is antidiuretic hormone) and vasoconstriction of arterioles and other smooth muscles.

LH is secreted by the anterior pituitary (not the ovaries). The normal period of human gestation is nine months; the second trimester of pregnancy begins after the third month of pregnancy, and the third trimester of pregnancy begins after six months. From the passage, the corpus luteum secretes progesterone until the second trimester. From the second to third trimester, the placenta continues to secrete the progesterone.

11. Very low levels of circulating progesterone and estrogen:

    A. inhibit the release of LH and FSH, thereby not inhibiting ovulation
    B. inhibit the release of LH and FSH, thereby inhibiting ovulation
    C. do not inhibit the release of LH and FSH, thereby not inhibiting ovulation
    D. do not inhibit the release of LH and FSH, thereby inhibiting ovulation

C is correct.

From the passage, high levels of circulating estrogen and progesterone present during pregnancy prevent ovulation (similar to the actions of birth control pills) by inhibiting the secretion of FSH and LH by the anterior pituitary. However, very low levels of estrogen and progesterone do not inhibit the secretion of FSH and LH, and ovulation occurs. After menstruation, estrogen and progesterone levels are very low. Because of these low levels, the negative feedback inhibition of FSH and LH secretion is removed. The subsequent rise in FSH and LH levels indicates the onset of a new menstrual cycle.

12. To confirm the pregnancy, which of these hormones must be present at high levels in a blood sample of a female patient who suspects to be 10 weeks pregnant?

    I. Estrogen and progesterone
    II. FSH and LH
    III. hCG

    A. I only   **B.** I and II only   **C.** II and III only   **D. I and III only**

D is correct.

From the passage, hCG (human chorionic gonadotropin) levels rise after fertilization and the presence of hCG in urine is the basis of some pregnancy tests. hCG is secreted until the 2nd trimester of pregnancy (through the 3rd month of pregnancy). Therefore, hCG could be used as an indicator for pregnancy between the 1st and 3rd months of gestation.

High levels of estrogen and progesterone are present throughout pregnancy. Estrogen and progesterone levels also rise during the menstrual cycle. Therefore, high levels of these two hormones alone do not indicate pregnancy. However, in conjunction with the presence of hCG, high levels of estrogen and progesterone are consistent with pregnancy.

II: FSH and LH secretion is inhibited (by high levels of estrogen and progesterone) during pregnancy to prevent ovulation.

> Questions 13 through 16 are not based on any
> descriptive passage and are independent of each other

13. Which of the following molecules is the site of NMR spin-spin coupling?

    A. CH_4 **B.** FCH_2CH_2F **C.** $(CH_3)_3CCl$ **D.** CH_3CH_2Br

D is correct.

Splitting pattern is determined by the formula $n + 1$, where n is the number of (non-equivalent) adjacent hydrogens.

CH_3CH_2Br has two peaks (two sets of non-equivalent hydrogens) with one peak ($-CH_3$) split into a triplet with an integration number of 3 and the other peak ($-CH_2$) split into a quartet with an integration number of 2.

A: CH_4 has a single peak with an integration number of 4.

B: FCH_2CH_2F has a single peak with an integration number of 4.

C: $(CH_3)_3CBr$ has a single peak with an integration number of 9.

14. Which of the following is correct about the hybridization of the three carbon atoms indicated by arrows in the following molecule?

A. C_1 is *sp* hybridized, C_2 is *sp²* hybridized and C_3 is *sp³* hybridized
B. C_1 is *sp²* hybridized, C_2 is *sp²* hybridized and C_3 is *sp* hybridized
C. **C_1 is *sp* hybridized, C_2 is *sp²* hybridized and C_3 is *sp²* hybridized**
D. C_1 is *sp²* hybridized, C_2 is *sp²* hybridized and C_3 is *sp²* hybridized

C is correct.

C_1 is in a triple bond of an alkyne. The carbon of alkynes has two σ (single) bonds and two π (the double and the triple) bonds. The carbon of an alkyne is *sp* hybridized.

C_2 is in a double bond of an alkene. The carbon of alkenes has three σ (single) bonds and one π (double) bond. The carbon of an alkene is *sp²* hybridized.

C_3 is a carbocation and *sp²* hybridized. The carbocation has a vacant unhybridized p orbital that corresponds to the carbocation.

The *sp³* hybridized carbon is part of a single bond in the alkane. All hybridized *sp³* hybridized orbitals create 4 σ (single) bonds.

The *sp²* hybridized carbon uses three orbitals for 3 σ (single) bonds and also contains an unhybridized p orbital. An unhybridized p orbital can be one of 4 species: a π of the alkene with a double bond to the adjacent carbon; a vacant unhybridized p orbital of the carbocation; a single electron of the radical; or two electrons of the carbanion. Carbanions are reactive species with the carbon having a negative formal charge due to the additional valence electron.

The *sp* hybridized carbon uses two orbitals for 2 σ (single) bonds and also contains two unhybridized p orbitals ($sp + p + p$). The unhybridized p orbitals can be one of 5 species: two π of the triple bond (i.e. most common variant); two π of the alkene with two double bonds on both adjacent carbons (cumulated double bonds); double bond with a vacant unhybridized p of the carbocation; double bond with a single electron of the radical; or double bond with two electrons of the carbanion.

Note: carbocations exist with vacant unhybridized p orbitals.

Radicals exist as a single (unpaired) electron in unhybridized p orbitals.

Carbanions (i.e. carbons with negative charges) exist with a pair of electrons in the unhybridized p orbital.

15. The extracellular fluid volume depends on the total sodium content in the body. The balance between Na^+ intake and Na^+ loss regulates Na^+ level. Which of the following will occur following the administration of digoxin, a poison that blocks the Na^+/K^+ ATPase?

A. Increased intracellular [H_2O] **C.** Increased extracellular [Na^+]
B. Increased intracellular [Cl^-]   **D.** Increased intracellular [K^+]

A is correct.

The Na^+/K^+ ATPase transports 3 Na^+ ions out and 2 K^+ ions into the cell.

Digoxin (also known as digitalis) is similar to ouabain since both disrupt the ATPase pump and therefore degrade the ion concentration gradient normally maintained (Na^+ ions outside of the cell and K^+ ions inside of the cell) by the ATPase pump. With the ATPase pump absent, 3 Na^+ and 2 K^+ ions move down their concentration gradient and in the direction of their natural equilibrium, where Na^+ enters the cell and K^+ flows out of the cell and into in the extracellular space.

Then water follows the Na^+ into the cell, causing massive swelling and, eventually, lysis (i.e. plasmolysis – rupturing of the plasma membrane) of the cell.

16. To selectively function on ingested proteins and avoid digestion of a body's proteins in the digestive system, pancreatic peptidases must be tightly regulated. Which mechanism activates pancreatic peptidases?

 A. osmolarity
 B. coenzyme binding

 C. carbohydrate moieties
 D. **proteolytic cleavage**

D is correct.

Zymogens are inactive enzymes that are synthesized in an inactive form at one location within the body and are then are transported to their target location, where they undergo *proteolytic cleavage* (i.e. cutting of the peptide bond that connects the inactive portion from the active portion of the functional protein) and convert into an active form. pH is often a controlling factor of proteolytic cleavage.

Pancreatic peptidases (enzymes end in ~ase) must be tightly controlled to prevent degradation of endogenous human proteins. The enzymes, once in the intestinal lumen, are activated by brush border enzymes. Pepsin (within the stomach) is the classic example of pH-dependent activation.

The pancreas secretes HCO_3 (sodium bicarbonate) to neutralize gastric (stomach) acidity. Once the chyme (food) enters the small intestine, HCO_3 adjusts the pH of the chyme exiting the stomach with a pH of 2 to a pH of 7.2 of the small intestine. The stomach has a low pH because HCl (hydrochloric acid) is secreted into the stomach for pre-digestion of dietary proteins. Once chyme leaves the stomach and enters the small intestine, there is a significant change in pH via HCO_3.

Temperature, ion concentration and osmolarity are all tightly regulated – homeostasis – within the body and, because they do not fluctuate widely, could not function as the triggers for proteolytic cleavage as zymogens move from the origin of synthesis to the site of activation.

Peptidases are enzymes that do not require coenzymes or cofactors. A cofactor is an inorganic substance bound to an enzyme and is classified depending on how tightly it binds to an enzyme. Loosely-bound cofactors are termed coenzymes, and tightly-bound cofactors are termed prosthetic groups.

Organic cofactors are often vitamins (or made from vitamins). Many cofactors contain nucleotide monophosphate (AMP) as part of their structure, including ATP, coenzyme A, FAD and NAD$^+$. Other examples of cofactors are magnesium in chlorophyll and heme in hemoglobin.

A prosthetic group is a non-amino acid component of a protein. Prosthetic groups are often bound tightly in a reversible manner to the enzyme and confer new properties upon the conjugated enzyme.

An apoenzyme is an inactive enzyme (without the cofactor bound). The complete (active) enzyme with the cofactor attached is a holoenzyme.

A coenzyme is a non-protein organic molecule that plays an accessory (but not a necessary) role in the catalytic action of an enzyme.

Passage 3
(Questions 17–21)

In pharmacology, a natural product is a chemical compound or substance produced by a living organism found in nature that usually has a pharmacological or biological activity for pharmaceutical drug discovery and drug design. However, a natural product can be classified as such even if it can be prepared by laboratory synthesis. Not all natural products can be fully synthesized, because many have very complex structures, making it too difficult or expensive to synthesize on an industrial scale. These compounds can only be harvested from their natural source - a process which can be tedious, time consuming, expensive and wasteful on the natural resource.

Enediynes are a class of natural bacterial products characterized by either nine- or ten-membered rings containing two triple bonds separated by a double bond. Many enediyne compounds are extremely toxic to DNA. They are known to cleave DNA molecules and appear to be quite effective as selective agents for anticancer activity. Therefore, enediynes are being investigated as antitumor therapeutic agents.

Classes of enediynes target DNA by binding with DNA in the minor groove. Enediynes then abstract hydrogen atoms from the deoxyribose (sugar) backbone of DNA, which results in strand scission. These small molecules are active ingredients of the majority of FDA-approved agents and continue to be one of the major biomolecules for drug discovery. This enediyne molecule is proven to be a potent antitumor agent:

Figure 1. Neocarzinostatin

Neocarzinostatin is a chromoprotein enediyne antibiotic with anti-tumoral activity secreted by the bacteria *Streptomyces macromomyceticus*. It consists of two parts, a labile chromophore (bicyclic dienediyne structure shown) and a 113 amino acid apoprotein with the chromophores non-covalently bound with a high affinity. The *chromophore* is a very potent DNA-damaging agent, because it is very labile (easily broken down) and plays a role in protecting and releasing the cleaved target DNA. Opening of the epoxide under reductive conditions present in cells creates favorable conditions and leads to a diradical intermediate and subsequent double-stranded DNA cleavage.

17. Which functional group is NOT present in the molecule of neocarzinostatin?

A. thiol   **B.** hydroxyl   **C.** ester   **D.** epoxide

A is correct.

The functional group not present on the molecule is a thiol (-SH).

The functional groups present in the molecule include: three hydroxyl (–OH of an alcohol) groups; one epoxide (a three-membered ring that has oxygen bridging the two carbons); a secondary amine group (–NHR); one ether (–COC–); two esters and a diester.

18. What is the hybridization of the two carbon atoms and the oxygen atom indicated by the arrows in Figure 1?

   A. C_1 is sp^2, C_2 is sp^2 and O is sp^2 hybridized
   B. C_1 is sp^2, C_2 is sp and O is sp hybridized
   C. C_1 is sp, C_2 is sp^2 and O is sp^2 hybridized
   D. C_1 is sp, C_2 is sp^3 and O is sp^3 hybridized

D is correct.

Carbon has 4 hybridized orbitals of $s + p + p + p$ for the sp^3 hybridization for single bonds. The C_1 atom has two σ (sigma) bonds and two π (pi) bonds with two electrons shared for each the double and triple bond. Therefore, the C_1 atom is sp hybridized, which refers to hybridized orbitals of s and p. Hence the other two unhybridized orbitals (p and p) are used for the double (two electrons in the p orbital) and the triple bonds (two electrons in the p orbital) for each of the π bonds.

The C_2 atom has 4 σ (single) bonds, and therefore is neutral. Variations from the neutral C atom could include a positively charged carbocation (vacant p orbital) or radical (single unpaired electron in the p orbital), or a negatively charged carbanion (with two nonbonding electrons in the p orbital).

The neutral oxygen atom has two σ bonds and two lone electron pairs and is therefore sp^3 hybridized.

19. How many chiral carbons are in the molecule of neocarzinostatin?

   A. 4   **B.** 8   **C. 10**   **D.** 12

C is correct.

The neocarzinostatin molecule has 10 chiral centers (as indicated by the asterisks in the diagram below).

The total number of possible stereoisomers is 2^n. The value of $2^{10} = 1,024$ possible stereoisomers. Among these 1,024 stereoisomers, one is the original molecule, one is the mirror image (i.e. enantiomer) and the others are non-mirror images (i.e. diasteriomers).

20. How many π bonds are in the molecule of neocarzinostatin?

    A. 7   **B.** 9   **C.** 11   **D.** 13

D is correct.

Single bonds contain only σ bonds.
Every bond, other than single (σ), contains a π bond. Double bonds have one σ bond and one π bond (with two electrons in each π bond). Triple bonds have one σ bond and two π bonds (with two electrons in each π bond).

21. Which of the following is correct about the absolute configuration of the carbon atom indicated by (*)?

    A. It has an *S* absolute configuration
    B. It has an *R* absolute configuration
    C. It is not chiral
    D. Absolute configuration cannot be determined

B is correct.

Since the order of the prioritized groups is clockwise, the absolute configuration is *R* (versus *S* for counterclockwise).

Note: there is no connection between the absolute configuration (*R vs. S*) and the rotation of the plane-polarized light (+ *vs.* −) when measured by the polarimeter. (+) is designated for clockwise rotation of plane-polarized light versus (−) for counterclockwise rotation of plane-polarized light.

For absolute configuration (*R vs. S* stereospecific) notation about a tetrahedral carbon atom, two bonds (i.e. lines) are in the plane of the paper, while one bond is pointing out (i.e. wedge) and one bond is pointing back (i.e. dashed line).

First, assign priorities to each moiety (i.e. group attached). When assigning priority (according to Cahn-Ingold-Prelog), use the first point of difference in the atomic number of the attached atoms and not the aggregate atomic number for all substituents attached to an atom.

Priority group #1 (a single oxygen) is higher in priority than group #2 (carbon attached to an oxygen, a carbon and a hydrogen) and is higher in priority than group #3 (carbon attached to three carbons). Group #4 is a H (not shown) pointing back into the plane as a dash line (not shown).

Passage 4
(Questions 22–26)

The human digestive system functions by a highly coordinated chain of mechanisms consisting of ingestion, digestion and nutrient absorption. Digestion is a progressive process that begins with ingestion into the mouth, continues with digestion in the stomach and then with digestion and absorption in the three sections of the small intestine.

Digestion involves macromolecules being broken down by enzymes into their component molecules before absorption through the villi of the small intestine. Nutrients from digested food, such as vitamins, minerals and subunits of macromolecules (e.g. monosaccharides, amino acids, di– or tripeptides, glycerol and fatty acids) are absorbed via either diffusion or transport (facilitated or active) mechanisms. These transport mechanisms may occur with or without mineral co-transport.

Digestive enzymes at the intestinal brush border work with digestive enzymes secreted by salivary glands and the pancreas to facilitate nutrient absorption. Digestion of complex carbohydrates into simple sugars is an example of this process. Pancreatic α-amylase hydrolyzes the 1,4–glycosidic bonds in complex starches to oligosaccharides in the lumen of the small intestine. The membrane-bound intestinal α-glucosidases hydrolyze oligosaccharides, trisaccharides and disaccharides to glucose and other monosaccharides in the small intestine.

Acarbose is a starch blocker used as an anti-diabetic drug to treat type-2 diabetes mellitus. Acarbose is an inhibitor of α–1,4-glucosidase (an enteric brush-border enzyme) and pancreatic α-amylase, which release glucose from complex starches. The inhibition of these enzyme systems reduces the rate of digestion of complex carbohydrates, resulting in less glucose being absorbed, because the carbohydrates are not broken down into glucose molecules. For diabetic patients, the short-term effect of such drug therapy is decreased current blood glucose levels and the long-term effect is a reduction of the HbA1C levels.

Figure 1. Acarbose molecule

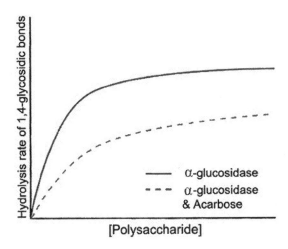

Figure 2. The kinetics of α-glucosidase in the presence/absence of acarbose.

22. According to the graph (Figure 2), how are α-1,4-glucosidase enzyme kinetics affected by acarbose?

    A. The concentration of available enzyme is reduced
    B. Enzyme specificity for the substrate is changed
    C. The K_{eq} binding of the ligand-enzyme complex is changed
    D. Covalent bonds that irreversibly inactivate the enzyme's active site are formed

A is correct.

The enzyme kinetics graph shows the reaction rate as a function of [substrate] and not acarbose (inhibitor) concentration. Note: [ ] signifies a reference to concentration.

Acarbose directly blocks the glucosidase enzyme's binding site and reduces the amount of free enzyme available to bind the ligand. A ligand is a molecule that binds to the active site of an enzyme (or to a receptor within a membrane). Specifically, a ligand that binds to the active site of an enzyme is called a substrate, and this is the molecule that the enzyme acts upon. Acarbose directly blocks binding of the substrate and decreases the observed rate, because there are fewer unbound enzymes available to bind to the substrate.

From the graph, acarbose is acting as either an uncompetitive or noncompetitive inhibitor, because the V_{max} (on the *y* axis) is reduced. Therefore, increasing the concentration of the acarbose decreases the relative rate (V_{max}) of the reaction.

Reversible inhibition involves weak bonds, such as hydrogen bonds (i.e. normally observed for enzymes). Noncompetitive, uncompetitive and competitive are reversible (not permanently bonded via strong covalent bonds), and they do not irreversibly inactivate the amino acid residues within the active site of the enzyme.

Irreversible inhibition involves strong bonds, such as covalent bonds. Poisons are a classic example of a molecule that binds irreversibly to enzymes.

Allosteric regulation means that the enzymes' shape changes due to conformational change. Conformational changes (e.g. chair conformers of cyclohexane or Newman projections) are examples of shape changes due to free rotation around single bonds.

23. Which type of α-1,4–glucosidase inhibition is most closely demonstrated by acarbose?

        I. competitive   **II. noncompetitive**   **III. allosteric**

  A. I only   **B.** II only   **C. II and III only**   **D.** I and III only

C is correct.

V_{max} and K_m are concepts of enzyme kinetics, and how they are affected by inhibition is important. V_{max} is the maximum rate achieved by the enzyme, and K_m is the substrate concentration where half of V_{max} is reached. In the graph (Figure 2), V_{max} has decreased due to the inhibitor because the curve that includes acarbose is lower on the *y* axis.

Competitive inhibition "directly inhibits" binding of the enzyme to the substrate. These inhibitors bind to the active site of the enzyme. Competitive inhibition can be altered by increasing or decreasing the relative ratio of [ligand] and [inhibitor]. Competitive inhibitors do not affect V_{max}; rather, they increase K_m, meaning that a higher concentration of substrate is required to achieve the same rate. Since acarbose decreases V_{max}, it cannot be a competitive inhibitor.

Noncompetitive inhibition is when the competitor binds to a site other than the active site (i.e. allosteric site) of the enzyme, which induces a conformational change (i.e. shape change) of the enzyme. Noncompetitive inhibition is not altered by increasing or decreasing the relative ratio of [ligand] and [inhibitor], because the competitor is not competing with the ligand for the same active site on the enzyme. A noncompetitive inhibitor always decreases V_{max}.

Uncompetitive inhibitors also decrease V_{max}, but this is not one of the options for the question. Uncompetitive and noncompetitive inhibitors are differentiated by their effect on K_m. A noncompetitive inhibitor has no effect on K_m, while an uncompetitive inhibitor decreases K_m. This is difficult to distinguish on the given Michaelis-Menten graph (Figure 2); generally, a Lineweaver-Burke plot (double reciprocal) is needed to accurately distinguish changes in K_m.

Noncompetitive inhibition is a type of allosteric inhibition, in which the substrate is either prevented (i.e. steric interference) or has less affinity (after the conformational change) for binding to the active site. However, some conformational changes actually result in increased affinity of the ligand to the active site, and this modulation is referred to as positive cooperativity.

24. Which condition most closely resembles the symptoms resulting from α-1,4-glucosidase inhibition by acarbose?

   A. Infection by *V. cholera*   **C.** **Deficiency of lactase**
   B. Deficiency of intrinsic factor   **D.** Deficiency of bile acid

C is correct.

If the glucosidase (i.e. enzymes end in –ase) is blocked, polysaccharides are not digested, and therefore are not absorbed. This is because only monosaccharides can be absorbed across the lining of the small intestine. If polysaccharides are not digested, they pass as indigestible material and, like indigestible dietary fiber from cellulose, are excreted in feces.

Lactase (ending in –ase) is an enzyme that digests the lactose (milk sugar) disaccharide. Normally, the intestinal villi secrete the enzyme lactase (β-D-galactosidase) to digest lactose into glucose and galactose monosaccharides that are absorbed across the wall of the small intestine. Without lactase, the disaccharide lactose cannot be cleaved into monosaccharides (glucose and galactose) to be absorbed within the small intestine, and is excreted in the feces.

Deficiency of lactase (commonly called lactose intolerance) is characterized by abdominal bloating, cramps, flatulence, diarrhea. Acarbose treatment of type 2 diabetes often produces similar side effects, because undigested carbohydrates remain in the intestine and pass through the colon where bacteria digest complex carbohydrates causing these gastrointestinal side-effects.

Lactose: β-D-galactopyranosyl-(1-4)-D-glucose

A: cholera is an infection of the small intestine caused by the bacterium *Vibrio cholerae*. Cholera affects ion channels in the intestinal mucosa resulting in profuse, watery diarrhea and vomiting.

B: an intrinsic factor deficiency results in vitamin B_{12} malabsorption (i.e. pernicious anemia). Intrinsic factor (IF) also known as gastric intrinsic factor (GIF) is a glycoprotein synthesized in the stomach by parietal cells (i.e. stomach epithelium cells that secrete gastric acid – HCl). Intrinsic factor is necessary for the absorption of vitamin B_{12} later in the small intestine.

D: bile acid deficiency results in fat malabsorption (i.e. steatorrhea). The main function of bile acid is to facilitate the formation of micelles to promote processing of dietary fat. Bile acids are steroid acids found predominantly in the bile of mammals. Bile is dark green to yellowish brown fluid, produced by the liver that aids the process of digestion of lipids in the small intestine. In many species, bile is stored in the gallbladder and, upon eating, is discharged into the duodenum.

25. Which molecule does NOT require micelle formation for intestinal absorption?

  A. vitamin A   **B.** triglycerides   **C.** cholesterol   **D. bile acid**

D is correct.

Bile acids are made in the liver by oxidation of cholesterol.

Cholesterol-steroid ring nomenclature

Only lipid components (e.g. cholesterol, triglycerides and fat-soluble vitamins such as A, D and E) are absorbed within micelles through the brush border of the intestine and enter the circulatory system. Bile acids function to stabilize micelle formation. Bile acids are stored in the gallbladder and may be excreted or reabsorbed via Na^+-dependent transport. The human body produces about 800 mg of cholesterol per day, and about half of that is used for bile acid synthesis. About 20-30 grams of bile acids are secreted into the intestine daily and about 90% is reabsorbed by active transport in the ileum and recycled in the enterohepatic circulation, which moves the bile salts from the intestinal system back to the liver and the gallbladder.

26. Glucosidase is best characterized as a:

  A. hydrolase   **B.** isomerase   **C.** ligase   **D.** phosphatase

A is correct.

The *y*-axis (vertical axis) of the graph is labeled hydrolysis, whereby a water molecule acts as a nucleophile with the lone pair of electrons on the oxygen breaking a bond; hydrolysis is the breaking (i.e. lysis) by the addition of H_2O.

There are six categories of enzymes:

- *Hydrolases* break bonds via hydrolysis (i.e. adding water).

- *Oxidoreductases* catalyze oxidation/reduction reactions.

- *Lyases* (commonly known as synthetases or synthases) catalyze the breaking of chemical bonds via hydrolysis and oxidation and often form new double bonds or a new ring structure (e.g. ATP $\rightarrow$ cAMP and PP_i). Lyases are unusual for enzymes because they require only one substrate in one direction, but two substrates for the reverse reaction.

- *Isomerases* catalyze the structural rearrangement of isomers.

- *Ligases* catalyze the joining of two large molecules (e.g. nucleotides in synthesis of nucleic acid) by forming a new chemical bond, usually via dehydration (i.e. condensation).

- *Transferases* catalyze the transfer of a functional group (e.g. methyl, phosphate, and hydroxyl) from one molecule to another.

  Two common examples include kinases and phosphatase. Kinases transfer phosphate groups from high–energy donor molecules (e.g. ATP) to specific substrates known as phosphorylation. Kinases function as the reverse of a phosphatase. Phosphatases remove phosphate groups (e.g. alkaline phosphatase) from its substrate. Phosphatases function as the reverse of a kinase.

Questions 27 through 30 are not based on any descriptive passage and are independent of each other

---

27. Which of the following is/are required for the proper function of the DNA-dependent DNA polymerase?

    I. DNA template strand   **III. 4 different nucleotides**
    II. primase (RNA primer)   IV. RNA polymerase

  A. I and II only   **B.** I and III only   **C. I, II and III only**   **D.** I, II, III and IV

C is correct.

DNA polymerase requires four different nucleotides (dNTPs) with A, C, G, T bases, a DNA template and a short strand RNA primer for the DNA polymerase to bind for initiation of replication.

DNA polymerase binds to a short segment of RNA (primer) and begins replication by complimentary binding to the DNA template strand. Without an RNA primer, the DNA polymerase cannot bind to the sense strand of DNA, and replication cannot occur. RNA primase (an enzyme that joins about 8 RNA nucleotides) synthesizes the RNA strand for DNA polymerase to bind. The DNA polymerase (after the short RNA primer) then adds individual nucleotides complementary to the DNA strand. In DNA, base A is a compliment to base T, while C is a compliment to G. The DNA polymerase catalyzes nucleotides to join along the sugar-phosphate backbone with hydrogen bonds between the bases of the nucleotide.

IV: RNA polymerase synthesizes mRNA from the DNA template during transcription.

28. Given that the availability of the carbon source determines energy yield, catabolism of which molecule will result in the highest energy yield?

    A. Short-chain unsaturated fatty acid   **C.** Long-chain conjugated fatty acid
    B. Short-chain saturated fatty acid   **D. Long-chain saturated fatty acid**

D is correct.

Acetyl CoA is an important 2-carbon metabolic intermediate entering the Krebs cycle in cellular respiration, and free fatty acids serve as a carbon source for acetyl CoA production. The longer the carbon backbone of the fatty acid, the greater the energy yield from the catabolism of the molecule due to the cleaving of a greater number of bonds.

Conjugation refers to a molecule with alternating single and double bonds. Both, the presence of unsaturation and the added stability of conjugation result, in less energy yield from conjugated fatty acids as the original molecule undergoes catabolism.

Double bonds refer to unsaturated (not saturated with Hs) molecules and result in a decrease in the potential (chemical) energy storage in the bonds. Therefore, unsaturated fatty acid catabolism yields less energy compared to saturated fatty acids of the same carbon chain length.

29. Which molecule has the closest to 3000-3500 cm^{-1} infrared (IR) stretch?

    A. $H_2C=CH_2CH_3$ **C. CH_3CH_2OH**
    B. CH_3CH_2COOH **D.** $(CH_3CH_2)_2CO$

C is correct.

CH_3CH_2OH is an alcohol which shows a broad, deep absorption in the region from 3000-3500 cm^{-1} of the infrared spectrum.

A: $H_2C=CH_2CH_3$ is an alkene that shows the absorption in the 2100-2300 cm^{-1} region of the infrared spectrum. This is characteristic of $C≡C$ and $C≡N$ triple bonds.

B: CH_3CH_2COOH is a carboxylic acid where the hydroxyl absorption shows a broad, deep absorption shifted to 2800-3200 cm^{-1} (compared to 3000-3500 cm^{-1} for alcohols) and it is also characteristic of strong, sharp absorption of the carbonyl in the region 1630-1740 cm^{-1}

D: $(CH_3CH_2)_2CO$ is a ketone which shows a strong, sharp absorption in the 1630-1740 cm^{-1} region of the infrared spectrum, which is characteristic of carbonyls. Carbonyls are present in seven molecules: aldehyde, ketone, acyl halide, anhydrides, carboxylic acid, ester and amide.

30. Which of these compounds has/have a dipole moment?

    I. CCl_4
   II. CH_3CH_2OH
  III. $CH_3CHBrCH_3$

  A. II only   **B.** III only   **C.** I and III only   **D. II and III only**

D is correct.

A dipole moment is the vector sum of the individual bond dipoles in a molecule.

I: is carbon tetrachloride and the individual C-Cl dipoles of the symmetric molecule cancel, so CCl_4 has no net dipole moment.

II and III: are asymmetric because they each have one highly polar bond (C-Br and C-O), and both have dipole moments originating from these polar covalent bonds.

Passage 5
(Questions 31–35)

Penicillins are one of the most successful classes of antibiotics derived from *Penicillium* fungi. They include penicillin G, penicillin V, procaine penicillin and benzathine penicillin. Penicillin antibiotics were the first drugs that treated serious diseases such as syphilis, staphylococci and streptococci. Penicillins are still widely used today, but many types of bacteria are now resistant to them. All penicillins are β-lactam antibiotics and are used in the treatment of bacterial infections caused by susceptible, usually Gram-positive, organisms.

The initial efforts to synthesize penicillin proved difficult with discrepancies in the structure being reported from different laboratories. In 1957, chemist John Sheehan at the Massachusetts Institute of Technology (MIT) completed the first chemical synthesis of penicillin. However, the synthesis developed by Sheehan was not appropriate for mass production of penicillins. One of the intermediate compounds was 6-aminopenicillanic acid (6-APA). Attaching different groups to the 6-APA allowed the synthesis of new forms of penicillin.

Figure 1. Penicillin biosynthesis

The structure of the penicillins includes a five-membered ring containing both sulfur and nitrogen (i.e. thioazolidine ring) joined to a four-membered ring containing a cyclic amide (i.e. β-lactam). These two rings are necessary for the biological activities of penicillin, and cleavage of either ring disrupts antibacterial activity.

Figure 2. Core structure of penicillins (beta-lactam ring highlighted)

A medical student performed three experiments as shown in Table 1 to elucidate how penicillin resulted in the death of bacterial cell.

	Method	Experimental results
Experiment 1	Two bacterial species were cultured and grown on agar plates. Both species had normal peptidoglycan cell walls. One population was exposed to penicillin, while the other was not exposed to penicillin.	About 93% of the bacteria treated with penicillin underwent cytolysis and did not survive, while the bacteria that were not exposed to penicillin were unaffected.
Experiment 2	Two bacterial species were cultured and grown on agar plates. One species had an intact peptidoglycan cell wall, while the other species had an incomplete cell wall. Both groups were exposed to penicillin on the agar plates.	The bacteria with incomplete cell walls survived, while 93% of those with intact peptidoglycan cell walls did not survive.
Experiment 3	The 7% who survived the treatment of penicillin in Experiment 2 were cultured and grown on agar plates. These colonies were repeatedly inoculated with penicillin.	The colonies grew continuously with no apparent effect from the antibiotic.

Table 1.

31. It is reasonable to hypothesize that penicillin causes bacterial death likely by:

    A. blocking the colonies' access to nutrients

    B. disrupting the integrity of the bacterial cell wall

    C. establishing excessive rigidity in the bacterial cell wall

    D. inducing mutations in bacteria from Gram-negative to Gram-positive strains

B is correct.

Peptidoglycan cross-linking of the bacterial cell wall is needed for the cell to resist osmotic pressure and the subsequent cytolysis of the bacteria. Penicillin inhibits the last step of cross-linking of peptidoglycan during the synthesis of the bacterial cell wall.

Peptidoglycan monomer

The peptidoglycan layer in the bacterial cell wall is a crystal lattice structure formed from linear chains of two alternating amino sugars. The alternating sugars are connected by a β-(1,4)-glycosidic bond (i.e. between the hemiacetal of one sugar with the hydroxyl on the adjacent sugar). One sugar is attached to a short (4- to 5-residue) amino acid chain, which helps protect the bacteria against attacks by most peptidases.

Bacteria constantly remodel their peptidoglycan cell walls, simultaneously building and breaking down portions of the cell wall as they grow and divide. β-lactam antibiotics inhibit the formation of peptidoglycan cross-links in the bacterial cell wall. The enzymes that normally hydrolyze the peptidoglycan cross-links continue to function, which weakens the bacteria's cell wall, and osmotic pressure increases – eventually causing cell death via cytolysis.

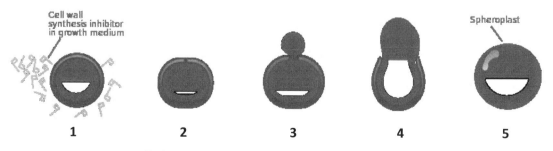

Penicillin's mechanism of action on peptidoglycan cell wall.

32. Knowing that penicillin G is rapidly hydrolyzed under acidic conditions, which limitation applies to its use?

   A. It is not active in the range of plasma pH
   B. It must be administered intravenously
   C. It must be taken 30 to 60 minutes before eating
   D. It should be avoided by young children and elderly patients

B is correct.

Benzylpenicillin, also known as penicillin G, is the "gold standard" type of penicillin (G in its name refers to "gold standard"). Penicillin G is typically given intravenously (injected directly into the venous circulation) or by other parenteral (not oral) route of administration, because it is unstable in the hydrochloric acid of the stomach.

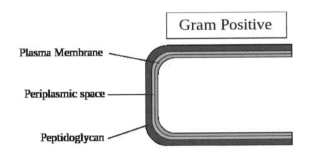

Phenoxymethylpenicillin (also called penicillin V) is an orally active penicillin type as it is more acid-stable than penicillin G, which allows it to be given orally. However, it is less active than penicillin G against Gram-negative bacteria.

33. From the experiments, which bacterial species are most resistant to penicillin?

   A. Species unable to transcribe DNA to RNA
   B. Species with complete peptidoglycan cell walls
   C. Species with incomplete cross-linked cell walls
   D. Species with the greatest intracellular osmotic pressure

C is correct.

From Experiment 2, bacteria with incomplete cell walls survived, while 93% of bacteria with a normal peptidoglycan cell wall underwent cytolysis.

Bacterial cell walls are composed of peptidoglycan, while plants have cell walls made of cellulose (i.e. dietary fiber) consisting of glucose monomers.

34. What causes the bacterial cells to undergo cytolysis upon the weakening of their cell wall?

A. Water enters the cells due to osmotic pressure
B. Proteins are not able to exit the cell through vesicles
C. Solutes are forced out of the cells through active transport mechanisms
D. Facilitated diffusion causes lipid-insoluble substances to cross the cell membrane

A is correct.

Osmotic pressure is a force that allows water to enter bacterial cells through the plasma membrane, because bacterial cells have a high solute concentration compared to the medium in which the bacterium is located. The cell wall with cross-linked peptidoglycan is a rigid structure that opposes this pressure and prevents the bacterial cell from swelling and undergoing cytolysis. In the absence of an intact peptidoglycan cross-linked cell wall, the osmotic pressure causes swelling as water enters the bacteria and lyses the bacteria (i.e. cytolysis or plasmolysis).

35. It is a reasonable hypothesis that 7% of the cell-walled bacteria treated with penicillin in Experiments 1 and 2 survived due to:

A. the bacterial cell wall's impermeability to penicillin
B. agar on the growth plates that hydrolyzed and degraded penicillin
C. plasmids that synthesized penicillinase
D. the limitation of diffusion, which resulted in select colonies not being exposed to penicillin

C is correct.

The variation of survival rate is not simply a matter of penicillin concentration. 7% of the bacteria that survived had the cells that were genetically different and not dependant on the penicillin. Plasmids are extrachromosomal pieces of DNA that confer antibiotic resistance to bacteria by synthesizing enzymes that cleave the antibiotic. Penicillinase is an enzyme that inactivates penicillin.

The resistant bacteria cells pass the plasmids and the corresponding antibiotic resistance to future generations during cell replication (experiment 3). Plasmids can also be transferred to other (non-daughter cell) bacteria by transformation (uptake of genetic information from the solution), transduction (viral vector) or conjugation (via sex pili). A plasmid within the bacteria that increases the expression of the penicillinase enzyme likely confers penicillin resistance in bacterial cells that survived.

Bacterium with chromosomal
DNA and plasmids

Passage 6
(Questions 36–41)

Adipose tissue is loose connective tissue composed of adipocytes and stores free fatty acids as triglycerides. A fatty acid is a carboxylic acid with a long aliphatic tail (often with even numbers of carbons between 4 and 28) that is either saturated or unsaturated. Saturated refers to the aliphatic chain which lacks double bonds, while unsaturated chains contain one or more double bonds.

Glycerol, a three-carbon molecule, contains three hydroxyl groups with a single OH on each of the three carbons. Glycerol is the backbone for triglycerides, and each hydroxyl group is the attachment point for a free fatty acid. The hydroxyl on the glycerol attacks the carboxylic acid group of the free fatty acid to form an ester linkage bond.

Figure 1. Glycerol

Figure 2. Fatty acid

Figure 3. Triglyceride

Triglycerides are released from adipose tissue into the circulatory system during high demands for energy by peripheral muscle tissue. The release of free fatty acids is controlled by a complex series of reactions tightly modulated by *hormone-sensitive lipase* (HSL). HSL hydrolyzes the first fatty acid from a triglyceride, freeing a fatty acid and a diglyceride. HSL is activated when the body needs to mobilize energy stores and responds positively to catecholamines and adrenocorticotropic hormone (ACTH), but is inhibited by insulin. Lipase activators bind receptors that are coupled to adenylate cyclase, which increases cAMP for activation of an appropriate *kinase* (PKA) that then activates HSL.

Free fatty acids targeted for breakdown are transported, bound to *albumin,* through the circulation. However, fatty acids targeted for adipose storage sites in adipocytes are transported in large lipid-protein micelle particles termed *lipoproteins* (i.e. LDL). During high rates of mitochondrial fatty acid oxidation, acetyl CoA is produced in large amounts. If the generation of acetyl CoA from glycolysis exceeds utilization by the Krebs cycle, an alternative pathway is ketone body synthesis. During the onset of starvation, skeletal and cardiac muscles preferentially metabolize ketone bodies, which preserve endogenous glucose for the brain.

36. Albumin is the most abundant protein distributed throughout the circulatory system and accounts for about 50% of plasma proteins. By which bond, and for what reason, does albumin bind to the free fatty acids?

A. Hydrogen bonding to albumin stabilizes fatty acid absolute configuration
B. Covalent bonding to albumin increases lipid solubility
C. Ionic bonding to albumin stabilizes free fatty acid structure
D. Van der Waals binding to albumin increases lipid solubility

D is correct.

Albumin is synthesized in the liver and is the most abundant plasma protein. It is very important because it provides substantial oncotic pressure (i.e. osmotic pressure in the circulatory system) in blood vessels, which maintains proper vascular pressure (due to osmolarity of the blood). Oncotic pressure from proteins (e.g. albumin) in the blood plasma attracts plasma (e.g. water) back into the circulatory system. Oncotic pressure counteracts the hydrostatic pressure (i.e. blood pressure) that forces blood into the interstitial space.

Without vascular osmolarity (from albumin and other proteins), fluid would leak out of the circulatory system (and cells) and flow into the interstitial space, causing swelling known as edema.

Some lipid-soluble (i.e. hydrophobic) molecules also bind to albumin, thereby increasing their solubility in the blood plasma (i.e. hydrophilic). Molecules transported by albumin are bonded *via* weak, non-covalent intermolecular bonds (e.g. hydrogen bonding, dipole-dipole and van der Waals attractions). In general, hydrogen bonding is used for attraction/dissociation for reversible reactions.

37. A person suffering untreated diabetes can experience ketoacidosis due to a reduced supply of glucose. Which of the following correlates with diabetic ketoacidosis?

A. High plasma insulin levels
B. Increase in fatty acid oxidation
C. Ketone bodies increase plasma alkalinity to clinically dangerous levels
D. Decreased levels of acetyl CoA lead to increased production of ketone bodies

B is correct.

Ketoacidosis is a metabolic state associated with high concentrations of ketone bodies. In ketoacidosis, the body fails to adequately regulate ketone production, causing such a severe accumulation of keto acids that the pH of the blood is decreased substantially, which, in extreme cases, can be fatal.

Ketone bodies are three water-soluble compounds that are produced as by-products when fatty acids are broken down by the liver for energy. Although termed *bodies*, they are substances dissolved in the plasma. Ketone bodies are produced from acetyl-CoA (i.e. ketogenesis), mainly in the mitochondrial matrix of hepatocytes (e.g. liver cells), when carbohydrates (i.e. glucose) are so scarce that energy must be obtained from catabolism of fatty acids (and also deamination of amino acids).

A: diabetes is characterized by the inability of the beta cells of the pancreas to synthesize insulin.

Insulin stimulates cell's uptake of glucose from the blood plasma within the circulation. Insulin-dependent diabetes results from either deficient or absent insulin synthesis by the β-cells of the pancreas. In diabetes type I patients, insulin production and the associated glucose uptake does not occur. Although the plasma glucose levels of a diabetic are very high, only a small amount of glucose is transported into the cells, because insulin is needed for the primary transport of glucose into cells.

As a result of the inability of the pancreas to synthesize insulin, the cell functions as though there were no plasma glucose and is similar to starvation mode. Therefore, ketone bodies are made, which causes ketoacidosis observed in type I diabetes.

C: ketone bodies are acidic and lower the pH, if untreated, to dangerous levels.

D: the passage states that increased acetyl-CoA levels lead to ketone body production.

38. Which of the following is the site of the breakdown for β-oxidation?

   A. mitochondria **B.** lysosomes **C.** the cytoplasm of the cell   **D.** the nucleolus

A is correct.

According to the passage, beta-oxidation occurs in the mitochondrial matrix, which is the location for the Krebs (i.e. TCA) cycle.

B: lysosomes are cellular organelles that contain hydrolase enzymes (i.e. catalysis via hydrolysis) for the degradation of waste material and cellular debris. They are used for the digestion of macromolecules from phagocytosis (i.e. ingestion of other dying cells or larger extracellular material such as foreign invading microbes), endocytosis (i.e. whereby receptor proteins are recycled from the cell surface) and autophagy (i.e. damaged or unneeded organelles/proteins, or invading microbes are delivered to the lysosome).

C: glycolysis occurs in the cytoplasm and begins with the catabolism (i.e. breakdown) of glucose, producing two 3-carbon pyruvates (i.e. pyruvic acid) per glucose. The pyruvate is shuttled through the double membrane of the mitochondria into the matrix that produces (via decarboxylation) acetyl CoA (2-carbon chain), which enters the Krebs cycle.

D: the nucleolus is a membrane-bound organelle located within the nucleus. The nucleolus is the site of the synthesis of rRNA, which are the main component (along with proteins) of the ribosome.

39. The main regulation point for fatty acid catabolism is *lipolysis*. All of the following are direct products of adipose tissue breakdown, EXCEPT:

A. acetyl CoA   **B.** glycerol   **C.** free fatty acids   **D. ketone bodies**

D is correct.

Lipolysis is the breakdown of lipids and is hormonally induced by epinephrine, norepinephrine, ghrelin, growth hormone, testosterone, and cortisol (its role in the mechanism is still being researched). Adipocytes comprise the adipose tissue as lipid storages (i.e. fat cells) within the body and function as the main storage site for triglycerides (e.g. glycerol plus three fatty acid tails).

Ketone bodies are produced from acetyl-CoA mainly in the mitochondrial matrix of liver cells (i.e. hepatocytes) when carbohydrates (e.g. glucose) are so scarce that energy must be obtained from breaking down fatty acids. The production of ketone bodies is not considered a direct product of lipolysis. Ketone bodies are produced only when levels of acetyl-CoA exceed the utilization capacity by the Krebs cycle.

Pyruvate (3-carbon chain) is oxidized into lactate (3-carbon chain) during anaerobic fermentation for the concurrent reduction of NAD^+ to NADH. In both cellular respiration (proceeding to the Krebs cycle) and lipolysis, acetyl-CoA (2-carbon chain) is formed by the decarboxylation (loss of CO_2) of pyruvate (precursor for Krebs cycle) or lactate (precursor for ketone bodies).

From the passage, the ester bonds within triglycerides are broken *via* hydrolysis by the hormone-sensitive lipase (HSL) to produce glycerol and free fatty acids. Free fatty acids are converted to acetyl-CoA that is either oxidized within the Krebs (TCA) cycle into ATP or used to produce ketone bodies.

40. Which organ is the last to use ketone bodies as an energy source?

A. kidneys   **B. brain**   **C.** cardiac tissue   **D.** skeletal muscle

B is correct.

Ketone bodies are formed by ketogenesis, when liver glycogen stores are depleted and fat (triacylglycerol) is cleaved to yield 1 glycerol and 3 fatty acid chains, in a process known as lipolysis. Ketone bodies are a group of ketones (carbonyl carbon linked between two carbon chains), including acetone, acetoacetic acid and β-hydroxybutyric produced in high levels during ketosis, as in diabetes mellitus and during starvation. The ketone body acetoacetate slowly decarboxylates into acetone, which is a volatile compound that is both metabolized as an energy source and lost in both the breath and urine.

Most of the cells in the body are able to use fatty acids as an alternative source of energy in a process known as beta-oxidation. One of the products of beta-oxidation is acetyl-CoA, which can be used in the Krebs cycle (citric acid cycle).

During prolonged fasting or starvation, acetyl-CoA in the liver is used to produce ketone bodies instead, leading to a state of ketosis, whereby the body starts using fatty acids instead of glucose. The brain cannot use long-chain fatty acids for energy because they are albumin-bound and cannot cross the blood–brain barrier. However, not all medium-length fatty acids are bound to albumin. The unbound medium-chain fatty acids are soluble in the blood and can cross the blood–brain barrier. The ketone bodies produced in the liver can also cross the blood–brain barrier. In the brain, these ketone bodies are then converted to acetyl-CoA and are used in the citric acid cycle.

According to the passage, cardiac and other muscle tissues metabolize ketone bodies to preserve any available glucose for the brain. The brain uses glucose preferentially as the molecule for oxidation into ATP. The brain, as starvation proceeds and after the depletion of residual glucose (i.e. initially from food and then from glycogen stores in liver and muscle cells), utilizes ketone bodies to sustain metabolic function. Therefore, under extreme conditions of prolonged starvation, the brain ultimately uses ketone bodies.

41. Which of the following bonds between glycerol and the free fatty acids is cleaved by phosphorylated *hormone-sensitive lipase* via hydrolysis?

   A. hydrogen bond   **B. ester bond**   **C.** ionic bond   **D.** disulfide bond

B is correct.

From the passage, *hormone-sensitive lipase* hydrolyzes the bond *via* the addition of water (hydrolysis). The free fatty acids bond to a glycerol molecule *via* an *esterification* reaction (i.e. the hydroxyl group on glycerol attacks the carbonyl carbon of the carboxylic acid of a fatty acid) to form an ester bond. These ester bonds are cleaved by *hormone-sensitive lipase* during hydrolysis of the triglyceride.

A common theme in biology is the breaking of bonds *via hydrolysis* (i.e. addition of water). The making of covalent bonds occurs *via dehydration* (i.e. loss of water) during bond formation involving condensation (joining of two subunits) reactions.

> Questions 42 through 46 are not based on any
> descriptive passage and are independent of each other

42. What is the correct sequence of organelles passed by the proteins targeted for the secretory pathway?

    A. ER → vesicle → Golgi → vesicle → plasma membrane
    B. ER → vesicle → Golgi → cytoplasm → plasma membrane
    C. Golgi → ER → vesicle → cytoplasm → proteosome
    D. cytoplasm → vesicle → Golgi → ER → vesicle → plasma membrane

A is correct.

The secretory pathway for a secreted protein is rough ER → vesicle → Golgi → vesicle → extracellular fluid (or to the plasma membrane or to the organelle within the cell).

Vesicular transport is used for the properly folded protein to migrate from the rough ER (site of protein folding using chaperones) to the Golgi. The Golgi is involved in protein modification (i.e. trimming of the properly folded polypeptide and/or adding of sugar moieties) and the sorting of proteins destined for the extracellular space (secreted from cell), the plasma membrane (as a membrane receptor or channel), or targeted for a cellular organelle (e.g. lysosome or nucleus).

Transport to the proteosome is not in the pathway for properly folded proteins. The proteosome is used for (misfolded) proteins that are destined to be degraded, because the protein failed to fold properly within the lumen (interior) of the endoplasmic reticulum.

43. During replication, which molecule do single stranded binding proteins (SSBP) attach to in order to maintain the uncoiled configuration of the nucleotide strands of the double helix uncoiled by the helicase enzyme?

    A. dsDNA   **B. ssDNA**   **C.** dsRNA   **D.** ssRNA

B is correct.

Nucleotides comprise the double helix of DNA. Helicase is an enzyme (along with topoisomerase) that uncoils the double stranded DNA molecule during replication (copying) of the nucleotides along the DNA. Once uncoiled and awaiting replication, the single stranded DNA strands are protected (coated with the SSBP) to avoid degradation by nucleases (enzymes that cleave nucleotides).

Replication occurs during the S phase of interphase. Transcription is the synthesis of an RNA molecule from the DNA template and is used for the generation of proteins (translation).

44. A biochemist hypothesized that the glucose transport protein is located only on the outer surface of the cell membrane. Is such hypothesis correct?

    A. Yes, because transport proteins are located only on the outer surface of the lipid bilayer

    B. Yes, because transport proteins are located only on the inner surface of the lipid bilayer

    C. No, because transport proteins are transmembrane and span the entire lipid bilayer

    D. No, because the hydrophilic heads of the lipid bilayer attract polar residues of the protein

C is correct.

Transport proteins are integral membrane proteins that span the entire phospholipid bilayer of membranes and allow molecules to pass through the membrane. By contrast, peripheral membrane proteins adhere only temporarily to the phospholipid bilayer with which they are associated and attach to integral membrane proteins, or penetrate the peripheral regions of the phospholipid bilayer.

Molecules are shuttled to the other side of the phospholipid bilayer by passage within the protein-lined channel of the transmembrane protein. Integral membrane proteins have membrane-spanning domains with hydrophobic amino acids projecting into the hydrophobic tail regions of the phospholipid bilayer. The presence of these hydrophobic amino acids allows the integral membrane protein to span the hydrophobic interior of the membrane.

45. Beta-oxidation occurs in the same location as:

    I. glycolysis

    II. the Krebs cycle

    III. pyruvate decarboxylation into acetyl-CoA

    A. I only   **B.** I and II only   **C. II and III only**   **D.** I, II and III

C is correct.

Beta-oxidation occurs in the same location as the Krebs cycle and pyruvate decarboxylation. The Krebs cycle, like beta-oxidation, occurs in the matrix of the mitochondria. Pyruvate (from glycolysis) decarboxylation into acetyl-CoA (Krebs cycle) also occurs in the mitochondrial matrix.

I: glycolysis occurs in the cytoplasm.

46. Which molecule has an infrared stretch closest to 1700 cm^{-1}?

    A. $CH_3CH_2CH_2CPh_3$ **C. $CH_3CH_2CH_2CH_2CHO$**

    B. $CH_3CH_2CH_2CH_2OH$ **D.** $CH_3CHClCH_2CH_2OCH_2CH_3$

C is correct.

An infrared (IR) absorption in the 1640–1750 cm^{-1} region is an absorption characteristic of the carbonyl (C=O) bond. Carbonyls are present in seven molecules: aldehydes, ketones, acyl halides, anhydrides, carboxylic acids (with a second spectra of hydroxyl absorption between 2500 – 3000 cm^{-1}), esters and amides.

Aldehydes (represented as ~CHO) contain a carbonyl.

Compare the ~CHO of the aldehyde

> ~CH$_2$OH of an alcohol
>
> ~COC of a ketone
>
> ~COX of an acyl halide (where X = F, Cl, Br or I)
>
> ~COOOC of an anhydride
>
> ~COOH of a carboxylic acid
>
> ~COOC of an ester
>
> ~CONH$_2$ of an amide

Passage 7
(Questions 47–52)

Esters are compounds consisting of a carbonyl adjacent to an ether linkage. They are derived by reacting a carboxylic acid (or its derivate) with a hydroxyl of an alcohol or phenol. Esters are often formed by condensing *via* dehydration (removal of water) of an alcohol acid with an acid.

Figure 1. Ester functional group (R and R' represent alkyl chains)

Esters are ubiquitous in biological molecules. Most naturally occurring fats and oils are the fatty acid esters of glycerol, while phosphoesters form the backbone of nucleic acids (e.g. DNA and RNA molecules), as shown in Figure 2. Esters with low molecular weight are commonly used as fragrances and are found in essential oils and pheromones.

Acid-catalyzed esterification is a mechanism of nucleophilic attack by the oxygen of the alcohol on the carboxylic acid (Figure 3). The isotope of oxygen, labeled in the alcohol as $R'^{18}OH$, was used to elucidate the reaction mechanism. The ester product was separated from unused reactants and side reaction contaminants in the reaction mixture. The water from the reaction mixture was collected as a separate fraction via distillation.

Figure 2. Two phosphodiester bonds are formed by connecting the phosphate group (PO_4^{3-}) between three nucleotides.

Figure 3. Esterification reaction mechanism

47. Which of these carboxylic acids has the lowest pK_a?

A. $ClCH_2CH_2CH_2COOH$

B. $CH_3CH_2CH_2COOH$

C. $Cl_3CCH_2CH_2COOH$

D. $CH_3CH_2CHClCOOH$

D is correct.

Carboxylic acids are strong organic acids (with pK_a ranges between 2.5 and 5), but are weak acids compared to the inorganic acids (with pK_a ranges between –10 and 3). The acidity of a carboxylic acid can be increased by the presence of electronegative substituents (e.g. F, O, N, Cl), because the electronegative substituents' bonds pull electron density along σ (sigma – single) bonds. This inductive effect (along σ bonds) increases the stability of the resulting anion (conjugate base) of the deprotonated acid.

This electron withdrawal along the σ bond (i.e. induction) stabilizes the conjugate base compared to the anions without electronegative moieties. Since the anion (i.e. conjugate base) is more stable (i.e. weaker base), the acid is stronger because it has an increased tendency to dissociate the proton. Overall, the more electron withdrawing groups present and the closer they are to the carboxyl group, the stronger the acid (i.e. lower pK_a).

Note: resonance structures (delocalization of π electron) are a much larger contributor to anion stability than induction (electronegative atoms pull along the σ bond).

Comparing resonance (i.e. π/pi electron delocalization) to induction (i.e. σ/sigma bonds), resonance has the greater effect on stabilizing the anion.

48. Given that esterification may occur between parts of the same molecule, which compound would most easily undergo intramolecular esterification to form a cyclic ester?

A. $HOOCCH_2CH_2OH$

B. $HOOCCH_2CH_2CH_2OH$

C. $HOOCCH_2CH_2CH_2CH_2OH$

D. $HOOCCH_2CH_2\ CH_2CH_2CH_2CH_2OH$

C is correct.

For an intramolecular attack, the stability of a ring structure is important. The least amount of ring strain (i.e. angle or Baeyer strain) occurs in structures that can form six-membered rings, as in cyclohexane (i.e. six-membered rings) chair conformational isomers. Angle strains occur when cyclic molecules are forced to deviate from the ideal sp^3 hybridized (i.e. tetrahedral) bond angle of 109.5°.

A: a four-membered ring produces a substantial bond angle (i.e. 90°) and an eclipsing steric strain.

B: a five-membered ring is not as stable as a six-membered ring.

D: an eight-membered ring is less stable than a six-membered ring because of the angle strain resulting from a larger bond angle, which deviates from the 109.5° bond angle of an sp^3 carbon.

49. An alternative method for forming esters is:

$$CH_3CH_2COO^- + RX \rightarrow CH_3CH_2COOR + X^-$$

The reason that this reaction occurs is because:

A. carboxylates are good nucleophiles   C. halide acts as a good electrophile
B. carboxylates are good electrophiles   D. halide is a poor conjugate base

A is correct.

This reaction occurs between a carboxylate (i.e. anion of the deprotonated carboxylic acids) and alkyl halides. This reaction is a nucleophilic substitution reaction with the carboxylate ion (i.e. nucleophile) and the halide (i.e. leaving group).

Leaving groups always dissociate with their electrons and become an anion if they are neutral before dissociation, or they become neutral if they are protonated before dissociation. A better leaving group dissociates more readily, because the conjugate base (e.g. leaving group) is more stable. Halides are very good leaving groups, because the anion is stable. The series of leaving group stability for the halides is I > Br > Cl > F. The same series is observed for nucleophilic strength of the halides.

50. The rate of the reaction is negligible without the acid catalyst. The catalyst is attacked by the:

A. carbonyl carbon and facilitates the attack of the carbonyl nucleophile
B. carbonyl carbon and facilitates the carbonyl oxygen electrophile
C. carbonyl oxygen and facilitates the attack of the alcohol nucleophile
D. carbonyl oxygen and facilitates the carbonyl carbon electrophile

C is correct.

Esterification of a carboxylic acid with an alcohol should be carried out under acid (H^+) catalysis, whereby (according to the mechanism presented in figure 3) the H^+ of the acid catalyst is attacked by the lone pair of electrons on the oxygen of the carboxylic acid. The protonated oxygen (with a positive charge), through resonance, produces a carbocation (positively charged carbon) of the carbonyl carbon.

The positively charged carbocation is susceptible to a nucleophilic attack by the lone pair of electrons on the alcohol. Thus, the reaction is between the lone pair of electrons on the alcohol oxygen (i.e. nucleophile) and the positively charged carbonyl carbon (i.e. electrophile).

51. Which alkyl halide most readily forms an ester with sodium pentanoate ($CH_3CH_2CH_2CH_2COO^-Na^+$)?

    A. CH_3Br
    B. $(CH_3)_2CHBr$
    C. $CH_3(CH_2)_6CH_2Br$
    D. $CH_3CH_2CH_2CH_2Br$

A is correct.

Pentanoate results from the deprotonation of pentanoic acid. The reaction between a carboxylate anion and an alkyl halide is an S_N2 mechanism. The sodium pentanoate reacts with alkyl halides to form an ester, according to the relative trend for alkyl halides: methyl > 1° > 2° > 3°.

As an S_N2 reaction (i.e. concerted mechanism), the reaction involves partial bonding between the attacking nucleophile (i.e. carboxylate) and the substrate containing the leaving group (i.e. alkyl halide). The reaction is favored with less bulky (e.g. methyl) substrates. Bulky substrates (i.e. 2° or 3°) sterically hinder the reaction by blocking (i.e. physically obstructing) the attacking nucleophile from approaching the carbon atom where the leaving group is attached.

The methyl bromide (CH_3Br) molecule has only hydrogens and the bromine substituent, while the other choices have bulkier alkyl substituents. The methyl bromide is the least sterically hindered and reacts most readily with sodium pentanoate.

52. Which statement is correct, assuming that only the forward reaction occurs (Figure 3)?

    A. Ester fraction does not contain labeled oxygen, while the water fraction does
    B. **Water fraction does not contain labeled oxygen, while the ester does**
    C. Neither the ester fraction nor the water fraction contains labeled oxygen
    D. Both the ester fraction and the water fraction contain labeled oxygen

B is correct.

The acid-catalyzed esterification of a carboxylic acid involves the carbonyl carbon (of the carboxylic acid) reacting with the alcohol oxygen to form an ester (R-COO-R') linkage. Therefore, the labeled oxygen of the alcohol is incorporated into the ester product.

The water fraction does not contain labeled oxygen, because the oxygen of the water comes from the unlabeled hydroxyl group (on the carboxylic acid) and not the labeled oxygen from the alcohol. Dehydration (-OH + H^+) is a common mechanism for condensation when two molecules are joined during biosynthetic processes.

> Questions 53 through 59 are not based on any
> descriptive passage and are independent of each other

53. Which of the following amino acids is an essential amino acid in the diets of children, but not adults?

    A. Asparate   **B.** Glycine   **C. Arginine**   **D.** Lysine

C is correct.

Arginine, a *semiessential* or *conditionally essential* amino acid in humans, is one of the most metabolically versatile amino acids and serves as a precursor for the synthesis of urea, nitric oxide, polyamines, proline, glutamate, creatine and agmatine (decarboxylated arginine). The sources of free arginine within the body are dietary protein, endogenous synthesis, and turnover of body proteins. At the whole-body level, most *de novo* arginine synthesis occurs in a metabolic collaboration between the small intestine and the kidneys in the intestinal-renal axis of arginine synthesis. The magnitude of endogenous synthesis is sufficient for healthy adults; therefore it is not an essential dietary amino acid. However, endogenous arginine synthesis cannot fully meet the needs of infants and growing children or of adults with certain metabolic or physiological conditions. This is why arginine is classified as a *semiessential* or *conditionally essential* amino acid.

54. At room temperature, triglycerols containing only saturated long chain fatty acids remain:

    A. oils   **B. solid**   **C.** liquid   **D.** unsaturated

B is correct.

55. Which of the following is an inactive precursor of protease enzymes synthesized in the pancreas?

    A. ribozyme   **C. zymogen**
    B. isozyme   **D.** allosteric enzyme

C is correct.

A zymogen (also called proenzyme) is an inactive enzyme precursor that requires a biochemical change (e.g. hydrolysis or configuration change to form the active site) to become an active enzyme. The pancreas secretes zymogens like pepsin in the form of pepsinogen (i.e. an inactive zymogen). When chief cells release pepsinogen into HCl, it becomes partially activated. Another partially activated pepsinogen completes the activation by removing the peptide and turning the pepsinogen into pepsin.

56. The most common naturally occurring fatty acids have:

    A. 12-20 carbon atoms with an odd number of carbon atoms
    B. 12-20 carbon atoms with an even number of carbon atoms
    C. 20-50 carbon atoms with an odd number of carbon atoms
    D. 20-50 carbon atoms with an even number of carbon atoms

B is correct.

57. The anticodon is located on the:

    A. DNA   **B. tRNA**   **C.** mRNA   **D.** rRNA

B is correct.

An anticodon consists of three nucleotides that correspond to the three bases of the mRNA codon. Each tRNA has a specific anticodon triplet sequence that base-pairs (*via* hydrogen bonds) to one or more codons for an amino acid. Some anticodons can pair with more than one codon due to the phenomenon known as wobble base pairing in the 3rd position.

58. Which disaccharide, when present in large excess over glucose, can be metabolized by *E. coli* through use of the operon?

    A. galactose   **B. lactose**   **C.** sucrose   **D.** cellobiose

B is correct.

59. Which mechanism is used to interconvert anomers?

    A. Isotopic exchange reaction
    B. Mutarotation
    C. Conformational change around carbon-carbon bonds
    D. Anomers cannot be interconverted

B is correct.

Mutarotation was described in 1846 by the French chemist Augustin-Pierre Dubrunfaut. Dubrunfaut observed that the specific rotation of aqueous sugar solution changed with time.

Mutarotation is the change in the optical rotation of plane-polarized light due to the change in the equilibrium between two anomers when the corresponding stereocenters interconvert (e.g. cyclic sugars experience mutarotation as α and β anomeric forms interconvert). The optical rotation of the solution depends on the optical rotation of each anomer and their relative concentration ratio in the solution.

We want to hear from you

Your feedback is important to us because we strive to provide the highest quality prep materials. If you have any questions, comments or suggestions, email us, so we can incorporate your feedback into future editions.

Customer Satisfaction Guarantee

If you have any concerns about this book, including printing issues, contact us and we will resolve any issues to your satisfaction.

info@onlinemcatprep.com

To access online tests at a special pricing visit:

www.MasterMCAT.com/bookowner.htm

Made in the USA
Lexington, KY
28 July 2019